MW00528754

SHORTCHANGED

SH RTCHANGED

How Advanced Placement Cheats Students

ANNIE ABRAMS

JOHNS HOPKINS UNIVERSITY PRESS

Baltimore

Johns Hopkins University Press
2715 North Charles Street
Baltimore, Maryland 21218
www.press.jhu.edu

Library of Congress Cataloging-in-Publication Data

Names: Abrams, Annie, 1984– author.
Title: Shortchanged : how Advanced Placement cheats students / Annie
  Abrams.
Description: Baltimore : Johns Hopkins University Press, 2023. | Includes
  bibliographical references and index. | Summary: "Every year millions of
  students take Advanced Placement exams hoping to score enough points
  to earn college credit and save on their tuition bill. But are they getting a
  real college education? This book shows how the AP program originally
  aimed to replicate the liberal arts experience for bright students, but over
  time became a testing behemoth and marker of student status"—Provided
  by publisher.
Identifiers: LCCN 2022030961 | ISBN 9781421446295 (hardcover) |
  ISBN 9781421446301 (ebook)
Subjects: LCSH: Advanced placement programs (Education)—History. |
  College Entrance Examination Board—History. | Democracy and educa-
  tion—United States. | Education, Secondary—Aims and objectives—
  United States. | BISAC: EDUCATION / Schools / Levels / Secondary |
  EDUCATION / Evaluation & Assessment
Classification: LCC LB2353.62 .A27 2023 | DDC 371.26/4—dc23/eng/20220812
LC record available at https://lccn.loc.gov/2022030961

A catalog record for this book is available from the British Library.

Special discounts are available for bulk purchases of this book. For more
information, please contact Special Sales at specialsales@jh.edu.

For Marlowe, whose worth is incalculable

Contents

SHORTCHANGED

INTRODUCTION

Collecting Data

You're an American public high school senior. It's May—AP exam season. Two hours before you sit for the Advanced Placement English Literature exam, anxiety hits. You're not sure whether the college you go to will grant the credit if you pass. You don't know if colleges will recognize your exam scores from last year or the one before that or the one before that, either. But it feels like there are high stakes regardless. Doing well on standardized tests is part of your identity.

You review the exam essay rubrics. "Sophistication" is worth only one point; you can definitely pass without "demonstrating sophistication of thought and/or developing complex literary argument." Relief.

You google "ap lit study guide." Resources for cracking the exam include reference books on Amazon, teachers' PDF worksheets, lists of tips, tricks, and sample questions from testing companies, and advice on Reddit. According to one Redditor:

> another kinda strange thing i did (but it ended up working) is very
> deeply analyzing the organizational patterns of high scoring previ-
> ously released essays. i ddi [*sic*] that for AP lang and found a nice
> formula to use (that might not be applicable to AP Lit) and then I
> got a 5 so even though it's kinda weird imitating other people's styles

1

of expression it definitely may improve your score nonetheless because you'd be writing exactly as they want you to.[1]

A classmate has done the work of "analyzing the organizational patterns" for you and posted the FRQ (Free-Response Question) formula for literary analysis in a shared Google doc:

- Five paragraphs, forty minutes
- Three body paragraphs, nine minutes each
- Organize chronologically because it's easier to write as you read
- Two pieces of evidence per paragraph, one sentence of analysis per piece of evidence

You glance at the list of transition words to use between chunks of evidence and analysis: "nevertheless," "additionally," "moreover."[2]

Write the introduction last (five minutes) so that your thesis statement can include a list of what you do in your body paragraphs. An enthusiastic guy on YouTube says to use this thesis template for all prompts: "In the (Genre) (Title), (Author's Name) presents* ——(Literary Element(s) 2x–3x)——in order to (choose one: highlight, convey, showcase, expose) textual understandings based on literary elements, ultimately illustrating that (universal idea) (specific insight about the idea based on the literary elements)."[3] Implicitly, you trust his sentence structure over anything you could come up with yourself. CliffsNotes reminds you, "A conclusion is not absolutely necessary in order to receive a high score."[4] Technically, the website is about AP Lang, but the scoring rubrics are all the same anyway.

One essay question will ask you to write about a text that's not provided. You didn't read any of the novels or plays for English this year because the money—and your future career—is in STEM (science, technology, engineering, math). You were pushed into this class because your district decided that more people should take APs.[5]

US News and World Report's rankings of high schools rely on participation and success in AP, and so does funding.[6] You suspect you can get a 5 on the exam, even if you get a zero on this one essay.[7] Still, to be safe, you search "best ap lit books." You learn that Ralph Ellison's *Invisible Man* is "the most frequently referenced title on the English book list since 1971" and is "as culturally relevant today as it was when published in 1954 [*sic*]."[8] With an hour left, you look at the book's Shmoop entry. You do your best to memorize some of the plot summary and skim the information on writing style. "Jazzy," you note. The tone is "frank, thoughtful." Shmoop's coverage of the book's themes tells you to "chew on this," so you memorize it: "In *Invisible Man*, everyone is invisible because everyone is deceiving one another as to their true identities."[9]

During the exam, you try to meet the College Board's standards. A prompt asks you to analyze a "character's idealism and its positive or negative consequences."[10] You regurgitate what you've just barely digested. "In the novel *Invisible Man*, Ralph Ellison presents a jazzy style and frank, thoughtful tone, in order to convey textual understandings based on literary elements, ultimately illustrating that everyone is invisible because everyone is deceiving one another as to their true identities, as his jazzy style and frank, thoughtful tone portray his perspective."[11] Does this make sense? Does it address the prompt? Doesn't matter, no time to think about it. Press on. You have no idea that the narrator of *Invisible Man* railed against "an increasing passion to make men conform to a pattern."[12] You pass the exam, place out of your college's introductory "cultural analysis" and "expository writing" requirements, and never take a literature course again.[13]

THE PROBLEM

Much of today's discussion about the decline of the liberal arts centers on the undergraduate experience: tracking applications to liberal arts colleges and enrollments in majors, navigating the relationship between humanities and STEM requirements.[14] But disregarding secondary schooling is a mistake. In 2016, I started teaching at a public high school, including one section of twelfth-grade Advanced Placement English Literature. I'd just finished my doctorate in that exact field, so I'd expected a relatively smooth transition from the college teaching I'd done as a graduate student to the new work I'd do teaching a "college-level" course in one of the nation's most academically competitive high schools. Nearly all graduates matriculate at a four-year college or university, so I thought I'd be preparing my classroom of bright, ambitious seniors for the kind of reading and writing I'd expected of undergraduates six months earlier.

I was wrong to assume continuity between the experiences of teaching liberal arts college courses and navigating the Advanced Placement program. As a college instructor, teaching writing was social. I sought to help students understand their papers as more formal extensions of ongoing conversations. In pedagogical training, I was encouraged to be liberal with praise and both open-minded and discerning about the values with which student writing aligned. Clarity, innovation, investment, and enthusiasm all contributed to an essay's quality. I tried to be empathetic to the fact that honing the ability to form thoughts required patience, simultaneous caution and persistence, and originality. As I understood the point of marking essays, it was to help students refine their thinking while instilling in them the confidence that they were capable of intellectual growth.

As a teacher of Advanced Placement, I tried to offer meaningful feedback in the context of relationships I worked hard to develop with students. But my literature course now had two goals: helping students take their own minds seriously and giving them the specific—and often competing—tools to perform well on a high-stakes test at the end of the year. Overwhelmed by the volume of papers I was expected to grade and the limited time in which I was expected to do it, there was definite appeal in rating a paper on the College Board's scale from 1 to 9 and using its canned commentary for each point value in place of customized feedback. But the context for the information teachers convey helps students understand how to integrate it into their own lives. Rubrics changed students' relationships to their writing, and to me, as their reader—the exercise became mechanical.

Over the next three years, then teaching eleventh-grade Advanced Placement English Language, the College Board revised the English essay rubrics. All rubrics for all essay types are now almost exactly the same.[15] And "grading" now consists of ticking boxes. One of my classes developed a running joke about the disconnect between developing meaningful thoughts and worrying about producing the requisite number of words per minute per point. This ethos concerns me. This book is the product of research I began in an effort to understand my new job and my own resistance to doing it "well."

SCALING

The AP is spreading and is being enshrined in law. Nearly 40 percent of American high school graduates in the class of 2020 took at least one AP exam. An *Arkansas Democrat-Gazette* article celebrating the state's participation in the program cited its company with "four Northeast states—New Hampshire, Massachusetts, New Jersey, Maryland"—that have "policies in place in which at least 70% of their public high schools offer clusters of four or more Advanced Placement courses."[16] Oklahoma already offers each public school one hundred dollars "for each score of three or better on an advanced placement test" and subsidizes testing fees for students taking more than one exam.[17] And in May 2020, Oklahoma Governor Kevin Stitt signed House Bill 3400, stipulating, "Beginning with the 2024–2025 school year, all public high schools in this state shall make a minimum of four advanced placement courses available to students."[18] Other states, like Indiana, already have such a policy in place. Even in states that rejected Common Core standards as a sign of federal overreach, lawmakers have supported the national program's growth. This is strange because the College Board's current CEO, David Coleman, was one of the chief architects of the Common Core, and the AP program has advertised alignment with those standards.[19]

The College Board is closing in on ownership of a national curriculum that holds not only high schools, but also universities, to the company's academic standards and its philosophy of education. A bill enacted in June 2021 stipulated that Oklahoma's public universities must grant credit for scores of 3 or higher—across dozens of disciplines, high schools *and* universities are now bound to the private corporation's definition of "college-level work." In Texas and Illinois, this structure has been in place since 2015.[20] Politicians in Massachusetts and Georgia are seeking to enact an identical policy.[21] Most states have formal statewide or systemwide AP credit policies.[22] Before Missouri mandated that universities "grant undergraduate course credit to entering freshman students for each advanced placement examination where a student achieves a score of 3 or higher," Paul Wagner, executive director of the state's Council on Public Higher Education, told the *Columbia Missourian*, "We're a lot more comfortable with saying, let's sit down and see: Where does the content of the test match to the content of the courses taught in our colleges campuses? That's different than just saying 'Thou shall award credit for a 3.'"[23] Now, the University of Missouri, like many other institutions, grants credit for all scores of 3 or higher.[24] The tail is wagging the dog. This consolidation of power over information and its dissemination is troublesome. Together, these laws and the College Board's exams comprise a structure in which the possibility exists for an abuse of power over a massive number of students.

A centralized curriculum can be automated and delivered at a discount. The same bill mandating Advanced Placement offerings in Oklahoma explains, "The Statewide Virtual Charter School Board shall maintain an online learning platform to provide high quality online learning opportunities for Oklahoma students." To meet this mandate for access to courses, schools can allow their students to enroll in "a program offered by the Statewide Virtual Charter School Board or one of its vendors." Oklahoma is recruiting in-state educators to help with this initiative. A handful of Oklahoman teachers will provide lectures and explanatory videos that align with the College Board's content, allowing the company to extend the number of students they reach in the name of choice without admitting that there is any cost to centralized, privatized control.[25]

Oklahoma's story fascinates me because in 2014, concerned that the new AP US History framework was overly negative about the nation's trajectory, Republican representative to Oklahoma's state legislature, Dan Fisher, introduced a reactionary bill. He wanted to mandate the study of "foundational and historical documents . . . for all United States history courses offered in schools in the state."[26] The list of texts—mostly beautiful articulations of ideals by white men who've held political power—makes some attempts at diversity: Abigail Adams's exhortation to "remember the ladies," "The New Colossus" by Emma Lazarus, Chief Joseph's surrender speech, Martin Luther King Jr.'s "Letter from Birmingham Jail," and Malcolm X's "The Ballot or the Bullet." Despite these additions, predictably, and rightly, liberals ridiculed Fisher's attempt to fix and dictate curriculum.

Critiques of Fisher's activism from journalists, students, and educators coalesced around rejection of overreach and insistence on academic freedom. Oklahoma newspaper *Tulsa World*'s editorial board wrote, "Members of the Oklahoma Legislature shouldn't try to write school curriculum. It politicizes the classroom and leaves their own ignorance on the table."[27] University of Oklahoma student Alli Hill accused Fisher of impropriety when she opined, "AP courses are not mandatory in schools, so kids choose whether to take the course. There is no need to govern its instruction model."[28] Gene Perry, a policy director at Oklahoma Policy Institute, explained away Fisher's perception of the program's encroachment on rights: "AP classes are voluntary."[29]

Fisher blinked. Two days after introducing the bill, he told *The Oklahoman*, "We're going to clear it up so folks will know exactly what we're trying to accomplish and it's not to hurt AP. We're very supportive of the AP program."[30]

Culture wars about course content distract from a broader point.[31] Expansion of Advanced Placement is part of a reimagining of education and the privatization of public services. In 2018, before remote learning replaced school for millions of students, during the same year students and journalists accused College Board CEO David Coleman of exploiting the victims of the Parkland shooting as an opportunity to advertise Advanced Placement, he gave a report on the College Board's future called "New Excellence, New Opportunity."[32] He highlighted the company's $80 million investment in "personalized learning" for AP, a label for the tools and structures I outline in chapters 4 through 6. He concluded the talk with the following: "The deep issue here is one of checks and balances."[33] The AP program and its attendant technologies would be reconfigured to provide students with feedback and scores from a source without bias, unlike human employees.[34] In April 2021, the College Board introduced the AP Alumni Network, which gives former AP students "a chance to build relationships and have thoughtful conversations with elected leaders at the state and federal level."[35]

In progressive districts, broadening access to a reputable program in the name of equity sounds like a no-brainer. Regardless of cost, who would want to deny students at historically disadvantaged schools access to the same opportunities as their more privileged peers? New York City's AP for All initiative sounds like a progressive step toward leveling the playing field. During the 2016–17 school year, the New York City Department of Education's Office of Equity and Access launched AP for All, a partnership with the College Board aimed at increasing participation in Advanced Placement courses in all schools across the city. The initiative was part of Mayor Bill de Blasio's Equity and Excellence agenda, which promised "every single child, in every classroom," a "rigorous, inspiring, and nurturing learning experience." Access to Advanced Placement, in particular, was intended to "increase college readiness."[36] In 2017, a record number of Black and Hispanic students sat for and passed exams. "These results show that we are making the right investments and moving in the right direction," said Chancellor Carmen Fariña in January 2017.[37]

A year after Fariña celebrated the program's initial success, eight elite private schools in Washington, DC, announced in the *Washington Post* that they would be dropping Advanced Placement courses. Following the lead of other affluent schools, they explained, "As schools devoted to nurturing students' potential, fostering their talents and preparing them to lead productive lives, we believe the flexibility we will gain from developing our own courses will better prepare our students for college and their professional futures."[38] If the Advanced Placement program is unnecessary to achieving those universal goals in private schools, why is its presence in public schools so desirable?

Brands can be powerful: enrollment in AP courses can help students see themselves as high achievers and can change the ways teachers understand their careers.[39] "For too long, the City wasn't doing its part to provide access to Advanced Placement programs, sending a message to students that they weren't college material," explained De Blasio.[40] On another occasion, he reiterated, "The presence of AP courses is a great equalizer. It sends a message to every student: college can be for you if that's the choice you make."[41] He displayed faith in the program's decades-old brand name, which is based on a promise to deliver college-level curriculum to high school students. It's an indictment of the school system to acknowledge that a brand can do so much to dignify an American classroom. But it's not clear that brand names always ensure high quality.

Part of the reason I've focused on Oklahoma and New York City here is the impossibility of navigating the total deluge of local and state legislation leading to the AP program's broad adoption. This book's conclusion consolidates an overview of the College Board's overall strategy, beginning with incentives for schools' participation in No Child Left Behind, but the details are in local government legislatures. At the federal level, Joe Biden mentioned Advanced Placement during his presidential campaign. On the trail in Iowa in 2019, he flubbed, "Poor kids are just as bright as white kids. . . . We should challenge students in these schools to have advanced placement programs in these schools."[42] His secretary of education has been praised for increasing access to the program in his home state.[43] The Progressive Policy Institute's Paul Weinstein is hopeful that "President Biden could use his executive authority to expand access to college (and make it more affordable) by making the process for earning college credit through Advanced Placement (AP), International Baccalaureate (IB) programs, and college courses taken in high school at community colleges, more transparent and accessible."[44] The Thomas B. Fordham Institute promoted AP as a cure for "bridging excellence gaps."[45] Bipartisan agreement!

In October 2021, Biden's "Executive Order on Advancing Educational Equity, Excellence, and Economic Opportunity for Black Americans" promised federal attention to "promoting a positive school climate that supports equitable access to and participation in college-readiness, advanced placement courses, and internship opportunities."[46] Historically Black private secondary schools like Mississippi's Piney Woods and North Carolina's Laurinburg Institute send graduates to college without offering Advanced Placement. Biden's policy won't give a leg up to Black students who want to go to Morehouse College, which stipulates that neither literature nor history requirements can "be earned by placement/examination."[47] It's clear that Advanced Placement represents, at best, one possible approach among many to "equity, excellence, and economic opportunity." This book is about the stakes of that approach.

As government at all levels bolsters the program's presence in schools, AP's academic substance remains out of the discussion. Its merit rests on the approval of six educators who form the AP content committee for each of the thirty-six subjects the program offers: three college faculty, three high school teachers. Each exam committee also has a "College Board advisor" and "chief reader." The College Board explains, "They represent a diversity of knowledge and points of view in their fields and, as a group, are the authority when it comes to making subject-matter decisions in the exam-construction process."[48] Their credentials don't matter. Even if the professors were giants in their fields, endowed chairs with prestigious peer-reviewed publications and lengthy lists of teaching awards, and if the teachers were the most earnest members of the profession, exquisitely attuned to their unique students' needs, the fact that they quietly control what constitutes college English credit for a staggering number of our country's public schools and universities would still be indefensible. I wish the minutiae mattered, but the structure of the Advanced Placement program makes clear that the enterprise is running on bankrupt authority. We've lost sight of what the program's initial promise was, and what delivering on it might mean for individual students and for the nation.

THE HISTORY

The disconnect between the original vision and its current shape is startling. The first part of this book outlines the Advanced Placement program's place in the broader history of Cold War education reform. In attempting to visit the College Board's archives, I've called several numbers posted on the company website and have never had success in reaching an archivist, or even a representative who understands what I'm asking to see. To the best of my knowledge, archivists acknowledged in other College Board histories have retired or moved on to other institutions. I'm not sure if they've been replaced. As I discuss in this book's epilogue, an email I sent to their reference address came back with an "access denied" message. A request to visit the Educational Testing Service (ETS) archives was likewise refused—maybe because of the pandemic restrictions the email cited. Or maybe because, as Merve Emre wrote of her own experience with the ETS in *The Personality Brokers: The Strange History of Myers-Briggs and the Birth of Personality Testing,* "secrets and lies and various strategies of bureaucratic obstruction" are to be expected of the agency's treatment of researchers.[49] Whatever the cause, in some ways, these limitations have made my research easy. The first part of this book focuses on how educators imagined the program before the College Board or the Educational Testing Service had direct control over it.

In 1956, 1,229 students from 104 schools sat for 2,199 exams that 130 colleges would consider for credit in freshman courses. The ETS had handled previous pilot examinations, but that was the first year of the College Board's Advanced Placement program.[50] The first part of this book is about how and why that happened. In *Learning in the Fast Lane: The Past, Present, and Future of Advanced Placement,* the most recent academic history of the program, the American Enterprise Institute's Chester Finn and Andrew Scanlan devote few scant pages to the history that comprises the first three chapters of this book. In decompressing this story, I build on other coverage of the program's origins, including journal articles by Eric Rothschild and Jack Schneider, a book chapter by Tim Lacy, and College Board employees' and affiliates' publications about their work, including compilations by Frank Bowles, John Valentine, and Michael Johanek.[51]

In the late 1940s and early 1950s, academics at some of the nation's most prominent colleges and universities conceived of the nation's expanding public education system as an instrument to strengthen the body politic. A constellation of Cold War educators, administrators, and philanthropists invested money and energy in a streamlined education system that held promise to sustain democracy and allow the country to compete economically on a global scale without squandering intellectual capital. This book does not argue for a wholesale recovery of the original program—this history demonstrates that the educators who designed Advanced Placement understood education as a human enterprise, which is to say that AP was never meant to be beyond reproach. Hubristic as its developers may have been about manipulating the nation's social order, they recognized the interests that drove their participation in the program's development to be historically specific, aligned with some goals and dismissive of others.

Those exams, and the courses they capped off, were the culmination of the work of many people, spanning many years, to rethink American education and especially the eleventh through fourteenth grades (see fig. 1). Before the College Board took over, the exams were most directly the product of a committee headed by Kenyon College president Gordon Keith Chalmers and Central High School principal William Hafner Cornog. Under the aegis of the Ford Foundation, they sought to humanize secondary schooling by setting high standards for liberal arts courses with distinct disciplinary approaches. Their committee's report, called the *School and College Study for Admission with Advanced Standing*, is the most immediate blueprint for the AP program. The Kenyon Committee incorporated and responded to the output of another committee that was also funded by the Ford Foundation. The Blackmer Committee, a group based at Andover, produced *General Education in School and College*, a report recommending that schools and colleges reconsider the role each kind of institution could play in making education more efficient and meaningful.

The members of both these committees wrote into the educational conversations of their time. James Conant, president of Harvard, was a major influence on their plans. Although he did not serve on either of those committees, those who did were shaped by his work on the Educational Policies Commission, his book *Education in a Divided World*, his support of both a Jeffersonian system of public schooling and of broad access to the liberal arts, and his role in shaping the Educational Testing Service. He had a large, if indirect, influence on the AP program and would become one of its champions on the national stage.

COMMITTEES LEADING TO THE ADVANCED PLACEMENT PROGRAM

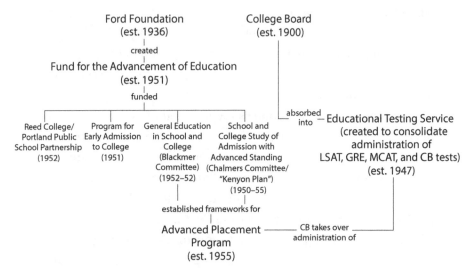

In part I, I tell this story in detail. Chapter 1 looks at Conant's intellectual influences and his early books on reform. Chapters 2 and 3 turn to the Blackmer and Kenyon Committees. The picture that emerges is one of ego, elitism, imperfection, zeal, and hope.

Many of the debates present at the program's inception are ongoing. In part II, I turn to the present and rely on journalism, legislation, and scholarship to inform arguments about the program's influence on student perception of the humanities. Chapters 4 through 6 build on the previous chapters' explications of ways the original Advanced Placement program represented an ideological argument about how to best navigate and possibly resolve some of the most pressing tensions present in American life. When I began work on this book, the top four best-selling exams were in English Literature and Composition, English Language and Composition, United States History, and US Government and Politics. The College Board has since removed information about the sales of specific exams from its website.[52] In part II, I give the arguments inherent to the AP program's navigation of the extant tensions as they relate to these exams and disciplines.

Chapter 4 explains how the College Board's new digital platform, AP Classroom, distorts the study of history as it distances high school and college work. By obviating the need for a teacher and encouraging the organization of information in discrete units, AP Classroom desiccates the course meaning in multiple ways. By focusing on the AP English courses, chapter 5 demonstrates how the program fails to align with the vision for the liberal arts outlined by contemporary thinkers. As of 2020, exams in English courses comprised the largest number of tests administered by the College Board. With 573,171 test takers, AP English Language was the most popular exam on offer; 380,136 students sat for an exam in AP English Literature. Taken together, these two subjects represent only a twentieth of the program's courses but nearly 19 percent of exams administered. This chapter demonstrates why the College Board's partnership with Finetune, a startup aiming to "objectively" grade essays using artificial intelligence, is a disaster for secondary English education. Chapter 6 describes changes to the Advanced Placement US Government and Politics course. In 2018, the College Board revised the course to mandate readings and a sequence. The company promises a "nonpartisan" approach that simultaneously meets requirements for high school civics and college-level political science. I'm unconvinced it does either.

As I've mentioned, the book's conclusion consolidates what I know about the current structure of Advanced Placement. The epilogue is about my experience trying to meet students' needs through a balance of the program's mandates, lessons from my own doctoral training, collaboration with a colleague, and concern for the always-fragile state of American democracy.

In 1954, the decision in favor of Oliver Brown recognized that high-quality education must be broadly accessible because "it is the very foundation of good citizenship. Today it is a principal instrument in awakening the child to cultural values, in preparing him for later professional training, and in helping him to adjust normally to his environment."[53] The decision codified equity as a formal educational value and, in the spirit of this decision, No Child Left Behind and the Every Student Succeeds Act have challenged the idea that academic success belongs to a select few. Those policies also secured financial support for the rise of Advanced Placement as a market-based solution to the problem of unequal access.

Notions of equity and progress drive my own politics. When I started researching the program's history, I sighed at the original committees' demographic makeup—privileged, white, Protestant men so self-assured about their rarefied understanding of the nation, its values, and its trajectory that they felt entitled to make prescriptions about its maintenance. True, Advanced Placement was designed as a shortcut for a population of students dominated by rich white boys to maintain their status. Aspects of the program's core philosophy are politically troubling. But surprisingly—not least of all, to me—there are intellectual orientations in the original vision that are worth perpetuating.

The current path is wrong. The Advanced Placement program's spread may sound like a step forward in terms of educational justice, but it represents a hoarding of power and wealth and the destruction of some of the "cultural values" *Brown v. Board of Education* sought to protect. As wealthy private schools and top-ranked colleges stop participating, public school students' success in the program relies on conformity to the increasingly rigid expectations of a powerful centralized authority. The College Board's approach to education is antidemocratic.

PART I
Validity

CHAPTER 1

Rational Reform

On September 18, 1936, Harvard president James Conant addressed an audience of administrators, faculty, staff, and guests at the school's tercentenary ceremony. Projecting confidence and responsibility, his authority bolstered by the pomp and circumstance of cap and gown, and a podium festooned with boughs, Conant offered a vision for the university's role in American life. Harvard would lead "the development of a national culture based on the study of the past," a task for which "one condition is essential—absolute freedom of expression, absolutely unmolested inquiry."[1] Disruptive as new discoveries and debates threatened to be, maintaining what Conant claimed to be a long national tradition of free, methodical truth-seeking would steady the country's thinking and secure its unity. So committed to rationality was Conant that he was reticent to condemn Nazism until after Kristallnacht in 1938. Regarding the Harvard tercentenary two years prior, he wrote, "We shall welcome the German scholars here as scholars whether they be Nazis in their hearts or not. We shall welcome the Italians here even if they be Fascists which, from my point of view, is equally objectionable. We shall welcome the rector of the University of Heidelberg in spite of his Nazism and as a representative of an ancient university." Conant's decision making was dispassionate.[2]

Throughout Conant's career in education, he tried to temper political and cultural chaos through different means—debate at Harvard, reform and standardized testing in public schools. By 1964, a
Crimson reviewer wrote that in his book *Shaping Education Policy*,
it had become clear that "he abhors the organizational mess that
is now American education," and "that Conant's whole heart is in
planning, order, effectiveness, and a perfect Weberian 'rationality.'"[3]
Calm, meticulous, and self-possessed, Conant liked things organized. He knew that some people faulted his "cold certainty," but
he insisted he was just shy.[4] A more sympathetic *Crimson* writer explained that his reputation as "Conant the Cold-Fish Chemist" was
only half-deserved—he was more than a stuffed shirt, even if he was
aloof.[5] Conant's composure should not distract from his dynamism.
He worked to shape the world he wanted to live in—one with a minimum of the kind of class-based social turmoil that, after his experience living through the Great Depression, he worried threatened
to upend the American experiment. Rationality was his best offense
against lawlessness.

Born to an old Massachusetts family of mixed financial fortune,
Conant had won a merit-based competition for admission to the Rox-
bury Latin School. His admission to Harvard as an undergraduate
with advanced standing in chemistry was a serendipitous opportunity granted "largely on the basis of one schoolteacher's judgment."[6]
He believed in economic and social advancement based on academic merit. He recognized his own path was one of contingency,
luck, and evolving notions of intelligence, and he hoped to clear
more rational, intentional paths for rising generations. In his autobiography, he wrote of shifting institutional expectations: "Only in the
1950s, with the introduction of the advanced placement program of
the College Board, did it again become possible to anticipate certain
college courses. . . . The similarity between this development and
the dispensation I was granted in 1910 needs no underlining. I must
admit to a certain chagrin that I record that it was only after I had left

the university administration that the advanced placement program was accepted."[7] Conant's appointment to the Harvard presidency was controversial. Some Brahmins worried that Conant's background— he was not born a blueblood—meant that he would be out of step with the mores governing the campus. He did flout the rules, but he did so in ways he hoped would promote stability, fairness, and the best of American heritage.

Conant's contributions to Cold War education reform were both theoretical and practical, and he was determined to manifest the ideas he believed would secure the continuity of American political and cultural traditions as well as the nation's prosperity. He understood education reform as the means to protect democracy from Communism by promoting both class fluidity and intelligent, humanistic liberalism. Although he did not serve on any of the committees responsible for AP, his work invited such a development. By 1961, he wrote, "The success of the Advanced Placement program in the last few years is one of the most encouraging signs of real improvement in our educational system."[8] He thought the AP program held the promise to uphold those values.

CONANT VERSUS DEWEY

Like all other reformers, Conant's most concrete, logistical recommendations arose from philosophical and historical contexts. When he entered into the public conversation about secondary schooling in the 1930s, John Dewey's influence was impossible to ignore.[9] By 1959, in *The Child, the Parent, and the State*, a history of American secondary schooling from 1905 to 1930, Conant wrote, "I am struck with the way the new ideas fit the new problems as a key fits a lock. . . . After closing John Dewey's volume, *Democracy and Education*, I had the feeling that, like the Austro-Hungarian empire of the nineteenth century, if John Dewey hadn't existed he would have had to be invented."[10] He argued that progressive education was a means of coping with the expansion and diversification of public schooling. He celebrated the optimism and public-spiritedness of the progressive reform movement but warned that "complex social and economic changes" had rendered Dewey's vision for public education outdated. Conant found Dewey's stance too unsophisticated and sentimental—too disorderly—to meet the country's needs.

The thinkers shared some values.[11] They both believed that American education should facilitate class mobility. Dewey had advocated for the amelioration of inequities through education, taking seriously the notion that "it is the aim of progressive education to take part in correcting unfair privilege and unfair deprivation, not to perpetuate them."[12] Like Dewey, Conant argued that American education should aid in the development of democratic attitudes, though they differed in approach. Dewey recommended "simplifying and ordering the factors of the disposition it is wished to develop; purifying and idealizing the existing social customs; creating a wider and better balanced environment than that by which the young would be likely, if left to themselves, to be influenced."[13] Dewey had also argued that goodness was innate in children, who were vulnerable to corruption by "evil institutions and customs." Instead, schools should "provide an environment in which native powers will be put to better uses." For Dewey, the best hope for American education was that, "by various agencies, unintentional and designed, a society transforms uninitiated and seemingly alien beings into robust trustees of its own resources and ideals."[14] In other words, Dewey advocated for citizenship through the fulfillment of one's unique potential. Harmony and concord would follow from a society of diverse individuals united by contentment, mutual respect, class mobility, and a sense of freedom.

By the 1940s, when Conant's work in school reform accelerated, public faith in Dewey's predominance was waning. Parents and teachers pinned their frustrations about schooling on Dewey, even if their complaints were traceable to a teacher's misunderstanding of his principles or faulty implementation of his suggestions. Later,

Conant theorized that in practice, the Deweyan emphasis on the child and on "learning by doing" had gained popularity among well-intentioned educators who found themselves helpless to offer meaningful instruction to an increasingly heterogeneous population of students, not because of the philosophy's enduring value.[15] In 1959, Fred Hechinger explained, "It is not so much that Dewey was singled out as hero or villain; he stood alone. He was the only major American philosopher to make education his domain. This condemned him to become the involuntary creator of the curse he warned most consistently against: an educational dogma."[16]

A chemist by training, Conant abhorred dogma.[17] By the 1940s, he was among a new class of reformers seeking to innovate.[18] Conant had spent his professional life searching for solutions, first to problems in the physical world, as a chemist, and later, to problems in the social and political realms, as an administrator and a diplomat. His experiences in academia and government led him to understand public education simultaneously as one of America's greatest assets and as a thorny, unsolved problem consummate in size to his ability to tackle it.

Like Dewey, he hoped that schools could become nodes of democracy in action, cultivating both academic and vocational talents under one roof while facilitating respect among students of diverse backgrounds, interests, and aptitudes. But unlike his predecessor, for Conant, maintaining liberalism also demanded a liberal arts curriculum on a broad scale.[19] Also contra Dewey, Conant was firmly attached to the maintenance of hierarchy. In Conant's vision, the "vast instrument," as he called the public education system, would be tuned to rational identification of the students who were intellectually capable of leadership and of making beneficial scientific advances. He wanted to pattern American higher education after German research institutions producing knowledge for national security and to align the rest of the system with those pinnacles.[20] Conant's advocacy for reform based on intellectual merit and technocracy set the stage for the Advanced Placement program.

CONANT'S JEFFERSON

Conant's argument for the historical specificity of Dewey's philosophy is surprising given the strength of his early commitment to Thomas Jefferson's ideology as timeless. Understanding what Jefferson represented to Conant is essential to appreciating his work in the field of education.[21] In *My Several Lives*, Conant's autobiography, he recalled speaking at a conference with conviction, but without much philosophical or historical grounding, about the necessity of developing scholarships for Harvard students who might otherwise have trouble paying tuition. An audience member pointed him to Jefferson as an intellectual role model. "From then on," Conant declared, "I was a Jeffersonian."[22] In other words, Conant's investigation into Jefferson began by reading backwards to justify his own convictions and to find rhetorical support for them. Of course, as is the case for any American, it is impossible to disentangle Jefferson's invisible and inescapable influence from the details of Conant's upbringing and intellectual orientation. But it is fair to say that he found in Jefferson a sort of guiding light for articulating the aims of American education, even if those ideals sounded cleaner and less complicated to implement than they would turn out to be in practice.

Critics of midcentury meritocracy like Nicholas Lemann and Michael Sandel have documented Conant's reliance on Jeffersonian schemes.[23] But "Jeffersonian" is an ambiguous word. It has always been possible to use Jefferson's writings to justify more than one narrative, more than one political agenda. He knew this himself. In 1823, Jefferson wrote to historian William Johnson, who was working on a history of American political parties, about his own letters and papers:

> Selections from these after my death, may come out successively as
> the maturity of circumstances may render their appearance season-
> able. But multiplied testimony, multiplied views will be necessary

to give solid establishment to truth. Much is known to one which is
not known to another; and no one knows every thing. It is the sum
of individual knoleges which is to make up the whole truth, and to
give its correct current thro' future time.[24]

Elusive in part because he was prolific, Jefferson never had a stable,
one-dimensional reputation in his lifetime, and it has remained dynamic centuries after his death. But Conant projected confidence in
his interpretation of the founder's legacy.

The educational scheme to which Conant most frequently referred
appears in several of Jefferson's works—his *Notes on the State of Virginia*, multiple revisions of his "Bill for the Diffusion of Knowledge,"
and a letter to John Adams all outline iterations of the same plan.[25]
According to Jefferson, the twin goals of American public education
were to be investing in the public's ability to safeguard itself against
power imbalances while channeling the right people into the right
social and economic positions. Jefferson's plans display his commitment to using math to solve social problems: communities were to be
divided into squared miles, young men were to be educated for a few
years "at the public expense" to protect their basic rights as citizens,
and a select few would continue on for advanced liberal arts and
professional training, relying either on family money or tax dollars
for support. Jefferson proposed the scheme to Adams as a way to
winnow from each generation a natural governing aristocracy based
on "virtue and talent." A hierarchical system of free schools would
identify "worth and genius . . . from every condition of life," and prepare its holders for self-governance by "defeating the competition of
wealth and birth for public trusts." While liberating the public from the
"aristocracy of the clergy," education would also raise "the mass of the
people to the high ground of moral respectability necessary to their
own safety, and to orderly government; and would have completed
the great object of qualifying them to select the veritable aristoi."[26] Inherent to the plan was optimism about the future, the transformative

power of education, and the potential for existence of good government. "Science," he wrote to Adams, "is progressive."[27]

The plans for education that Jefferson—and Conant—took to be rational and straightforwardly democratic are thorny. From the start, John Adams was unconvinced. He replied to Jefferson's letter, "Your distinction between natural and artificial Aristocracy does not appear to me well-founded." Adams skewered Jefferson's idealism. Both Jefferson and Adams despised the concept of inherited power, but Adams mocked the enslaver's obsession with purity as part of a romantic view in which, as Adams put it sardonically, "our pure, virtuous, public Spirited federative Republic will last forever, govern the Globe and introduce the perfection of Man." Adams argued that the nation was already corrupted by "sacrifice of national interest and honor to private and party objects." To him, there was not enough meaning in the distinction between Jefferson's natural and artificial aristocracies because too much power was corrosive no matter how it was attained. Adams would not endorse replacing one corruptible hierarchy with another, and he replied to Jefferson with a challenge to confront the injustice inherent to the country's emerging system of banks and property.[28]

Today, scholars warn about the dangers evident in Jefferson's impulses to organize American life. Jefferson's logic relied on, in the words of Karen Fields and Barbara Fields, "self-deceiving" rationalizations about the nature of race. In *Notes on the State of Virginia* and in letters, Jefferson invented racial difference and justified subjugation through scientific and algebraic argument.[29] Historian Alan Taylor has offered one possible reconciliation of Jefferson's idealistic plans for education with his reliance on the existence of a slave caste. Jefferson's scheme for public education was an antidote to his description of what the children of enslavers, "nursed, educated, and daily exercised in tyranny," experienced at home. In *Notes on the State of Virginia*, Jefferson warned, "The whole commerce between master and slave is a perpetual exercise of the most boisterous passions, the most unremitting despotism on the one part, and degrading submissions on the other. Our children see this, and learn to imitate it. . . . This quality is the germ of all education in him."[30] In Taylor's account, Jefferson pressured rising generations to remediate the consequences of their ancestors' shortcomings, an end requiring high levels of autonomous thought. This plan to make Virginia more democratic backfired.[31]

Conant could not have had access to these critiques. His consistent allusions to Jefferson grew out of the voguish interpretations of the third president's work during the early twentieth century.[32] Throughout the 1930s and 1940s, Conant was far from alone in calling for unification behind Jefferson's vision for American life.[33] In 1939, Franklin Delano Roosevelt committed to the establishment of a Jefferson memorial, in part because he was so impressed by journalist Claude Bowers's popular *Jefferson and Hamilton: The Struggle for Democracy in America*.[34] Without acknowledgment of contradiction, Bowers simultaneously celebrated Jefferson as "a humanitarian ahead of his time" and "a master who loved his slaves." Bowers painted Jefferson as anti-aristocratic, citing his "interest in democracy and popular rights" and emphasizing the influence of his father's background as a farmer. Despite the unabashed enthusiasm for Jefferson the book evinces, the *New York Times* praised Bowers's account for being objective and unsentimental. In 1945, Bowers published a biography of Jefferson that sought to "rescue a very human being from the wilderness of myth and fable," after decades of accounts that offered him up as a "symbol, a flag, a steel engraving, a philosopher in an ivory tower, or, more often, a cunning politician spinning his web of intrigue in dark corners."[35] But by then, Bowers had already been instrumental in contributing to the mythos that informed the ways readers like Roosevelt and Conant could make the past usable on a broad scale.

In 1927, six years before Conant's appointment as president of Harvard, Vernon Louis Parrington's *Main Currents in American Thought* won the Pulitzer Prize for History. The sprawling three-volume study delineated an outline of American intellectual history based on brief sketches of thinkers Parrington admired. "A barely controlled resentment of Harvard and of the Brahmin culture it served lingered in his mind and occasionally broke through the surface of his history," wrote Richard Hofstadter. Like Conant, as a Harvard undergraduate, Parrington had felt like an outsider on campus, and, as was also true for Conant, his critiques of the establishment would go on to shape the institution's essential functions.[36] Parrington's history encouraged what Hofstadter would call "the democratic idealism of the Progressive tradition."[37] In Parrington's account, Jefferson's biography demonstrated that the unknown and the powerless could win in a struggle against the established and the powerful.[38]

The values informing Parrington's account are visible in Conant's work. In what today reads as an outrageous disregard for slavery, Parrington wrote, "The America of Jefferson's day was a simple world, with a simple domestic economy," with "no closely organized class groups."[39] Conant parroted this description, explaining in a lecture that Jefferson's vision for education was, in part, a response to "the simpler society of his day."[40] Parrington argued that Jefferson fought against "the inequalities which spring from the progressive monopolization of natural resources, with augmenting corruption and injustice."[41] Conant blamed "ruthless and greedy exploitation of both natural and human resources" for increasing stratification.[42] Parrington found Jefferson's idealism inspiring: "That Jefferson was an idealist was singularly fortunate for America; there was need of idealism to leaven the materialistic realism of the times."[43] The very notion of idealism guided Conant's reform efforts: "If we as educators accept the American ideal, then this acceptance must be the major premise for all our thinking."[44] For some, the word "Jeffersonian" might conjure up an aristocratic statesman in a velvet waistcoat, detached from practical concerns about money because of his mother's (Jane Randolph) family fortune and his wife's (Martha Wayles) inheritance.[45]

But for Parrington, and for Conant, what historians Charles and Mary Beard called "the magic of Jefferson's name" represented democracy, concern for the common good, and a principled, rational form of idealism rooted in a distinctly American philosophy. Jefferson's life was proof positive that it was possible to translate radical ideas about political equality into living institutions—or at least it was possible to do so rhetorically.

Throughout the 1920s and 1930s, Jefferson's legacy also represented a uniquely American strain of intellectualism. Parrington's chapter on Jefferson ends with the same quotation that would eventually appear on the memorial's frieze, dedicated in 1943: "I have sworn upon the altar of God eternal hostility against every form of tyranny over the mind of man." Connecting Jefferson's political and educational philosophies was faith in the polity's interest in and ability to make rational decisions for itself by engaging with the information available to them. In Roosevelt's address laying the memorial's cornerstone, he celebrated Jefferson's "transcendent" political philosophy and the complexity of his thought, his commitments to art, architecture, invention, and science, and his role in establishing schools and universities as part of the nation's infrastructure. Education and erudition were to be neither elitist nor detached. Roosevelt emphasized that Jefferson "lived, as we live, in the midst of a struggle between rule by the self-chosen individual or the self-appointed few. . . . He believed, as we do, that the average opinion of mankind is in the long run superior to the dictates of the self-chosen."[46] In Roosevelt's last words to the American people before his death on Jefferson's birthday in April 1945, he opened with an appeal "to the living memory of Thomas Jefferson—one of the greatest of all democrats; and I want to make it clear that I am spelling the word 'democrats' with a small 'd.'" Jeffersonian contemplation was individualistic but not selfish—it was in service of the public good. By 1940, Conant worried that "popular enthusiasm for enlightenment, for overturning dogmas, for intellectual exploration, has temporarily waned," and with it, the individualism that was crucial to democratic governance. Preventing "the extinction of the Jeffersonian tradition" was a matter of preserving a form of American identity that embraced both empowerment of masses and intellectual autonomy.[47]

Jefferson's philosophies had the added benefit of providing strong support for Conant's own belief in the necessity of an intellectual, social hierarchy. His commitment to the concept is unsurprising for a man who understood his own autobiography in terms of climbing from childhood obscurity into an adulthood defined by a privately endowed position with vast public influence. He wanted to pave the way for what Lemann called "little Conants."[48] Like Jefferson, Conant believed that hierarchy was not only necessary but vital to the American way of life, as long as it was not based on heritable wealth. In the *Atlantic,* he continued that his ideal third-party American

> believes in equality of opportunity, not equality of rewards; but, on the other hand, he will be lusty in wielding the axe against the root of inherited privilege. To prevent the growth of a caste system, which he abhors, he will be resolute in his demand to confiscate (by constitutional methods) all property once a generation. He will demand really effective inheritance and gift taxes and the breaking up of trust funds and estates.[49]

Conant put a tremendous amount of faith in a public system of education's ability to guard against the development of a caste system. For Conant, slow, limited class mobility within a hierarchical framework was an indisputable American ideal.

Conant appreciated how Jefferson's educational system hypothetically aligned with and supported his political one, as part of a complete social and political scheme for American life—in Conant's words, a "total plan."[50] Parrington had celebrated Jefferson as "our first great leader to erect a political philosophy native to the economics and experience of America."[51] In his 1940 lecture on the potential for a Jeffersonian education system to keep America afloat, Conant enumerated this philosophy's guiding principles:

> a belligerent belief in individual freedom; complete confidence in the powers of man's intelligence to overcome all obstacles; the assumption of a society without hereditary classes, without an aristocracy; a differentiation of labors with a corresponding differentiation in the types of education (but no ruling caste, no hereditary educational privileges, everyone to be "as good as everyone else"); widespread education for all citizens so that political decisions might be "rational."[52]

Without a trace of irony or awareness about the presence of slavery and disenfranchisement during the eighteenth and nineteenth centuries, Conant mourned the passing of time and urged a return to that century, in which he believed, "Dominating all was the doctrine of the maximum independence of the individual, the minimum of social control by organized society."[53] As a liberal in the classical sense, both the idea of teaching future generations to lead and the Enlightenment-era rationality that is a hallmark of Jefferson's scheme appealed to Conant. So did the notion that it was possible to help organize a society without controlling it in the style of an authoritarian or a totalitarian.

APPLYING IDEALS

Conant's interest in understanding what he came to call "human organizations," and in turn, his investment in a healthy, democratic public education system, grew out of his academic and diplomatic work and his role as a consultant for the Manhattan Project. His experiences navigating difficult moral decisions with wide impact led him to believe that human behavior could—and should—be studied with the remove of a scientist. At the same time, he advocated for an understanding of science that foregrounded the social interactions and intellectual frameworks that made discovery possible. For Conant, both the social and the physical worlds were full of patterns and systems waiting to be uncovered, experimented upon, and analyzed in the name of progress.[54]

Conant described much of his work in education as "in harmony with the EPC," a group to which he had been appointed chairman in 1941. The Educational Policies Commission was a private council of educators—later, Columbia president Dwight D. Eisenhower would join—that made research-based policy recommendations to government officials. Conant's tenure with the group was formative. As the Second World War challenged Americans to define and defend their ideological and moral boundaries, the group produced a report called *Education for All American Youth* that sought to provide stewardship in perfecting a national intellectual infrastructure.[55] The book began with a "strong and unanimous" rejection of federal control over curriculum but a demand for federal aid.

Linking the values and the tangible results the group hoped to promote, the report offered a history of the future they hoped to avoid through their work. Warning against declining public interest in education, they wrote that in a dystopian American future, citizens would think, "each added bit of federal activity in education seemed desirable and, taken by itself, quite harmless. The common man was beset by many economic and political problems which seemed, at first glance, far more important than these issues of educational control." But eventually, federal overreach "assumed a rigidity of pattern and procedure," and "the locally administered high school, for so many years the center of the American dream of equal opportunity through education," would find itself "in the great wastebasket of history."[56] The group hoped to maintain a sense of initiative in local communities. They wrestled with how to make education meaningful and beneficial for a diverse range of students, like "Edith of Suburbia," "Max, born in Metropolis," and "Gilbert, who lives across the street from the post office in Farmville." Authors imagined that George, "a Negro boy," "superior" in "intellectual ability," might have different needs from Gertrude, "who is rarely dressed attractively."

For all the group's insistence on autonomy, it acknowledged the need for some degree of coherence. In attempting to conjure a system that might work for all of its imaginary students, the commission tried to focus not only on differences but on potential commonalities. In so doing, they limned the borders of American identity from on high. "All American youth are citizens," "all American youth are now living in the American culture," "all American youth have the capacity to think rationally," they declared, without concern for the ways these stipulations could exclude immigrants, people of color, students with learning disabilities, and other minorities. And yet, there is tenderness in the group's stated aims: "These youth—all of them—are to be the heirs and trustees for all that is good or bad in our civilization.... Each of them is a human being, more precious than material goods or systems of philosophy. None of them is to be carelessly wasted."[57] And so, the group advocated for comprehensive high schools that would offer, at minimum, two years of enriching, unifying "liberal education" and then options for further academic study or vocational training. The Educational Policies Commission resisted standardization and imagined a cheery democratic education system as an integrated network, with all of its constituents imbued with vitality, ambition, and agency.

HARVARD'S RED BOOK

In 1945, the year after the Educational Policies Commission published its vision for a public education system that would nimbly, righteously, and magically balance federal, state, and local interests, authority, and money, Conant wrote the introduction to *General Education in a Free Society*. In 1943, he had appointed a faculty committee to consider the "continuance of the liberal and humane tradition" for "the great majority of each generation, not the comparatively small minority who attend our four-year colleges." Conant's introduction, titled "Objectives of a General Education," promised the book would address the "entire problem of providing adequate education for all American youth" from the vantage of Harvard's faculty. In support of the committee's humanistic definition of adequacy, he wrote, "Unless the educational process includes at each level of maturity some continuing contact with those fields in which value judgments are of prime importance, it falls far short of the ideal."[58] As Jamie Cohen-Cole writes, "The democratic society that the committee imagined would be held together by right-minded people who could speak to and judge one another according to universal rational standards." Holding up Harvard (home base for the committee members) as a model, the report's authors imagined the country as "a disparate community of experts held together by the rational abilities of citizens to communicate across the boundaries of expertise."[59] The report, which aligned secondary and university education, was intended to serve as a model for schools and colleges across the nation.

The authors of *General Education* were entering into a long-standing national debate over the place of the liberal arts in secondary schools.[60] In 1893, the "Committee of Ten," chaired by then president of Harvard, Charles Eliot, had issued recommendations for "uniformity in school programmes and in requirements for admission to college."[61] All American students were to have access to streamlined, standardized, modernized coursework aligned with college-level academics. According to Diane Ravitch, "Almost immediately, the [Committee of Ten's] report came under fire from opposite directions. On one side were the traditionalists, who saw the report as an insult to their own field. . . . Attacking from the other extreme were critics who objected to the report's support for academic education for all students, even those who did not plan to go to college."[62] The report's publication precipitated decades of debate among critics and reformers about the proper function of public schools and their responsibilities to individual students, colleges, the workforce, and the project of self-governance. Some detractors resented the imposition of a ruling class's will and its conception of success. Some argued that the primacy of academic subjects would make school irrelevant to a majority of American students, who had neither the inclination nor the use for such an education.[63] The scheme's popularity waxed and waned, and high schools varied in their commitments to its prescriptions.[64]

By the 1930s and 1940s, influential defenders of a humanistic approach to education at the secondary level included Columbia's Jacques Barzun, Stanford's Sidney Hook, and reporter Walter Lippmann.[65] Robert M. Hutchins and Mortimer J. Adler, the president and a professor of philosophy at the University of Chicago, respectively, were some of the most vocal champions of centering the transmission of a coherent American cultural heritage.[66] In a series of book reviews, John Dewey rejected Hutchins's call to "purify" curriculum by wresting apart general and vocational education and insisting on a hierarchy of texts and values. Dewey warned that "culture and vocation" were inseparable, and that it did a disservice to students to treat them otherwise while endowing institutions with the authority to promote narrow visions of "truth" about human nature. By 1952, Hutchins elucidated the principles of "liberal education" and clarified that, in agreement with Dewey, he believed a major goal of American education should be helping students become workers with firm understandings of the meaning of their work, both personally and for the sake of society. But he argued that this mooring could come only from dedicated time away from vocational training and other practical concerns.[67]

The authors of *General Education* sought a middle path. In a chapter titled "Unity Conditioned by Difference," the authors revealed their central concern, echoing Conant's introductory note and his work with the Educational Policy Commission: "How can general education be so adapted to different ages and, above all, differing abilities and outlooks, that it can appeal deeply to each, yet remain in goal and essential teaching the same for all? The answer to this question, it seems not too much to say, is the key to anything like complete democracy."[68] The men responsible for the report professed fidelity to humanistic study as they supported a society organized on the basis of "common standards" and the sorting of students according to the intelligence and ability evident in their responses to a universal—but flexible—curriculum.

As the *Crimson* reported, committee members such as Raphael Demos and Arthur Schlesinger Jr. wanted broad-reaching "general education" programs "to prepare men for citizenship by making them aware of their common cultural heritage. Through required courses in the humanities, social sciences, and natural sciences, students would become acquainted with disciplines other than their own, and would be the richer as individuals, no matter what their occupation."[69] For the men on this committee, and others like them, as campuses across the nation, including Harvard, welcomed increasingly heterogeneous freshman classes, general education requirements could unify students, regardless of where they were coming from or where they were going. Attempting to institutionalize that kind of transformation was an ambitious project. It seems easy enough to critique a committee of white, male Harvard professors for perpetuating fantasies of a common national culture as an antidote to Communism. But the same year they issued their recommendations, Richard Wright published *Black Boy*, which includes a celebration of books as a "cultural transfusion" that imbued him with the sense that "America could be shaped nearer to the hearts of those that lived in it."[70] To Wright, the notion of a creedal American identity was worth perpetuating.

Conant's support for liberal education was part of a broader geopolitical strategy. In 1945, he delivered a series of lectures at Yale on the teaching of science in school and college. Drawing an analogy between careers in science and the military, he encouraged his audience to think of both in terms of strategy and tactics rather than dogma. "Whether we have . . . intelligence enough to proceed with the next stage in the development of civilization will in part depend on education," he warned. "This fact in itself would be justification enough for all of us who spend our lives trying to explore new and better ways of 'perpetuating learning to posterity.'"[71] Intellectualism was crucial to Conant's vision for defense.

EDUCATION IN A DIVIDED WORLD

Education in a Divided World was Conant's attempt to foster public agreement and national planning on pedagogical philosophies and goals as a means of combating totalitarianism. In that volume, he sought to reconcile many of the tensions that still persist in American education—meeting national, local, and individual needs; attaining the proper balance of vocational and liberal arts education for each student; navigating teacher autonomy; and determining concrete academic standards and attendant standardized testing. In 1949, Conant wrote the following to Educational Policies Commission chairman John K. Norton: "By the time a person is a young man he is a product of a cultural pattern and his thinking and acting is heavily conditioned by this pattern."[72] He was joining a long line of reformers who sought to reshape what those patterns were and how schooling formed them.[73]

Conant expanded on how education could maintain the distinction between what he called "early American type" and the "Russian model" of "classless society." In *Education in a Divided World*, Conant made clear that, to him, the public education system was bound up with questions of national identity. He invited readers to "imagine a society in which each citizen, be he a skilled worker, a manager, a storekeeper, a professor, or a farmer, would have the minimum interest in his own or other people's occupational status, the maximum interest in how far his own or other people's conduct approximated the universally recognized ethical ideal," involving such traits as "individual integrity in dealing with other people, human sympathy, and moral courage."[74] Bound by what Jefferson had called, in the Declaration of Independence, "the laws of Nature," citizens would be honest, kind, and brave. Conant's firsthand experiences of the social cleavages caused by the Great Depression and World War II, compounded by the threat of communism, meant that, to him, sustaining democracy entailed limiting resentment about and increasing access to class mobility within a capitalist system.

Conant was not only concerned about mediating the nation's internal struggles but about using the system to defend against a foreign ideological threat. He hoped the same system that he understood to be fundamentally American would protect that national identity in the face of totalitarianism. In *Education in a Divided World*, he defended the public education system as "the product of our special history, a concrete manifestation of our unique ideals, and the vehicle by which the American concept of democracy may be transmitted to our future citizens. The strength of this republic is therefore intimately connected with the success or failure of our system of public education."[75] Conant promoted schools as potential sites for translating ideals into reality and training future generations to understand the American project in light of those values.

In terms of realizing greater opportunity for all American students, Conant argued in *Education in a Divided World* that academic and curricular control over schools must be local, in keeping with the recommendations of the Educational Policies Commission. At the same time, he again advocated that the basis of tax support should be federal in order to equalize opportunity and maximize fluidity for students of diverse backgrounds. Although the concept of educational equity had not yet crystallized, Conant had some understanding of entrenched bigotry as a threat to the American way of life before the passage of *Brown v. Board of Education*. Especially in the wake of Swedish sociologist Gunnar Myrdal's *An American Dilemma: The Negro Problem and Modern Democracy*, which quantified and laid bare racial inequalities for a global readership, international demands illuminated America's hypocrisy regarding the treatment of its Black citizens.[76] Conant addressed this tension explicitly when he wrote, "Our national idealism and our social practice are in head-on collision in these areas. . . . In competition with the Soviet philosophy our present social mores on these matters are perhaps the most vulnerable spots in our armor."[77] For Conant, domestic tranquility was a matter of foreign policy. He hoped to increasingly put American ideals into practice, both at home and globally. But he envisioned incremental change.

This view met with resistance. In a review, Black philosopher Alain Locke wrote that Conant's "very moderate and commonsense approach" to ameliorating inequality of opportunity was "perhaps . . . the right prescription, since American public opinion likes its social medicine optimistically sugar-coated." Locke explained, "Fair educational practices must be federally reinforced and guaranteed; otherwise, in the realities of our present situation, a truly democratic educational system cannot be anticipated in the near future."[78] In Locke's view, under local control and initiative, change would be too slow and too painful for Black Southerners to bear. But Conant did not share Locke's sense of urgency. Instead, he urged patience with the system's ability to churn the nation's classes: "We must recognize the necessity of evolution rather than revolution in this field of equalizing advanced education." His concern for devising a system to identify and cultivate America's raw intellectual talent ignored the lost potential of underserved students.[79] Conant elevated the interests of the lower classes above those of the current elite, but his approach to redistributing resources was conservative.

At both the secondary and collegiate levels, Conant insisted that such an ideological war must be fought with ideas, and that students ought to be trained in the production of those ideas. He also was a vocal advocate for the development of "scientific manpower" in order to maintain the most sophisticated armament to protect those ideas.

Unlike fixed economic and social classes, academic stratification was not only socially acceptable but, to Conant's mind, necessary. He argued that tracking was beneficial to learning, whereas he believed "the alleged development of democratic spirit by mixing different types together . . . to be largely an illusion."[80] He believed in selective schooling that was rational above all else and complained of teachers and administrators who balked at the suggestion to turn education into the kind of system he envisioned. He dismissed schoolteachers who disliked the idea of "rational selectivity."

In keeping with Conant's vision for codified American identity and a rationally selected intellectual elite charged with maintaining and protecting it, his plan for curriculum was comprehensive inasmuch as it accounted not only for the science to which he had special allegiance but also for social science and the humanities. As proposed by the Harvard Committee's report, academic fields would work in tandem to produce a well-rounded citizenry. Conant wrote that in order to avoid catastrophe, "we must be better students of human nature than were our predecessors in this century . . . and that human beings do not behave like economic symbols. We must analyze our problems not only as economic questions but in terms of human motives, of social ideals, and the relation of these ideals to a well-formed picture of the future of the nation." While the humanities would aid in "cultivating enduring satisfactions" for workers in a "mechanized civilization," Conant hoped that the social sciences could provide answers to human problems. He put stock in anthropology, sociology, and psychology to use the same methodologies he trusted to develop a "new strategy" for curing the country's ills. With optimism and faith in rationality, he wrote, "Once this [strategy] is formulated and accepted there will be a rush of able pioneers to exploit the field. Confidence in our intellectual leaders will again surge upward. The Jeffersonian tradition will move forward."[81]

Since Conant understood science as a social enterprise, he advocated a humanist approach to the discipline. He proposed the division of knowledge into three disciplines: the humanities, the study of man, and cumulative knowledge. This final category included not only science but history, because he advocated for a scheme in which science teachers would "show the frame of reference in which they now operate." He took the teaching of science as a necessity for twentieth-century schools, given the development of careers in technology. But he cautioned, "To put the scientist on a pedestal because he is an impartial inquirer seems to me quite erroneous." Reinforced by the professional norms and strictures of a laboratory, Conant believed a scientist had no choice other than rationality, but "once he walks out of the door of the research institute—then he is as other men."[82] He argued that teaching science could not guarantee the transferability of the mindset to other realms of experience, and that such transference might not even be beneficial. Instead, it was important to learn about the relative benefits and drawbacks to the maintenance of the relevant habits of mind—all part of a process of uncovering and ameliorating gaps in knowledge.

THE EDUCATIONAL TESTING SERVICE

Despite Conant's repeated insistence on viewing education as a human endeavor, he often spoke about public education in technical, mechanized terms. In his view, realizing a more enlightened society meant adherence to technocratic solutions to social problems. He wrote, for instance, "In this century we have erected a new type of social instrument. Our secondary-school system is a vast engine which we are only beginning to understand. We are learning only slowly how to operate it for the public good."[83]

As Conant was writing *Education in a Divided World*, the Carnegie Foundation for the Advancement of Teaching appointed him chair of its new Committee on Testing.[84] That committee issued a recommendation for the Carnegie Corporation to sponsor the consolidation of the nation's major testing companies. ETS would produce tests with scientific precision and the other organizations would guide the programs of testing. The College Board, the American Council on Education, and the Carnegie Foundation would come together under the aegis of the Educational Testing Service. The new agency's trustees elected Conant chairman of the board. Conant waved off concerns about monopoly in his group's recommendation. By 1951, ETS won a lucrative government contract, increasing its influence and empowering its administrators.[85]

The consolidation of ETS also represented the resolution of a contest over the nature of college admissions. Conant's position of power represented a victory by believers in the notion of quantifiable IQ— ETS's aptitude tests would identify George from Detroit as a potential nuclear physicist, worthy of winning a spot in Harvard's incoming freshman class. Conant was obsessed with testing and admitting students on the basis of "aptitude" instead of "achievement" because he believed that money conferred an unfair advantage to students with access to better test preparation.[86]

During this "democratization" of college admissions, the College Board was thrown into an identity crisis about its mission. Historically, the group had been committed to determining criteria and standards for college admissions for a like-minded group of schools and students. But since 1944, the GI Bill had expanded the horizons of higher education, and even institutions that had been the preserve of the wealthy and well connected were reconsidering their admissions practices.[87] An expanded, more geographically diverse College Board membership forced a reckoning with the elitism that had bonded its stalwarts. And then newly subsumed under this larger agency, director Frank Bowles had to clarify its purpose given the changed landscape. Testing was becoming more "objective," and talk about best practices for assessing content knowledge gave way to discussion of standard deviations and means.[88]

There is an unresolved paradox at the heart of Conant's philosophy. Convinced of the need for renewed optimism about American progress and intellectual leadership from liberated minds, Conant's rejection of tyranny and desire to facilitate maximum mobility led to his support for standardized testing on a mass scale. For Conant, an objective metric like the SAT would ensure rational, impartial selection of the next generation of leaders based on intellectual merit, which tests would be able to identify. He did not indicate concern that the scheme he envisioned would, decades later, be criticized as a "regime."[89] For Conant, a system of standardized tests would be the best, most fair, objective arbiter of who belonged in which social strata. Despite his repeated insistence that schools prepare the nation's most gifted students for nuanced intellectual work, he held fast to a preoccupation with measuring reductive, tangible signs of belonging to distinct social classes.

Conant was successful in articulating a set of mutual concerns (strengthening national senses of identity and purpose without resorting to base nationalism, identification of talent, and well-rounded education before professionalization) among schools and colleges. His work invited public discourse about each of these problems. By 1960, the American Association of School Administrators presented him with their Distinguished Service Award because "more than any other man, by his logic, keen analysis, patriotic sacrifice, and courageous vision [Conant] rekindled the nation's flame of faith in free men's basic human values and rebuilt confidence in the public schools of America."[90] Conant was optimistic about the movement. "We are now beginning to set as our goal an education system through which the future members of the learned professions will be recruited from the able youth irrespective of family income," he wrote. "When we have moved further [in that direction], we will have attained an educational posture which is completely Jeffersonian."[91] *Education in a Divided World*'s influence on midcentury thought about American education and the growing impact of the Educational Testing Service cemented his values in schools and colleges. Conant's zealous faith in a technocratic, hierarchical public education system motivated widespread debate about how to best modify or realize the scheme he imagined.

By the time Conant published *Slums and Suburbs* in 1961, he acknowledged that idolatry of Jefferson was dangerous. In the book's introduction, he admitted, "Even the author of the Declaration of Independence, who advocated emancipation, also advocated the colonization of the freed Negro slave outside the United States." He was clear about his departure from his hero when he wrote, "The idea of the Negro and the white living together peacefully on equal terms in a free society was literally inconceivable to Jefferson. Yet after nearly two hundred years we are endeavoring to accomplish the building of just that type of society."[92] The civil rights movement forced a reckoning with what a "completely Jeffersonian" school system would be and do. After Conant's death in 1978, the *New York Times* lamented the loss of a leader who understood that "not even the best of universities could preserve the Jeffersonian concept of an aristocracy of talent unless the public schools provided a durable foundation."[93] His acute, cautionary 1960s writings about the best methods for building that base with heightened social awareness were too late. The AP program had already taken flight as a manifestation of the ideas he had championed throughout the 1940s and 1950s: America's school system would form a pyramid of both intellect and social class. Performance on standardized tests would determine ascension to its peak—Harvard.[94]

CHAPTER 2

Common Standards
and Common Purposes

In March 1930, when Alan Blackmer was 28, he contracted tuberculosis. He had to give up coaching tennis at Phillips Academy Andover that spring, but even chest pain and bed rest did not stop him from hosting Saturday night salons for his students.[1] Energized by cookies and cider, the boys would sprawl on the floor, listening to Tchaikovsky and solving the world's problems. By all accounts, Blackmer was an electrifying teacher and students sought opportunities to find themselves in his company. In his English class, students trusted him to help them articulate their inchoate thoughts about Shakespeare. Blackmer poured his heart into coaxing them to read and to write with more insight, clarity, and depth, and they reciprocated to the best of their abilities. When he revived the long-forsaken campus literary magazine a few months before falling ill, the school newspaper reported with affection, "Mr. Blackmer has been able to extract reasonably good material from a school apparently barren of all literary ambition."[2] An alumnus cited "the exciting and valuable experience of associating with him as a man" as one of the highlights of his academic career.[3]

When Blackmer retired in 1968, John Kemper, Andover's headmaster, celebrated the way he had "elevated the tone of manners and morals," and "performed so many unrecorded acts of kindness and goodwill."[4] Kemper's words made clear that many of Blackmer's efforts as an educator lived on in the minds of his students, even if his formal historical record is scant. His presence in the classroom inspired some published testimonials, and his administrative work on the Andover course catalog and revision of the curriculum is in the campus archives. He also worked on annotated editions of a few works of literature and published a smattering of articles about life at Andover. But like most teachers, much of his work was evanescent and intimate.

Blackmer's *New York Times* obituary did not commemorate these accomplishments. It did, however, name him as the "principal author of 'General Education in School and College,' [and] chairman of a university-school committee to study the transition of strong students from school to college." The obituary continued, "The result was the Advanced Placement Program now in effect in schools and colleges."[5] Although Blackmer was essential to the program's founding, the story is not so straightforward—his involvement in the program's development was one part of a much larger mosaic of competing interests. Organizations including private schools and colleges, the College Board, the Carnegie Corporation, and the Ford Foundation worked to change the nation's educational structures. As private funding insulated them, they made proclamations about serving the public good.

ELITE, GENERAL EDUCATION

Blackmer's pedagogy reflected the vogue for liberal education promoted by Conant and other university administrators. Conant had called for a reformed national program of "general education" (a term he considered interchangeable with "liberal education") that was soulful, democratic, and multidimensional.[6] As I explained in the previous chapter, Conant was at the fore of protecting and promoting the liberal arts on the national scene. By 1945, in response to the

Second World War, Conant had already delegated Harvard professors from a range of disciplines, including philosopher Raphael Demos and historian Arthur Schlesinger Jr., to produce a report outlining the university's plan for public schooling that would advance democracy. In the introduction to this report, *General Education in a Free Society*, Conant explained, "The heart of the problem of a general education is the continuance of the liberal and humane tradition. Neither the mere acquisition of information nor the development of special skills and talents can give the broad basis of understanding which is essential if our civilization is to be preserved."[7] The education Conant and his committee envisioned entailed developing relationships, habits of mind, and intellectual processes—not rote memorization. Schools and universities were the "ways and means by which a great instrument of American democracy can both shape the future and secure the foundations of our free society."[8] The committee sought to provide stewardship in erecting a national intellectual infrastructure while making a public argument about the relevance of the liberal arts to the nation's political health.

In the body of the report, the committee grappled with balancing an emphasis on autonomy for both students and educators with schematization and standardization that could promote equity and social cohesion. While insisting on the necessity of some sense of national unity, they admitted that the country was far too diverse for a prescriptive plan. "The question of common standards and common purposes," they wrote, could "help young people fulfill the unique, particular functions in life which it is in them to fulfill, and fit them so far as it can for those common spheres which, as citizens and heirs of a joint culture, they will share with others."[9] In navigating the tension between individual and collective, they were careful to align their recommendations with democratic practice:

> Unless teachers are free to enjoy the privileges of citizenship . . . and
> to carry on in the classroom the spirit and practice of inquiry and

discussion, the rights of teachers and students will have been sacri-
ficed to a principle of enforced conformity which has been far more
productive of the spirit of revolt than of intelligent participation in
the democratic process.[10]

Other studies of postwar American education have demonstrated
that wrestling with how to best uphold a democratic mindset was a
key feature of the political climate precipitating the development of
the Advanced Placement program.[11] Given fears over communism,
protection of free thought and speech was an urgent concern. Some
parents, administrators, and politicians thought this meant limiting
teachers' first amendment rights; this committee fell on the side of
protecting them.

Following the report's publication, Conant issued independent
calls for aligning secondary education with national security in ways
extending beyond the liberal arts. As discussed in the previous chapter, *Education in a Divided World*, Conant's influential, book-length
plea for his fellow citizens to consider education reform as an anti-
totalitarian measure, proposed blueprints for reinventing the school
system as a national intellectual, meritocratic, data-driven contest for
university admission.

FORD AND THE FUND FOR THE ADVANCEMENT OF EDUCATION

As Conant led efforts to reform education in line with his own values
and priorities, so did the Ford Foundation. There was quite a bit of
overlap in terms of concern for promoting intellectualism and individualism. The foundation, which galvanized and started funding
projects in earnest in 1950, was careful about articulating the relationship between its private interests and the public good. Rejecting
authoritarianism, in which "human rights and truth are subordinated
wholly to the state," the Ford Foundation's trustees positioned their

work as complementary to government because "the most important problems in contemporary life lay in man's relationship to man."[12] The foundation's first report spelled out its vision for maximally democratic education. In the trustees' estimation, "Perhaps the greatest single shortcoming of our school system is its tendency to concern itself almost exclusively with the dissemination of information. School should be the most important influence outside of the home for the molding of whole persons." The report called for a renewed emphasis on individuality and human potential. As the philanthropy exerted increasing influence on the shape of American schooling in the name of reconfiguring students' relationships to authority and to each other, it attracted some criticism for interfering in democratic processes.[13]

It deflected these concerns with appeals to anti-Communism. The Ford Foundation was zealous about innovation. The organization would support democracy by giving "fresh forms to its underlying principles," sponsoring projects that were too risky or time-consuming for government agencies. In the field of education, this meant funding endeavors like "the clarification of the goals of education and the evaluation of current educational practices and facilities for the better realization of democratic goals."[14] A *New York Times* article on the new foundation summed up this philosophy—or justification: "Governments cannot afford to risk mistakes, foundations can."[15] Alvin Eurich, vice president of the Ford Foundation's new committee, the Fund for the Advancement of Education, argued with regard to Ford that "a foundation, not embroiled in factional disputes, independent of the educational system, and not forced to yield to public pressure, might encourage new approaches and support experiments, demonstrations, and pilot programs too uncertain or too controversial to be paid for by public tax money."[16] Robert Hutchins, the first director of the foundation's education division, expressed hope that its Fund for the Advancement of Education would "ultimately result in the reorganization of the educational system."[17] Between 1951 and 1953, the fund gave away more than $100 million for education projects. The *New York Times* praised its "maverick spirit." Private funding held the potential to liberate students by forcing confrontation and resolution of public problems. If the means were antidemocratic, at least the ends would justify them.

Articulating the relationship between school and college had, by the 1950s, already long been a dilemma in American education. Addressing the issue at a conference, Eurich said, "Of efforts to make the transition from school to college easier and more meaningful educationally, some progress has been made. I hasten to add, however, that the problem has by no means been solved. It remains one of the most critical and baffling problems in education."[18] Beginning in 1951, the foundation's Fund for the Advancement of Education supported four experimental "alternative approaches to the same goal" of enriching education for the "superior" students whose aptitudes would help the nation navigate its new "heavy burdens of world leadership." The foundation's report on this initiative, titled *Bridging the Gap between School and College*, lamented inefficiency for three reasons: "dulling of student interest in learning, a downgrading of educational results, and a waste of human resources." Concern for promoting individualism by unlinking academic progress and chronological age, "making education as rich, as continuous, and as efficient as possible for each individual," was as much about domestic cultivation of liberalism as it was about capitalizing on students' abilities for a global fight. The Fund for the Advancement of Education imagined an innovative, holistic education from grades 11 to 14, "unmarred by wasteful repetitions, gaps, and disruptions."[19] By yoking individualism and efficiency instead of age and academic progress, the foundation aimed to accelerate the development of an intellectual elite capable of leading the nation.

Even as these men (always men, always white) worked for private organizations, their rhetoric did echo public figures' concerns for defending democracy against both Communism and McCarthyism.

On November 25, 1952, Hutchins testified on behalf of his organization's anticommunist activity:

> The civilization which I work and I am sure, every American is working toward, could be called a civilization of the dialogue, where instead of shooting one another when you differ you reason things out together. In this dialogue, then, you cannot assume that you are going to have everybody thinking the same way or feeling the same way. It would be unprogressive if that happened. The hope of eventual development would be gone.[20]

Less than a month later, Supreme Court justice Felix Frankfurter, a former Harvard professor, cited Hutchins's testimony to support his own understanding of the alignment between the rights and responsibilities of American educators. Teachers were to be conduits for "those habits of open-mindedness and critical inquiry which alone make for responsible citizens. Teachers must fulfill their function by precept and practice . . . they must be exemplars of open-mindedness and free inquiry. They cannot carry out their noble task if the conditions for the practice of a responsible and critical mind are denied to them."[21] And just before Eisenhower's inauguration in January 1953, he marked the end of his tenure as Columbia's president with a farewell address that echoed the aforementioned sentiments. "As we preach with conviction and teach with integrity, that is the true defense against communism," he proclaimed. "We are engaged in a war of great ideologies. This is not just a casual argument against slightly different philosophies. . . . No man flying a war plane, no man with a defensive gun in his hand, can possibly be more important than the teacher."[22] Since the threat of Communism was ideological, alternative intellectual orientation was a proper defense. In an age of suspicion and paranoia, educational institutions could train citizens in the skills necessary to peaceably and rationally resolve domestic conflicts while limiting the government's power.

Despite public proclamations about ways in which the struggle against Communism was one of ideas and words, the Harry S. Truman administration privately outlined a dire geopolitical landscape that resulted in tripling the defense budget and shaped the nation's response to the Korean War.[23] By June 1951, following the outbreak of the Korean War, the US government had passed the Universal Military and Training Act.[24] Men between 18 and 26 could file for deferments for up to a year on the basis of their enrollment status. In school or out of it, whether in a "civilization of dialogue" or armed and deployed, young men were to work toward protecting American interests.

THE BLACKMER COMMITTEE

In 1950, after a lunch with Alan Blackmer discussing possibilities for delivering a more organized liberal education in a chaotic world, John Kemper, Andover's headmaster, wrote to the Fund for the Advancement of Education's Alvin Eurich about dividing the responsibilities of the school and college. He outlined four possible approaches:

1. An integrated sequence of courses spanning eleventh to fourteenth grades, limited in participation to "a few preparatory schools and a few colleges."
2. Schools might "prepare able boys to enter college as Sophomores, simply skipping the Freshman year."
3. The schools could take full responsibility for liberal arts, while colleges could focus on specialization.
4. Somehow shrink the last two years of high school and four years of college into four years total, details to be decided.[25]

All involved recognized that the suggestions were protean.

In October 1951, the *Phillips Bulletin* reported to Andover alumni that the school would be home to a study, involving colleagues from

Exeter, Lawrenceville, Harvard, Yale, and Princeton. The group was to examine the relationship between high school and college curricula. It would aim to eliminate inefficient repetition of coursework, which "is costly enough at any time. Present national emergencies offer additional reason for a new attempt to help able and ambitious boys to make the best possible use of their brief years of liberal education before military service."[26] The bulletin continued, "The motivating force was the thinking stimulated during the past two years by the task of revising the Andover curriculum," and the committee was operating "on the assumption that creative, pioneering leadership is part of Andover's obligation to national education."[27] The announcement in the bulletin framed the streamlining of college preparatory curriculum as a service to the country. Kemper appointed Blackmer to chair the committee and released him from teaching duties to do so.

Blackmer, who had been appointed as an English teacher in 1925, had concluded by 1939 that the school's curriculum needed an overhaul to meet the needs of the students in attendance. "Looking back over a period of five years," he wrote in that year's bulletin, "steadily and with increasing effectiveness we are adapting our education to Bill Smith or Tom Jones, whom we know and like as persons and whose unique capacities, weaknesses, ambitions, temperaments, hopes, and fears must determine the kind of education which they receive."[28] Blackmer expressed concern for reviewing the Andover curriculum not only for each boy's private enrichment but for the sake of the nation. He continued on to express the faculty's frustration with the student body's privileged remove from public life: "Many teachers are still wondering . . . if there is anything more which they or the school as a whole can profitably do to awaken in Andover boys a keener sense of their social responsibilities. . . . Many of us would like to see more of them thinking in terms of social and civic service . . . acquiring knowledge of the sore spots in American life."[29] Blackmer revealed an eagerness to revitalize the school's philosophy in line with his understanding of both students' needs and national demands. On June 18, 1951, Kemper wrote about Blackmer to Eurich: "He is a particularly alert and forward-looking man. His interest and preoccupation with the teaching and curriculum end of education have caused him to turn down several headmasterships which have been offered him."[30] Blackmer loved the substance of English education and, for decades, had shown little interest in abandoning it for administrative power.

During the early 1950s, several philanthropic initiatives sought to blur the lines between business executives and devotees of the liberal arts. By 1952, Blackmer and other Ford-sponsored educators concerned with the problem of integrating school and college had been invited to attend the Aspen Institute for Humanistic Studies. The conference was founded in 1950 by philanthropist Walter Paepcke to provide the managerial class with space to reflect on "the whole galaxy of perplexities of man to man."[31] Like the Ford Foundation and the Fund for the Advancement of Education, the Aspen Institute would support humane study for the sake of the nation. At Aspen, industrialists would use liberal arts training to grapple with a problem under consideration at places like Harvard Business School during Donald K. David's tenure as dean: "Is Private Enterprise Undermining Our Citizenry—and Itself?"[32]

The Blackmer Committee's members focused on teaching, not management, but they comprised a distinct upper class. To understand the Andover committee's output, it is imperative to know that its members' resistance against imposing dogma on teachers and students ran deep and shaped the plans. At the same time, the group's rarefied, overlapping background experiences, in combination with the similarity of their professional affiliations, enabled them to see themselves as unified and poised to understand and to transmit the American creed.

In a volume of essays reflecting on intersections between Christianity and history, committee member and Princeton Reformation historian E. Harris Harbison—Jinks, to friends—grappled with what he understood to be a centuries-old tension between open-mindedness to new truths and commitment to and faith in God. He warned that regardless of the balance of religious and secular interests in a classroom, the aim should always be liberation: "If you try to turn the classroom into a space for dogmatic instruction, I should say you are wrong. . . . You are not going to accomplish your end and you are going to destroy many of the values you are trying to save."[33] For Harbison, there was no fine line between academic and moral instruction.[34]

In an obituary, Massachusetts Historical Society curator Frederick Allis celebrated Exeter history teacher and committee member Henry Bragdon's American history textbook, *History of a Free People*, revised over four decades, as a work of bold, original thinking: "The author refused to knuckle under to pressure to produce a universally acceptable textbook. . . . Compared with the bland texts produced by educational prostitutes writing for the market, his book was a triumph: throughout, it stressed the concept of freedom in American history."[35] Bragdon made his pedagogical commitment to freedom and fluidity of thought clear when he explained in an essay on teaching history that "external tests . . . too often dictate method and content. Fearing for their students and for their own reputations, teachers tend to teach for the examinations." More than thirty years of teaching had convinced Bragdon "that the best way to prepare for external tests is to ignore them." He pleaded with teachers to "emancipate themselves from the tyranny of testing" because the practice of teaching to the test was inconsistent with his sense for how to make students appreciate the discipline's import.[36]

The effects of McGeorge Bundy's worldview on foreign policy are well documented; however, their effects on education are largely unexplored. But both before and after Bundy was national security advisor to Kennedy and Johnson, he was involved in education reform. In an article on controversy surrounding the SAT, even the

most aloof and mathematically inclined of the technocrats admitted
that "among the recognized experts, both friendly and critical, there
is something close to agreement that [exams] do not constitute an
absolute guide to later performance."[37] On his own college entrance
exams, Bundy refused to follow the instructions and instead wrote
an essay about constructing a better question. Two readers gave him
top marks; the third gave him no credit. He was unafraid of how challenging authority would affect his college prospects. He went to Yale,
where he majored in math. Then, despite his lack of a relevant termi-
nal degree, Harvard hired him as a professor of government.

Rounding out the committee were Wendell Taylor, a Princeton
graduate and head of the science department at Lawrenceville, and
Yale art historian Charles Seymour, who was "descended from Yale
teachers going back to the Colonial period, as well as three former
Yale presidents, most notably his father, Charles Seymour, president
from 1937 to 1950."[38] The Blackmer Committee produced a scheme
that was self-assured about the necessary components of a college-
prep curriculum for "able" students and about the heritage to be
transmitted to the next generation's guardians.

The Fund for the Advancement of Education was hesitant about
facilitating exchange among a broader coalition of teachers and
professors. "The plan of having a companion project between high
schools and State universities and the possibility, at a later date, of
conducting a similar study, with reference to our colleges for women,
adds greatly to the scope of what we can accomplish together. This
approach whereby the major elements are tackled separately seems
to me better than expanding the Andover Group," wrote one administrator to another. When the *Boston Herald* reported on the group's
formation, the superintendent of Brookline schools wrote a letter
requesting an invitation to participate. He was perplexed: "Surely, the
public schools which send large numbers of graduates to the colleges
of the country every year would make every effort to cooperate in
providing 'a general liberal education which will fit a boy for a happy,

useful life.'" In meetings, the group considered "additions to the central committee," including "a broad-gauge public school man," a "foreign language man," and "a 'layman' of the right type."[39] On Sunday, October 7, 1951, the small group convened at the Peabody, an archaeological museum on Andover's campus founded at the bequest of Robert S. Peabody, nephew of famed philanthropist George Peabody. Despite their earlier considerations, the committee "decided that in general all Saturday meetings should commence at 4:30 PM, run for about two hours, and then resume after supper." There, too, the group made clear one of its commitments: "The Ford people and Mr. Kemper are against doing too much research involving too many people."[40] With the counsel of guest speakers, colleagues, and students, the six of them would protect democratic norms.

THE BLACKMER COMMITTEE'S PLAN

The committee's stated goal was to customize education for a targeted population, and to liberate specific teachers and students in the process. The November 1952 issue of the *College Board Review*, the organization's quasi-academic journal, focused on "the able student" and offered a collection of articles "on new school to college transition patterns." All of the essays were inspired by the Ford Foundation's new interest in articulating the relationship between the school and university systems. Blackmer contributed a paper titled "The Three School, Three College Plan," a nod to the narrow focus of the committee's work on which he reported. Blackmer's essay introduced to College Board stakeholders the precepts the report would expand on later that year. Writing to a community of educator colleagues, Blackmer warned, "The study should be considered as an inquiry into the relations between programs of study in *these* three schools and the colleges of *these* three universities."[41] The report would make the institutions' shared academic values public knowledge without being dictatorial.

When Blackmer retired from Andover in 1968, the school newspaper provided a glimpse inside the committee's meetings: "The six
men met in exhaustive hearings, attempting to find a way to integrate high school and college education on a national basis, *without
having to standardize it.*"[42] Meeting notes reveal that the committee
members discussed potential constraints. On February 22, 1952, they
asked, "Are some books or literary materials essential to a liberal education? If so, with what should a college Freshman be equipped
on entering college? If not what should be the criteria for choice of
texts?" Collecting input from their home campuses, they recorded
one Harvard English professor complaining, "They aren't well read."[43]
But the committee resisted the urge to fix course content. Their conception of "curriculum" had to be flexible enough to win over the
contentious faculties at their home institutions.

Meeting minutes reveal eagerness to consider creative approaches
to organizing curriculum. The group drew on colleagues' research
about the goings-on in various disciplines and programs across institutions. Wendell Taylor's preliminary proposal to the group for
science education cited Harvard's report on general education and
Conant's independent writing on the subject.[44] It opened with consideration of "four classes of individuals": the "non-scientist," "the
boy of general all-around ability," "the boy of clear math-science aptitude and interest," and "the pre-medical student." Rejecting, after
some discussion, the notion of an adolescent "non-scientist," Taylor
proposed three distinct sequences of courses based on levels of ability and interest. For the least interested, there would be a "general
course in the methods and implications of science, presumably more
or less historical." For the others, there would be varying amounts of
lab work. In approaches to history and social science, the group con-
templated organizing courses by thematic questions: cooperative in-
terdepartmental teaching by various specialists offered "fructification
through cross-fertilization" in helping students to think about social
problems. They considered the best ways for schools and colleges to

balance the teaching of ethics, values, and religion. They consulted psychiatrists and pediatricians. Sex education would wait until at least grade 13. A physician, Dana Farnsworth, warned against too small a program—"preciosity" could be alienating. The committee consulted with students, and their reflections formed an appendix that served to justify the enterprise. Henry Bragdon prepared several charts with different academic schemes for a seven-year school-college experience. Obsessively, dutifully, the group discussed the ways in which students might maximize their time in school and college. In an interim report to the fund, the committee explained, "The basic weakness . . . is a failure of the school and college to view their going enterprise as a whole and decide what is the proper business of the school and the proper business of the college."[45]

The interim report warned against denying teachers' professionalism and autonomy, even as it outlined a concerted effort to strengthen the kind of education that, in the minds of its writers, would lead to cultured, conscientious, civic minded, innovative, individualistic citizens. Its primary recommendations to strengthen American education were to "give top priority to the job of recruiting and encouraging imaginative, enthusiastic, creative teachers. Take practical, concrete action to enhance the prestige and rewards of teaching," and, "to the greatest possible extent within the resources of the institution, make education a more personal, individual affair . . . increase the opportunity for 'mind to meet with mind' on a personal basis."[46] The impulse to lead lives of inquiry and analysis, innovation and dynamism was part of the committee's anti-authoritarianism, and central to their understandings not only of education but of American life. Given the group's understanding of teaching as a serious profession and their commitment to independent thought, it is unsurprising that they resisted standardization in education.

The full Blackmer Report, titled *General Education in School and College*, was published by Harvard University Press in 1952.[47] The slim volume outlined the committee's main objectives given their understanding of the specific "weaknesses and failures" confronting American education. The project's political import becomes clear in a chapter titled "The Essentials of Liberal Education," and the authors repeat their understanding of their "single most important" observation: "our frequent failure to communicate the meaning and purpose of a liberal education and to make students care about getting it."[48] The book offers both general principles and specific areas of focus for a proposed slate of courses, as well as a number of seven-year programs for students with a variety of interests and career goals. Since the project was based, in part, on the results of a survey administered to alumni of the schools represented by the committee members, the book also includes an appendix compiling some of the students' reflections on inefficiencies or missed opportunities in their own educational careers.

The committee's sense of liberation, limited to the intellectual freedom of wealthy white boys attending their institutions, did not align with the one that emerged into the mainstream during the civil rights movement in the ensuing decades. As was true for Conant, the committee's original purpose was to ensure equity only in the Jeffersonian sense—with a nod to the existence of an invisible underlying hierarchy of intelligence that a meritocratic educational system could reveal. The report's introduction explained that the program was not for the masses: "As individuals we are proud of the quantitative achievements of education in America. We believe in the 'Jacksonian' ideal of extending the benefits of education as far down the scale of ability as it is possible. But our task in the present study is to emphasize the 'Jeffersonian' concept of the right of every able student to the *best* education from which he is capable of profiting."[49] The committee was blunt: "While we have tried to outline a program of study which would offer all students of college caliber a better education, *we have been particularly concerned about the superior student.*"[50] Taking up the charge of one small part of Conant's call for reform— and the part the authors of the Red Book had rejected as an explicit priority—the program was more concerned with reproducing habits of mind in the emerging ruling class than it was with understanding the American education system as a mechanism for rapid social restructuring.[51]

Despite the educators' pointed lack of concern in this study for students beyond the narrow boundaries of their own lives, they still understood their work in terms of emancipation. Their program would have philosophical coherence but rely on "progression in strength," a custom course schedule for each student. "Individual persons are ends in themselves," they wrote in justification of their project. "Liberal education and the democratic ideal are related to each other in a thousand ways. It is not too much to say that they stand and fall together."[52] The committee's vision for an empowered, united citizenry was rooted in an understanding of humanism that required nuanced communication. In defense of teachers' individuality, they wrote, "A love for learning depends overwhelmingly upon the personality, skill, knowledge, and communicable enthusiasm of the individual teacher. In a sense, all else is peripheral."[53] The writers conceived of the program's liberal arts emphasis as an explicit anti-totalitarian measure. "A liberally educated man demands freedom," they declared. "When totalitarian dictatorship triumphs in the modern world, truly 'liberal' education is the first object of attack, since it is one of the most obvious bulwarks against the brutalization and atomization of the individual."[54] A plan for an English course modeled on Blackmer's own anti-propaganda teachings took pride of place among the curricular offerings. They explained, "For his own sake and for the sake of the democracy of which he is a part, the individual must be able to distinguish between the false coin and the true in the talk and writing to which mass media of communication now subject us all."[55] American students needed training to be able to organize their thoughts. The program promised to help students understand themselves as free participants in the public conversation about the nation's past, present, and future.

The liberal arts focus extended to the committee's understanding of a student's overall health. As the Cold War called for a rapid marshaling of the nation's intellectual resources, they believed in pushing their students to grow. They wrote, "We believe first of all in individual excellence. We think that higher education should be even more concerned than it is about encouraging our more capable students to excel, to develop their mental abilities to the very utmost."[56] But they expressed concern about driving students to the point of breakdown. A draft of the plan warned against "the hothouse forcing which would defeat the purposes of education."[57] In the final report, the committee admitted that both mind and emotions were vital considerations. "We are modern enough to be concerned with the intimate connection of the mind and the emotions," they wrote.[58] Their students were to flourish—to understand themselves as well-rounded human beings.

After the committee completed their work, Bundy scoured Boston and New York for a gift to Blackmer from the rest of the committee—a first edition of Alfred North Whitehead's *The Aims of Education*. On December 26, 1953, Blackmer wrote to Bundy, "The wonderful committee gift is the nicest thing that has happened to me in my working life, and I am left with a terrific mixture of feelings—gratitude, surprise (complete), a sharpened realization of what all of you achieved and meant to me individually and collectively. While undeserved by me personally, the gift stands as a symbol of very precious values."[59]

Understanding the frame implied by the report's epigraph throws into even sharper relief its educational philosophy. The epigraph reads, "In the conditions of modern life the rule is absolute, the race which does not value trained intelligence is doomed."[60] Whitehead, this sentence's author, was a British mathematician, philosopher, and education reformer. *The Aims of Education* came out of his work teaching at Harvard. In the same essay on education reform from which the authors of the study chose their guiding words, Whitehead said, "The uniform external examination is deadly. We do not denounce it because we are cranks, and like denouncing established things. We are not so childish. . . . Our reason of dislike is very definite and very practical. It kills the best part of culture."[61] Whitehead believed that assessments should grow out of conversations between teachers and students—that they should reflect the vital relationships at the heart of the experience that give it meaning.

Whitehead was aghast at the direction of educational systems in England and America during the first half of the twentieth century. He felt it necessary to remind his audience that "the students are alive, and the purpose of education is to stimulate and guide their self-development. It follows as a corollary from this premise, that the teachers also should be alive with living thoughts. The whole book is a protest against dead knowledge, that is to say, against inert ideas."[62] Attuned to the dangers of dehumanization by World War I, Whitehead hated the external examinations that were developing on both sides of the Atlantic. He was adamant: "We are dealing with human minds, and not with dead matter. The evocation of curiosity, of judgment, of the power of mastering a complicated tangle of circumstances, the use of theory in giving foresight in special cases—all these powers are not to be imparted by a set rule embodied in one schedule of examination subjects." To Whitehead, the teaching of mathematics was a cultural enterprise and he denounced mechanical pedagogy.[63] The committee echoed Whitehead's idea that education should be a creative, emboldening project.

After articulating the expansion of both mind and spirit that they believed a liberal education should afford, the authors wrote, "Above all, the liberally educated man is never a type. He is always a unique person, vivid in his distinction from other similarly educated persons."[64] Ralph Ellison's *Invisible Man* was published in 1952, the same year as the Blackmer Report. The novel is about a Black American's treacherous quest to resist stereotypes and develop a unique identity in his own mind and in the eyes of others. In the summer of 1953, Ellison gave a talk at Harvard on American literature. He wrote to friends about the experience: "The atmosphere there is so thick with learning, scholarship, and freedom that most other schools I've seen are like imitations."[65] Of course, some educators exercised discretion and experienced agency in other places—and some insisted on doing so despite burdensome restrictions. But unspoken in the Blackmer Report was the notion that institutional and financial support for the cultivation of individuality—over seven years or otherwise—was a privilege.[66]

The high-flying ideals animating the body of the report contrast sharply with its provisions for testing. The committee insisted that in terms of implementation, "the one principle we should like to see rigidly adhered to in any seven-year program is that the essential values of a liberal education shall not be lost or compromised."[67] The appendix that follows the report is hard to square with the Blackmer Committee's promotion of free thinking and their commitment to improving the "spirit and atmosphere of the classroom."[68] On May 13, 1952, Blackmer had written to Eurich about a meeting with the "college deans and school headmasters" regarding their "very promising" interim report. The "deans were strongly of the opinion that examinations for advanced credit should be set by some agency such as the College Board rather than by college departments. We shall deal with this practical problem with Mr. Dyer."[69] On February 9, 1953, after the report was published, Blackmer apprised Eurich of progress on examinations. He reported that at a meeting with College Board employees, "there was not time to study our particular proposal in detail; the idea was merely approved in principle after an hour's discussion of our draft." Regarding the appended proposal for a slate of exams, Blackmer wrote, "It may be so modified in the future that the present draft will have no more than historic interest."[70]

DYER'S APPENDIX

By 1953, Blackmer was eager to return to teaching, and to hand off the program's administration to another entity. In that same letter, he had written to Eurich, "For psychological as well as for practical reasons, you almost need two teams—a 'think' team and implementing team. Not exactly the ill-favored two platoon system but something like it." Blackmer, like many of the colleagues he knew, had consulted for the College Board as it sought to innovate. They were skeptical of the organization's ability to capture a student's aptitude or ability and eager for technocracy to facilitate a rational, liberal society. In 1950, Blackmer had corresponded with Frank Ashburn, Paul Diederich, Frank Bowles, Louis Zahner, and William Fels about composition exams. When the University of Chicago's Earle G. Eley suggested grading essays on the basis of five variables, and that "separate judgments on these variables will greatly increase reader reliability," Blackmer had scrawled in the letter's margin: "Maybe."[71] As part of the technocratic experiment, Blackmer's committee recommended outsourcing to the College Board the development of "Advanced Subject Matter Examinations" with the following guidelines:

1. To give an incentive to the ablest students in secondary schools to progress in fields of particular interest and strength at a rate commensurate with their ability.
2. To stimulate the secondary school to provide the best possible teaching, as well as other opportunities, for top-level students.
3. To attack wasteful duplication of work between school and college.
4. To give the college an effective way to keep superior, and potentially superior, students fully stretched before admission.

These goals—to motivate students, to strengthen teaching, to eliminate tedium and repetition, to maintain students' intellectual agility in the transition from high school to college—were humanistic in nature. Blackmer and his team weren't experts in implementation.

For that, they turned to Henry S. Dyer, who authored the report's appendix on examinations.

Dyer's professional priorities and inclinations help explain a sudden shift in tone and purpose between the report and its appendix.[72] The introduction to the body of the Blackmer Report credits Dyer, "a pioneering expert in psychometrics, the measurement of mental processes through psychological tests," with leading a panel on the development of the AP exams in advance of the report's publication.[73] He was not part of the main committee—his role was administrative. Dyer understood "educational measurement" as a "rational process in which the behavior of pupils is observed and judged in respect to some system of values."[74] He believed in testing as a tool to uncover and then ameliorate gaps in knowledge and other problems in social systems, as it helped teachers come "closely to grips with those modifications of human behavior we call education."[75]

In Dyer's framing, determining eligibility for advanced placement could be accomplished by using scores on two other ETS products— the scholastic aptitude test and the College Entrance Examination Board's "achievement tests." Despite the College Board's decades of unsuccessful efforts to develop uncontroversial tests of writing ability, Dyer insisted that new placement exams could "measure a student's maturity in those intellectual processes required by each subject."[76] Dyer worked backwards from the fact of tests, even as he understood that the committee's values should guide their development.

By the time the report was published, Dyer had spent the better part of a decade as director of Harvard's Office of Tests, where he grappled with how to best advise a heterogeneous incoming freshman class about their academic and professional paths.[77] At the outset, the appendix makes clear, "It should be understood that these examinations would be used, not for admission to college, but for placement after admission." In a direct response to the Harvard General Education report's insistence on strengthening academic advising, he pioneered the use of testing and technology to guide freshmen in course selection. Dyer told the *Crimson*, "What we're trying to do at present is to explore individual differences by means of statistical research. We predict the academic rank of each freshman after registration and then follow up his record. Our predictions are usually 78 percent accurate within a certain area."[78] These predictions were to help faculty advisors guide students into courses of study that offered the best chances at success—both in terms of personal fulfillment and career options.

Dyer's experiences at Harvard informed his work at the College Board, and that organization's interest in refining its postwar research program influenced his plans. In 1952, Dyer was appointed associate director of the College Board, where he continued to think about both quantification and issues surrounding placement of freshmen. An author biography from the *College Board Review* explained that he occupied three positions: "Associate Director of the Board, Research Vice President of [the] Educational Testing Service, and a seat on the express which runs between Princeton and New York," where the companies had their respective offices. As discussed in the previous chapter, in 1947, at the behest of Conant and the Carnegie Corporation, the College Board had "turned over its laboratories, its equipment, and all its tangible assets" to ETS, as well as "all its contracts and agreements for test development, construction, administration, and research, not directly connected with its college entrance examinations."[79] The board was now a purchaser, not a producer, of tests. Even as the merger limited the board's scope, an ever-widening constituency of colleges introduced new potential projects. Discussing the board's new research agenda, Dyer explained that as greater numbers of students from a diverse range of hometowns applied to colleges, "instead of drawing a homogenous group of students from a few well-controlled schools, the colleges began to get a more and more heterogeneous but no less able group of students from schools that had never heard of the College Board." Conant aimed to measure merit for admission through aptitude testing, while Dyer understood this new problem of discontinuity as an opportunity to invent, for the College Board, the Tests of Developed Ability (TDA).

In opposition to Conant, Dyer wrote about the ways in which measures of aptitude, such as IQ, could skew educators' perceptions of both testing and students' potential, and advocated instead for the testing of achievement.[80] He held out hope that testing could reflect students' success in liberal arts subjects. For the TDA, he worked with a committee of academics in the three fields of "general education"—humanities, social sciences, and natural sciences—to produce a six-hour battery of tests that would give public secondary education a sense of direction without imposing "any serious restrictions on the subject matter content of secondary school curricula" and cover "a number of different intellectual abilities which are important for the college preparatory student and which at the same time can be developed under a variety of instructional patterns." After a brief trial period, college administrators agreed that shorter achievement tests in specific fields were enough to demonstrate candidates' academic promise.[81] But Dyer was zealous about the potential for standardized achievement testing as the board was in a moment of flux in terms of its mission and purpose.

It would seem that Dyer bore much of the responsibility for the eventual development of Advanced Placement exams, and for the program's home at the College Board. But when Frank Bowles, the head of the College Board from 1948 to 1963, reflected on the organization's shifts in purpose and function he helped to facilitate in a history of his tenure, Dyer's name did not appear. Bowles admitted, "The tendency of the Board as an organization in reality—as a power structure—is to subordinate the humane to the technical."[82] He credited Secretary William Fels with maintaining humanism and insistence on liberal education as the College Board sought to redefine its purpose in an inclusive era. Fels was "the individual who patiently put together bits and pieces of separate programs into what became the Advanced Placement program."[83] As College Board director, Bowles was resistant to taking on the program, which carried "shocking" financial losses of over $80 per candidate in its first year. But Fels won him over, even operating at a loss. They shared hope that in a democratized educational landscape, making accessible to a broad range of secondary schools the standards and practices of the nation's preeminent colleges would be liberatory for students.[84] Financial statements and other records from the archives of the College Board and the Educational Testing Service might tell a different story.

THE REPORT'S AFTERMATH

The Blackmer Committee disbanded after the report's publication. Bundy recommended that the group put the rest of their budget toward a social gathering, but Blackmer sent the money back to the Fund for the Advancement of Education. By 1953, the College Board was at work on "development and validation of a new series of advanced placement tests."[85] By the fall of 1954, a preliminary bulletin outlining course descriptions and potential examinations appeared in print. In private exchanges, the committee members celebrated their accomplishment. Blackmer wrote to Bundy, "Before the report appears and we start ducking various flying objects, I am enough of a sentimentalist to want to tell you how grateful I am for the major part you played in getting the job done."[86] E. Harris Harbison reported to Bundy that, at Princeton, "all is sweetness and light here on the report."[87] Within a year of the publication of the Blackmer Committee's report on the necessity of such a program, Bragdon wrote to Bundy: "Sensational! The twelve-college study has voted to back our plan in advanced placement examinations. See the last *College Board Review*."[88]

Optimistic as the Blackmer Committee was about their project's success, reception to their vision was mixed, even among the parties who would bear responsibility for its implementation. The group to which Bragdon referred went by several names, and it was also sponsored by Ford: "The Kenyon Plan," "The Twelve-College Study," "The School and College Study of Admission with Advanced Standing." William Cornog, director, wrote on February 9, 1953, to Gordon Keith Chalmers, chair: "I enclose the revised proposal of the Andover group. . . . You will note that we have been dealt a hand. From my remarks you will also note that I am inclined to take a long, poker-faced look at the cards." He was wary of "those old Mississippi gamblers at the Fund for the Advancement of Education."[89] As I explain in the next chapter, Chalmers and Cornog had wanted to retain control of the structures they'd built to facilitate collaboration and alignment. Blackmer knew this. He had written to Eurich in 1952: "If we wait until Bill Cornog's definitions of college Freshman work are out—and discussed by the twelve faculties involved, momentum generated by our report may be lost. And I don't know whether Bill's group is working towards common national examinations anyway. Bill and I have kept in very close touch, but neither of us knows how our projects can be fitted together for maximum effectiveness."[90] But if the final scheme was incoherent, at least it would be fast and new. Speed and innovation were the order of the day.

The Blackmer Committee's report provided important ideological grounding for the program while validating the enterprise as a legitimate one in the eyes of an academic community dazzled by prestige.[91] Affiliation with the "Big Three" validated the notion that it was possible to reinvent the liberal arts for a new age. The particular schools and colleges represented by the Blackmer Committee established the project as academically sound in the minds of colleagues and students. In a letter pleading for Harvard's continued involvement in the Advanced Placement program, Cornog explained to Harlan P. Hanson, the graduate student and administrator in charge of the college's new Office of Advanced Standing, that "endorsement of 'top-ranking colleges' is our way of keeping our 'currency on a gold standard.'" The upholding of confidence in the program was more than a hypothetical issue. Hanson explained to faculty in 1955, "We have received more than twice as many candidates as the next most popular college in the program."[92] Undergraduates were aware of the extent to which the program's success relied on name recognition, and on Harvard's ability to supply it. By 1961, the *Crimson* criticized Harvard's involvement with the program: "The College's privileges of leadership have given rise to serious and somewhat unpleasant obligations. The Administration feels, for example, that abandoning Soph Standing is absolutely out of the question because it would impair the prestige of the national advanced placement program."[93] Beyond its role in establishing the testing framework, the Blackmer Committee's involvement was crucial to establishing "Advanced Placement" as a reputable brand.

High-profile institutional backing also muffled the influence of individual critics and dissenters. Luke Steiner, Oberlin chemistry professor, declined the opportunity to chair his field's curriculum development committee. He wrote to Cornog on August 5, 1953, that at Central High School in Philadelphia, "Your chemistry teachers can ignore the outside examinations because they are above the examinations," but that teachers at less reputable institutions would not be so fortunate.[94] School headmasters were hesitant to endorse the program for "social and emotional" reasons. Even on and around the Harvard campus, support was not unanimous. One faculty dissenter, J. Douglas Bush, told the *Crimson*, "Liberal education should not be viewed as a prison term with one-fourth off for good behavior. I'm aware of the pressures of time and money, but these should not be the real consideration." But these critics were no match for Harvard, fashioned by Conant over the previous decade as a beacon for rectitude, innovation, and purpose in American education—the apex of the Jeffersonian intellectual pyramid.[95]

The year after the Blackmer Report's publication, McGeorge Bundy was promoted to dean at Harvard and he led the initiative to implement the program. Harvard undergraduate David Halberstam, who would go on to skewer Bundy as a "glib, smug, insensitive" member of a group he blamed for the catastrophes of the Vietnam War and sardonically dubbed "the best and the brightest," wrote for the *Crimson* during his senior year about the controversy surrounding advanced standing. Of the meeting during which Bundy prevailed in convincing the faculty to adopt measures recommended by the report, Halberstam wrote, "By voice vote, despite loud objection, the Faculty approved plans which encourage unusually able students to move quickly into advanced level work."[96] In 1954, Halberstam wrote that the "proposal passed by faculty with unexpected speed"; by 1972, he characterized Bundy as "the supreme mover of papers," who "thought that there was always a straight line between two points."[97] In a 1951 meeting with the Blackmer Committee on the prospect of a "values" course requirement, Bundy complained, "The student visualizes a world where things happen to him; he should be shaken into imagining himself as happening to the world."[98] In foreign policy, his failure to evolve past this false dichotomy would prove disastrous. In the context of AP, Bundy's effectiveness as an administrator helped secure the program's presence at Harvard despite colleagues' concerns about its implications.

In 1953, the Ford Foundation issued a report on the status of four projects it had funded in the name of improving education for gifted students, the Blackmer Report and the Kenyon Plan among them. In the introduction to this volume, the authors were careful to make clear the difference between the endeavors of the Ford Foundation and the Ford Motor Company:

> The procedures that the automobile industry has developed to hold down costs by pushing thousands of cars of identical design through the same production line are not adaptable to education, at least not in a democracy which depends for its fruition and survival upon the cultivation and free exercise of varying individual abilities. An educational system that fails in this respect is a hazard to democracy.[99]

As a result of its origins in the Cold War zeal for establishing and maintaining a democratic intellectual framework, the Advanced Placement program was designed to uphold liberal ideals.

It was also designed to consolidate and propagate the influence of an academic, social, and economic elite. In 1955, Bundy gave a talk at a College Board meeting. Instead of focusing on schools' failures, as he said his colleagues often did on such occasions, he offered reasons for hope. Chief among them was the development of academic standards. He said, "In this welter of cross-currents of communication . . . if we cannot have some standards which have meaning to large numbers of schools and to large numbers of colleges, we shall indeed be unable to communicate our concern for real learning about real things." He admitted to not knowing much about the development of ETS and College Board exams, but he was glad for their existence in the struggle to maintain order. In response to his colleagues' anxiety about waning relevance and influence, he acknowledged that millions of school students were "beyond our reach," but that competitive college admissions could be "a kind of pressure at the point of admission" to change schools' academic quality because "the colleges represented in the College Board have in the letter of admission a pearl which is of very great price to a very large number of students." Because of student demand for admission to institutions promising transformation into the very academic, social, and economic elite he was addressing, he expected that among "a limited but still considerable number of schools and colleges, there may be real communication and great progress."[100]

As Jack Schneider has noted, "despite the resistance of school leaders and those at the College Board, the meaning and purpose of AP" began to change almost immediately after it was implemented.[101] But Blackmer's commitment to Whitehead's articulation of pedagogical ideals held steady. In 1962, he spoke about his vision for Andover's future. He gave full-throated support to the continuance of "great, imaginative teaching" and liberal education. In closing, he remarked,

"I shrink from prediction and can only voice a concern and a hope. Whitehead's dictum is true: 'In the conditions of modern life, the rule is absolute; the race which does not value trained intelligence is doomed.'"[102] I agree with Blackmer: liberal education can be a perennial good. But, as Bundy made clear, the structures that shape school's meaning and import are subject to change.

CHAPTER 3

The Blueprint

In May 1956, two weeks after Kenyon president Gordon Keith Chalmers died of a cerebral hemorrhage at the age of 52, the *Kenyon Collegian* paid homage to his leadership of a staggering number of institutions. "The deep impress he has left upon everything and everyone he touches remains," wrote political science professor Raymond English. Among Chalmers's multitude of honors and achievements, his involvement with the founding of the Advanced Placement program received special mention. English continued, "His influence on public and secondary education was subtle and pervasive . . . above all through the seminal scheme for Admission with Advanced Standing [i.e., the AP program], popularly known as 'The Kenyon Plan.' With what skill and tact and elaborate care he pursued this scheme to bring back efficiency to education can be known only by those who cooperated with him."[1] In the decades since Chalmers's death, the extent and nature of his role in American history has gone largely unrecognized. As one of the chief architects of the Advanced Placement program, however, he is among the most influential figures in the history of American education.

Described in his *Kenyon Collegian* obituary as "an ardent horseman and sailor," Chalmers spent his childhood on the East Coast. He enjoyed several decades of education at elite institutions. He went

75

to Brown University, then to Oxford as a Rhodes Scholar, and, for his PhD in English literature, Harvard. At 30, he became president of Illinois's Rockford College and was a member of the National Committee on Fulbright Awards, a lay reader in the Episcopal Diocese of Ohio, and president of the College English Association. Principled and confident, the establishment empowered him and he advocated for its promise to maintain an appropriate balance of order and freedom.

This upbringing provides context for a faith in institutions and their ability, properly organized, to mete out rewards and consequences for citizens' aptitudes and behaviors. Chalmers understood himself as well positioned to participate in the Ford Foundation's midcentury effort to expand possibilities for American education. That effort, which produced the AP program, was an immediate response to concerns about the Korean War, Communism, and increased demands for a well-educated polity. To develop an educational scheme in line with his vision for the nation, in 1951 Chalmers joined forces with William Hafner Cornog, then president of Philadelphia's Central High School. As I demonstrate in this chapter, the men shared a set of concerns about the direction of postwar American public life. In addition to Cold War commitments to maintaining democratic norms and resisting communistic ones, their letters and publications reveal acute fears about dehumanization in what they worried was becoming a technocratic, nuclear age. Both men championed the maintenance of qualitative thinking and believed that conceiving of education primarily in terms of economics, customer service, and data clashed with academic integrity and civic ideals. These advocates for the liberal arts argued in favor of divorcing education from economic outcomes in the name of maintaining American civilization. In keeping with midcentury traditionalist conservatism's focus on the transformative power of culture, Chalmers and Cornog pushed for liberal education—and humanities coursework in particular—that held the potential to uphold the sanctity of the individual while teaching students about the human condition as an antidote to Communism's threats of collectivism and mechanization.

Although an obvious admirer of Chalmers's independent spirit, cheerful confidence, and clear sense of vision, Professor English described his employer's temperament as "autocratic." Chalmers liked things done his way. In 1948, early in the civil rights movement, before any mandates required he do so, he insisted that Kenyon College matriculate its first two Black students. One of the students, Allen Ballard, went on to write of his Kenyon experience, "We were . . . forced to suppress our natural inner selves so as to conform to the mores of a campus dominated by upper-middle-class Americans."[2] In 1949, when Sewanee's football team expressed reluctance to play against Kenyon's integrated team, Chalmers canceled their scheduled game.[3] Across contexts, he did not capitulate to authority he deemed unjust. Uncompromising about the rectitude of his own standards, Chalmers could be intimidating. But even English did not predict that the administrator's power over education would be as widespread or imposing as the Advanced Placement program is today. By 1960, Bayes M. Norton wrote to Richard Pearson, executive vice president of the College Board, "One of Gordon Chalmers's great concerns was that [the Advanced Placement program's] significance might be lost in the structure of 'proficiency' examinations."[4]

DEWEY'S PROGRESSIVISM AND CONANT'S TECHNOCRACY

To understand the choices Chalmers made on the committee that formulated the Advanced Placement program, we need to situate him within the broader debates about education and democracy in which he participated. Like Conant, he was wary of Dewey's impact, especially in terms of humanistic education. Dewey admitted that "cultivation" brought with it "greater promise for a social service which goes beyond the supply in quantity of material commodities."[5] He hoped to reconcile individualistic and collective goals for educational systems, as when he wrote: "It is the particular task of education at the present time to struggle on behalf of an aim in which social efficiency and personal culture are synonyms instead of antagonists."[6] But when it came to cultivating students' minds, he warned against teaching "aristocratic" cultural traditions and texts that "represented the intellectual and moral outlook of the class which was in direct social control."[7] Dewey proposed balancing studies of literature with appreciation for the working conditions that had produced the texts under discussion. What we might now call his historicist lens was also part of his pragmatism: understanding the work in context could help students see cultural products as part of a whole social organism.

In 1935, Dewey published a critique of liberalism, painting the framework as fractured and outdated. He warned about liberals' lack of awareness of "the historic relativity of . . . interpretation[s] of the meaning of liberty" and argued that, in fighting absolutism, liberals had the tendency to become too fixed themselves in the meaning of such concepts. In the Revolutionary era, "The instruments of analysis, of criticism, of dissolution, that were employed were effective for the work of release. But when it came to the problem of organizing the new forces and the individuals whose modes of life they radically altered into a coherent social organization, possessed of intellectual and moral directive power, liberalism was well-nigh impotent."[8] Against adherence to a tradition that no longer suited the nation's needs, Dewey advocated a new kind of liberalism. He called for "organized social planning, put into effect for the creation of an order in which industry and finance are socially directed on behalf of institutions that provide the material basis for the cultural liberation and growth of individuals." To some, what Dewey called "the sole method of social action by which liberalism can realize its professed aims" sounded like socialism.[9]

In developing these ideas, Dewey debated with journalist and Harvard alum Walter Lippmann about the most realistic, democratic vision for the distribution of both money and knowledge.[10] While Lippmann advocated for technocratic experts who would consolidate and act upon information in the citizenry's interest, Dewey pushed for a more participatory model in which a broader swath of citizens would share information and other resources. In some ways, this distribution of responsibility was aligned with the conservative interest in decentralization. But still, by the 1940s and 1950s, some critics took Dewey's definition of liberalism, his insistence on ameliorating injustice, and his focus on pragmatism as more threatening to democracy than in alignment with it. Concern about Communism led to conservative commentators like Mortimer Smith, an education writer who complained that, for Dewey, education was too instrumental. Smith disagreed with what he took to be an anti-intellectual notion that the value of metaphysical thought must be rooted in the present, that "there are no ultimates or any universal, timeless human values" worth studying on their own terms.[11]

Meanwhile, Conant had begun facilitating a reorientation of the national education system as an instrument for producing an intellectual elite.[12] As I've discussed, contra Dewey, Conant insisted on the preservation of liberal education to achieve this end. Conant's ideas about restructuring the school system garnered praise from professional educators and gained popular appeal. Chalmers engaged with Harvard's 1945 report, *General Education in a Free Society*, which Conant had commissioned. He complained, "The sentimental language of the times creeps in on occasion, and the humanities are said to be concerned with visions and ideals." Despite his misgivings about the portrayed value of humanistic work, he wrote: "On the whole, the report is realistic, talking sense about the nature of mankind, of learning itself, and about the job of teaching and keeping school." At the very least, the report represented an invitation to contribute to a public conversation about liberal education. He celebrated its defense of "the idea of the individual as one capable of approximating, despite the violent war in his own breast, the norm of manhood."[13] For Chalmers, the idea of self-governance in this sense was the defining feature of American democracy. He appreciated that citizens had responsibilities to each other, but his primary concern was the maintenance of a kind of individualism that would be mutually beneficial—a thoughtful society. He supported the Harvard Committee's position that reading literature and philosophy could cultivate common values and attitudes while avoiding dogma.

Chalmers worried that post-Dewey, even for Conant, "education as a social technique is preoccupied with group behavior. It seeks not human values, but political or economic or institutional ones because they are collected together. It is based on the sentimental belief that the individual can best be served by neglect of his character and by attention to the circumstances which surround him."[14] For Chalmers, liberal education could ameliorate the collectivism he worried would eclipse the school's potential to foster democratic dialogue and self-governance. He was skeptical of the emerging technocratic impulse to quantify norms. In *The Republic and the Person*, he wrote of the Kinsey Report, which in 1948 had challenged conventional thinking about sexuality: "The logic of the Kinsey report would hold that forty million Frenchmen can't be wrong; but how wrong they, or one hundred forty million Americans, can be!" Against the ascendency of social science in general, he railed, "Statistics are mistakenly thought in our lifetime to prove something about quality or value, provided you have enough of them."[15] Chalmers believed in norms and standards, but his approach to uncovering them relied on qualitative evidence. In his view, "the whole effort of mind called liberal education may be described as the approach to the norm of human conduct."[16] He wrote, "The need for stories, reflection upon these, for human facts and a skeptical analysis of the record to determine where it is inadequate or false is the same for every man, as every man must have protein." This faith in an invisible natural, moral law underpinning all of human affairs was in line with the conservative tradition. More progressive was his sense that "the ability to judge these matters with shrewdness seems distributed without reference to father's occupation."[17] In 1956, Chalmers was scheduled to give the convocation address at Brown University's graduate school ceremony, but he died shortly before the occasion. He devoted much of that speech to questioning the wisdom of Conant's vision for American universities—he was positioning himself as a humanistic counterweight when his life ended.[18]

LOCATING CHALMERS AS COLD WAR CONSERVATIVE

In the middle of the 1950s, Chalmers received acclaim from peers whose reputations would go on to eclipse his own. In "The American Conservative Character," Russell Kirk listed Chalmers and his book-length study of American education, *The Republic and the Person*, as part of a cohort of thinkers and works marking a watershed moment in the conservative intellectual movement, alongside Daniel Boorstin's *The Genius of American Politics* and Richard Weaver's *Ideas Have Consequences*.[19] In 1963, Kirk published a tribute to Chalmers in which he celebrated how he had "kept the notions of Dewey and Counts and Kilpatrick and that breed from sweeping everything before them." He concluded, "His influence will be felt in subtle ways, but it will endure long. . . . He does not expect that legions will spring up where he stamps his foot. The work of the humane scholar of high talent, instead, resembles what the Apostle said of the seed—unless they die, they cannot quicken."[20] Peter Vierick's *Conservatism: From John Adams to Churchill* identified Chalmers as "slightly older" than the emerging cohort of "New Conservatives," instead placing him in a group of cultural critics "generally Burkean in approach."[21]

Recent scholars of midcentury conservatism's evolution have not agreed on Chalmers's relevance to the tradition. Even within the more expansive historical accounting of the political right's intellectual development now available, it is difficult to locate Gordon Keith Chalmers among his influences, contemporaries, and students.

George Nash cited Chalmers as an intellectual contemporary of Richard Weaver's, whose humanism bore the influence of the Southern agrarians, and as a critic of Dewey like Arthur Bestor and Mortimer Smith.[22] Despite Nash's grouping of him with conservative education thinkers, Chalmers does not appear in Andrew Hartman's more recent account of conservatism's role in shaping Cold War education.[23] Nor does he have a place in Patrick Allitt's survey of twentieth-century American conservatism.[24] Despite the lack of uniform recognition as a thinker who shaped conservatism, Chalmers's impact still resonates. His publications may have played a minor part in intellectual conservative history, but in the words of Richard Weaver, his ideas had major consequences for the history of American education.

Looking at Chalmers's key intellectual influences will be useful in understanding his work as part of a constellation of writers emerging in the middle of the twentieth century. In 1953, Russell Kirk published *The Conservative Mind*, now a touchstone for traditionalist conservatives. In a *New York Times* review, Chalmers celebrated it as a "brilliant and eloquent" articulation of an "affirmative tradition of Burke, de Tocqueville, and Irving Babbitt." The book helped Chalmers to conceptualize himself as a thinker in a long line of humanistic, "independent lovers of liberty throughout the past century of expanding democratic collectivism," not merely as a reactionary anti-Communist.[25] Kirk advocated for the study of "serious poetry" as a means to see past the "ideological dogmas of this century," and to "reinterpret and vindicate the norms of human existence."[26] These notions are embedded in a worldview committed to both elitism and insistence on universal individual dignity.

Kirk held specific ideas about how universities and, more particularly, humanities departments, should function. He expected campuses to enrich students' lives by divorcing education from the expectation of financial reward. By promoting comfort with fluidity and humanism, Kirk hoped that schools would expand America's capacity for self-governance while reducing dependence on the kind of mechanization he equated with soullessness. Left unchecked, industrialization would enslave Americans. In the Christian mold, Kirk saw the liberal arts as a path toward redemption and liberation.

Chalmers also kept company with and synthesized the thoughts of other conservative thinkers, including John Crowe Ransom, now best known as the leading advocate for New Criticism and as the founder of the *Kenyon Review*. In 1930, Ransom published a defense of Southern agrarianism titled *I'll Take My Stand*, in which he painted progress as a threat to humanism: "The intention of Americans at large appears now to be what it was always in danger of becoming: an intention of being infinitely progressive. But this intention cannot permit of an established order of human existence, and of that leisure which conditions the life of intelligence and the arts."[27] Although Ransom moved away from his early conservative views, throughout his career he remained defensive about the maintenance of culture in an industrial age. In 1937, Chalmers hired Ransom to pursue multiple projects geared toward protection of "culture." Ransom envisioned a literary theory that would, as Kirk believed reading should, get at hard, universal truths about the human spirit, but he was less sentimental about the project. In Ransom's essay "Criticism, Inc.,"—credited with bringing New Criticism to prominence—he insisted that "Criticism must become more scientific, or precise and systematic." The essay details his concerns about historicism eclipsing literary study and science obscuring its value. In an effort to protect English departments and to help professors and their students "define and enjoy the aesthetic or characteristic values of literature," he proposed that criticism "shall be objective, [and] shall cite the nature of the object rather than its effects upon the subject."[28] Contra Dewey, Ransom hoped to shift students' attention away from a work's context and toward some inherent, enduring, aesthetic meaning.

Key to Chalmers's conservatism was his deep well of faith in the type of human organization offered by the Protestant church. When Chalmers was president of Kenyon College, it was an Episcopal institution, comprised of the college and the Kenyon Divinity School. Reverends numbered among its faculty, administrators, and trustees. As Chalmers spoke out against indoctrination, he believed that faith "should be implicit in the aims of the whole system of schools and universities in America. The faith there described is a limited thing, founded on common experience, not derived from what is commonly called religion." In 1955, the last year of Chalmers's presidency, the Kenyon College *Bulletin* included a description of the school's philosophy and attendant practices. In line with its history as a school to prepare clergy, "Kenyon has never aspired to hugeness, for it has grown up in the collegiate rather than the university tradition. Numbers are deliberately limited to preserve the social unity of the college, to make it possible for every member to know intimately most of the students and all of the faculty. . . . Such intimacy is acknowledged by all to be a valuable part of the educational process."[29] At Kenyon, the approach to learning was humane. Chalmers worried about the "intrusion of sociological considerations" that would distort the meaning of education and warned: "Numerous managerial problems of the nation appear susceptible of the same treatment."[30]

CHALMERS, THE REPUBLIC, AND THE PERSON

Writing into the ongoing national conversation about the purpose of American schooling, Chalmers framed education as a political problem but not a sociological one. His sense for the challenges confronting American education and his attendant proposals and recommendations were informed by and helped to shape his conceptions of democracy and liberty. Historian Andrew Hartman wrote the following of midcentury education reform: "As Americans variously experienced the crisis of the Cold War as a crisis in education, both consciously and subconsciously, the schools, in turn, facilitated the construction of 'cold warriors' conditioned to fear and loathe Communism, the Soviet Union, and more nebulously, leftist ideas in general."[31] Like many of his contemporaries, including Kirk and Ransom, Chalmers was indeed obsessed with how to best mount an ideological attack against anti-American thought structures.

In *The Republic and the Person* (1952), Chalmers warned about ruinous repercussions for what he argued was the disintegration of American liberalism during the 1920s and 1930s. He aimed to reorient education toward the production of "responsible American liberalism of a kind adequate to our obligations abroad and at home."[32] With conviction, he continued, "All provision for order and common welfare must not only avoid violating the rights of the individual but must positively serve the maximum opportunity for the individual to exercise his civil rights." Chalmers revisited what, over a decade earlier, Louis Mumford warned was a developing "disintegrated" American liberalism. Mumford argued that during the Second World War, liberalism's tendency toward moral equivocation, its insistence on dispassionate rationality and debate, and its dismissal of emotion prohibited the nation's timely attendance "to the overwhelming duty of the moment, in a spirit of clear-sighted understanding." Mumford worried that "in a disintegrating world, pragmatic liberalism has lost its integrity but retained its limitations."[33] Chalmers argued that restoring integrity to liberalism was a necessary goal for American education given the nation's postwar vulnerability to alien ideology.

Chalmers knew that he was not alone among academic leaders in reconsidering the relationship between education and democracy in the face of the Communist threat, but he did not wholly agree with the loudest of college presidents. In the penultimate chapter of *The Republic and the Person*, he engaged with Harvard president James Bryant Conant's popular solution to the preservation of democracy—using the national system of education to realize a technocratic national order, in which rational leaders would make political decisions with profound moral implications on the basis of statistics and social science. Chalmers argued that in *Education in a Divided World*, Conant had misunderstood the point of studying language, literature, and history.[34] In addition to a public equipped to read editorials and form what Walter Lippman, borrowing from Jefferson and Madison, called "public opinion," Chalmers imagined a kind of education that would teach students "how to think responsibly and fruitfully about our nature in order that we may not only understand but fulfill the urgent request of our friends abroad that America provide the world with moral leadership."[35] In his view, "mastery of the humane knowledge necessary for liberal and democratic government" should "stand at the center of the objectives of higher education; every device and plan, for the schools as well as the universities, should be made in the light of it."[36] Chalmers argued that Conant misunderstood humanistic study as a source of pleasure and enrichment; its true value was in broadening access to a sophisticated, firm understanding of "human nature" that could restore integrity to liberalism and, in turn, save democracy.

Chalmers's simultaneous devotion to Protestantism and his position of power within the academy demanded reckoning with *God and Man at Yale* (1951), William F. Buckley's politicized crusade against secular liberalism.[37] Chalmers understood school as a microcosm of the kind of community he hoped to promulgate throughout the country and devoted a chapter in *The Republic and the Person* to arguing in favor of incorporating Protestant worship into collegiate life as an antidote to both New Deal state control and the moral relativism he worried was emerging from the Second World War. In the fashion of other conservative thinkers, he worried that "the theological ignorance of American humane learning has contributed to ethical ignorance and moral decline."[38] But in a direct refutation of Buckley's polemic about academic freedom as a superstition that would undermine religious life in America, Chalmers wrote, "The improvement would come not because dogma and conformity to creeds had influenced common education. Far from it, for that describes neither the Protestant nor the liberal relation of faith to learning. The improvement would be effected because the purely human principles on which many men may agree at the level of action would not be analyzed in ignorance." He continued, "For while it is true that throughout the ages and at present there has been earnest disagreement about these ultimates, it is also true that belief in their existence is of paramount importance to all men."[39] Even as Chalmers remained committed to the notion of religious education, he argued that responsible citizenship—and the education attendant to it—was both intellectually liberal and guided by faith in morality.

In articles and essays, Chalmers expounded on his positions pertaining to the relationship between liberalism and the best system of education to sustain it. Echoing Ransom's call for professionalized, serious attention to reading habits, Chalmers denounced "relaxed, friendly, sentimental, and humanitarian education," blaming it as both a symptom and a cause for "our unwillingness as a people to discipline ourselves."[40] He mocked the nation's lack of intellectual preparedness to fend off the Soviet Union's un-Christian ideological threat: "Having gone to school in institutions which are boyish, relaxed, imprecise, and sentimental, we are acting like boys in the face of intellectualized evil."[41] Like Ransom, Chalmers advocated instead for a mode of reading that uncovered hard truths. The aim was not to reform or to expand democracy in the progressive sense but to protect constitutionalism and uphold high intellectual standards. Chalmers envisioned individuals with the autonomy to self-govern according to the strictures of the nation's founding documents.

While Chalmers did acknowledge and celebrate the social progress arising from Dewey's efforts at reform, he disagreed with Deweyan framing of the child as a sentimental "Rousseauen innocent." Chalmers's view of the humanities might seem cold, but it was far from detached. Rather, in his view, reading was deeply personal: "If the law for man is the center of studies, the child must begin to read literature not as an aesthetic picnic of the sensations but for what it is, the contest within men's own hearts. If he is to do this, his teachers must respect language and the word."[42] Active, lively, sharp moral imagination was crucial to his traditionalist conservative worldview because it could liberate Americans from what Chalmers viewed as dogmatic pragmatism or overemotional reaction. In an open jab at Dewey, he dismissed teachers and professors who concerned themselves with "developing 'attitudes' rather than by coping with the hard job of increasing the number who can read critically." He was resistant to the idea of mass consensus at the expense of individual thought. Instead, he imagined that "the social objective for popular education" could be "to bring a large number of people to the point where they can read accurately the editorials of the day."[43]

Chalmers defended the concept of constitutionalism—the idea that the nation is held together by adherence to the document outlining its governing ideals. In line with New Humanists like Babbitt and the next generation of academic conservatives like Richard Weaver, he rejected valuing sentimentalism, feeling, and generalities over critical thought and specificity because he worried that these tendencies left students susceptible to weak ideas. Chalmers echoed Kirk's insistence on protecting an invisible, universal natural order: "In a time in world history when the great organized forces both of intellect and of military power are mobilized against the universality of law and due process, it is clear that the central intellectual task of lovers of freedom is the understanding and exposition of these things." In keeping with his experience as both a Protestant and a humanist, Chalmers understood American democracy as a text-based tradition upheld through exegetical study and rigorous debate. Chalmers was concerned about the diminishing role of the humanities not only in universities but in public life. He linked the failures of American education and political life: "The reason for all the failure of thinking in the political sphere has been poor humanities. These errors of national policy are the price we have paid for starving them, for forgetting what the humanities are for, and for failing to re-define and re-discover their purpose and content."[44] Chalmers defended humanistic study as a legitimate means to navigate the human problems students would face in an automated, industrialized, and globalized world.

Despite what Chalmers described as his own "conservative" mindset, it's important to understand him as a proactive reformer. Chalmers's emphasis on notions like character and universality of human experience fell in line with Kirk's brand of conservatism, and his approach to reading literature as a sort of science leading to universal truths aligned with John Crowe Ransom's New Criticism. Against his understanding of the prevailing purposes for studying literature, he fumed, "The humanities are not culture; they are not escape; they are not antiquity; they are not texts; they are not art history; they are not philology; they are not tradition. They are materials and method by which we understand the ethos of modern American life."[45] As Dewey had promoted pragmatic reforms and Conant was working to promote the power of social science, Chalmers would fight for the maintenance of qualitative, individualistic thinking.

THE KENYON PLAN

As previous chapters have discussed, Korean War conscription, the ideological lure of Communism, and grappling with postwar uncertainty animated much of the national conversation about education reform in the early 1950s. In 1951, the Ford Foundation established its Fund for the Advancement of Education to promote its postwar mission of the "achievement of peace."[46] That same year, the faculty of Kenyon College discussed the possibility of revising bachelor's degree requirements to accommodate "able students in strong secondary schools to pursue a liberal arts education at a pace appropriate to their ability and their teachers' interest and skills."[47]

Recognizing that they were addressing issues with ramifications far beyond Kenyon, Chalmers convened a committee of leaders from elite liberal arts colleges and well-respected public and private school administrators to discuss solutions to the simultaneous problem of inefficiency and protection of the liberal arts. Beginning in 1951, meetings involved faculty and administrators from the Massachusetts Institute of Technology, Bowdoin College, Brown University, Carleton College, Haverford College, Kenyon College, Middlebury College, Oberlin College, Swarthmore College, Wabash College, Wesleyan University, Williams College, and school representatives from Brookline High School, the Brooks School, Central High School, the St. Louis Country Day School, the Germantown Friends School, Lower Merion Senior High School, Horace Mann, Western Reserve Academy, Oak Park and River Schools, Evanston Township High School, the Bronx High School of Science, the Providence school district, and Newton High School.

By 1952, the group, now calling itself the School and College Study for Admission with Advanced Standing, had appealed to the Ford Foundation's Fund for the Advancement of Education for support. Clarence Faust and Alvin Eurich, president and vice president of the Fund for the Advancement of Education, respectively, were excited to hear from Chalmers, in part because they were "disappointed at the slowness of Al Blackmer's committee."[48] Over the next three years, the fund would go on to award Chalmers's group $189,000—almost $2 million in 2022.[49] The School and College Study produced several reports on areas of mutual agreement and a concrete scheme for improving college preparation for gifted high school students rooted in the ideology Chalmers expressed in his writing. The group's publications included a 1953 report on subcommittees' progress toward defining courses, a 1954 announcement and course bulletin building on that work, and a 1956 "final report and summary" advertising the program's vision for secondary school and college alignment. In each discipline, the subcommittees' recommendations differed: English language and literature committees did not suggest specific readings while the Latin committee did. All offered general outlines of their discipline's contours and the ways college freshmen could benefit from them.

In 1952, Chalmers published a report in the *College Board Review* apprising fellow educators of the project excerpted from the group's book-length announcement. He wrote, "The colleges cooperating in the study might be called conservative in the sense that they have not abandoned liberal for general education nor adopted the university device of the core curriculum."[50] Whereas Conant had conflated "liberal" and "general" education, Chalmers believed his endeavor to be staking space for traditional disciplinarity. "In one way and another," he wrote, "the subject-matter committees are considering how to define and describe this central core of required knowledge and the ability to use it."[51] He expressed the School and College Study's view that if students could transfer credits between colleges, they could transfer credits from high school to college, and that these decisions would need to be made by academic departments. He never mentioned Robert Hutchins by name in *The Republic and the Person*, but two years into the School and College Study, Chalmers explained to John W. Hallowell, headmaster of Ohio's Western Reserve Academy, "The basic philosophical reason for all this has not been stressed, largely because it is much more controversial than the instructional part of the problem. . . . Graduates [from the general education programs at the University of Chicago and Columbia University] fascinate and amaze people with their pat dismissal of subtle and complex human problems. This is what comes of easy and early generalization."[52] Inviting collaboration around this intellectual orientation, whether it was explicit or overt, represented an investment in a particular philosophy of education.

The group's ideological framework was apparent in the plans. As an administrator, Chalmers was committed to strengthening Kenyon's humanities program.[53] Cornog, then president of Philadelphia's integrated Central School and Chalmers's cochair, also had a doctorate in English. Given the broader goal of aligning high school and college, the School and College Study echoed its leaders' dedication to language and literature. Although neither of the men were

on the subject committees, the plans stipulated, for instance, that AP
English Language class sizes be limited to fewer than twenty students
so that each teacher could "know and deal with each of his pupils as a
thinking individual." The aim of the course was neither transactional
nor career-oriented: "The student should be led to regard his theme
writing not as means to an end, but as an intrinsically valuable process of mental self-exploration and orientation."[54] The AP English
Literature course description repeated this defense of the inherent
worth of engaging with words. The committee authoring the bulletin articulated their "fixed belief that the basic aim of all teaching of
literature is to broaden comprehension and enhance enjoyment of
literature, the greatest single criticism of life."[55] In keeping with this
humanistic ethos, they are also careful to note that "there is nothing
mechanical about the full reading of a piece of literature, and there is
no slide-rule by which to compute its dimensions."[56] The emphasis
was on qualitative, rather than quantitative, outcomes, and on maintaining the integrity of the discipline over concerns about measurement and credentials—the point was to make education meaningful,
not to make it easily calculable.

Concern for distinguishing between vocational training and liberal arts education is apparent throughout their group's work. In a
prefatory note to the 1954 *Bulletin* explaining the program's structure and courses, this committee expressed that it "wholeheartedly
supports the values of a liberal education, and would caution school
advisers not to let these opportunities for advanced work become
vocational."[57] They warned that individual growth should be the goal,
not credentialing or vocational training. "We deplore but accept the
necessity of measuring scholastic progress by credit counts," they
wrote, "but we do not accept the mere acquisition of credit as the aim
of our plan."[58] But there was a tension implicit in the program from
the start. The bulletin concludes with some notes on the small pilot
program undertaken during the previous academic year: students
were eager to participate because they "recognized the benefit . . . in

the prospect of an earlier start in their professional careers following graduation from college."[59] As the committee's plans materialized, practical concerns challenged the idealism at the core of their vision.

The notion of a national system of examinations made critics uneasy. Vocal detractors warned about the dangers inherent to ceding to such a system. Oberlin chemistry professor Luke Steiner rejected an offer to chair the examination committee in his discipline, explaining to Cornog that he supported the notion of advanced placement and inter-institutional exchange, but that "it is to be expected that administrators—both in the colleges and the secondary schools—should think in terms of standards as automatic in operation as possible. Examinations act as such standards. However, [he believed] that formal examinations, if emphasized, tend to distort the learning process." In correspondence with Steiner, Cornog explained that teachers at his own school "don't give a hoot" about external measures of success, and that examinations were the quickest possible way to ensure the program's success. According to Cornog, the Fund for the Advancement of Education invested in the program because of "its broad applicability, and in the influence which it may have in American education, especially on secondary education. The only way in which a system of advance credit may have currency, at least in its first years, is by means of a series of validating examinations."[60]

While addressing the "problem of communication" among faculties in schools and colleges, the Central Committee stated directly, "The college teachers have no wish to standardize courses and restrict the freedom and initiative of the teachers." Still, some worried that the plans for examinations would do just that. Charles M. Coffin, chairman of Kenyon's English department, called the plans for the English literature course "over-elaborate and confining," and warned that the sample examinations in the field were "too prescriptive and mechanical."[61] On behalf of his colleagues, he advised against offering "any program which would impose a stereotype or pattern of uniformity upon their work." The group made clear in their report their respect for the judgment of individual educators when they provided the qualification to their plans that "definitions and examinations can never be allowed to be the sole criteria for determining the granting of advanced credit. Much weight must be given to other evidence of unusual ability and valued personal qualities."[62] In tacit acknowledgment that there was tension between the Kenyon Plan's pedagogical philosophies and plans for implementation, Cornog wrote, "I think that after a few years of experience and with the growth of mutual confidence and respect among schools and colleges, much can be done for improvement of instruction on both levels, and a system of accreditation of schools or school departments may well eventuate."[63]

In the meantime, exams were central to the School and College Study's plans. In 1953, Bayes Norton, Kenyon chemistry professor, School and College Study Chemistry Committee member, and eventual chairman of the College Board's Commission on Advanced Standing, expressed concern to a fellow committee member "about the singular emphasis on the examining program for this year. The examining committees are merely sub-committees. Perhaps the over-emphasis comes from the Andover report's recommendation causing the examining problem to be dropped in the lap of SACS."[64] With irritation, Cornog said of the Blackmer Committee's work, "Their plan is a beatitude, ours is a blueprint."[65] While the Blackmer Committee focused on the six institutions with which its members were affiliated, the group from Kenyon had hoped to generate conversation about a more transcendent sense of mission and standards. Exams would externalize expectations and facilitate communication as they preserved liberal education.

CHANGING HANDS

In February 1954, two years after Blackmer had expressed faith in "a 'think' team and implementing team" to Fund for the Advancement of Education vice president Alvin Eurich, the fund denied a request from Chalmers for an additional "$40,000 to support the development of teaching in the schools and two-day regional conferences of school officials of more than 400 schools." Despite "recognizing fully the need for the type of activities outlined" in the proposal, Eurich had disappointing news. The fund "had a firm policy from the outset of our operations not to provide funds for special conferences or work periods designed to advance any particular program in education." Eurich explained, "We have attempted to utilize the funds for exploration and demonstration purposes on the assumption that once the worth of an idea has been demonstrated, it could be advanced most effectively through the usual channels provided by educational organizations and institutions."[66] He suggested that independent universities might sponsor the kinds of organic exchanges Chalmers envisioned—institutes where teachers and professors would clarify and hone their shared sense for the disciplines in which they comprised two halves of education between grades 11 and 14.

When Chalmers and Cornog submitted their "third and final report" to the fund in 1954, they knew the program would be out of their hands soon and they were clear about their vision: "The plan entails a public promise by a group of colleges to strong schools and strong students. It is that if the schools will organize college freshman level courses in any of the ten subjects central to the first years of liberal college education, the colleges with school help will examine graduates of these courses."[67] Unlike Blackmer's insistence that his group's study concerned six specific institutions, Chalmers's group imagined a vaster reach. On May 27, 1954, as Chalmers faced the end of his control over the program, he was explicit in a letter to Eurich: "The center of this whole program is the teaching. The examination is merely an available and objective method of setting standards for the teaching and standards for general acceptance and recognition of the teaching by a great many colleges."[68] In February of that year, the College Board's William Fels explained in a speech to the

National Association of Secondary School Principals that testing could not compete with the nation's mobility, its multiple philosophies of education, and the meaning of subject matter in defining the structure of American education. Still, the title of his talk was "How Tests May Be Used to Obtain Better Articulation of the Total Educational System."[69] Cornog himself, along with Frank Ashburn, B. Alden Thresher, Archibald MacIntosh, members of the Study's Executive Committee, were also College Board officers, but the organizations' priorities were distinct.

Chalmers and Cornog were not among those present for a New York City meeting on November 14, 1955, for members of the School and College Study and representatives from the College Board and the Educational Testing Service. Minutes from this first meeting "under the Board's sponsorship" are vague about the transfer of power between the entities: "At the request of the Fund for the Advancement of Education, which had financed the Program under the School and College Study of Admission with Advanced Standing, the Board agreed to assume responsibility for the Program upon the condition that this sponsorship was agreeable to the Study. Since the SCSAAS could not continue its work, it was agreed that the Board should continue its operation."[70] Of course, the School and College Study had stopped its work, at least in part, for lack of support from the Fund for the Advancement of Education. "It was agreed" that the College Board should take control of the program, but by whom? And why?

From the start of the College Board's management of the program, it was clear that it would evolve away from the School and College Study's blueprints. On December 30, 1955, the College Board's Advanced Placement director Charles Keller wrote to Chalmers, "The College Board has an over-all Program which is a continuation of, a development from, the School and College Study of Admission with Advanced Standing." In a paragraph about concern for Harvard's outsized influence on American education, Keller was clear that as he and Chalmers made plans to promote Advanced Placement along the West Coast, "the Board's program should not be confused with the practices of any one college or university."[71] Keller was optimistic about the ways the program could strengthen relationships between and among teachers and professors.[72] The scheme would represent consensus about schools' standards and missions, not the goals of any particular academic institution.

CORNOG'S REFLECTIONS

Chalmers did not survive to see the practical implementation of his ideas. For reflection on the program's effectiveness at translating ideas into practice, I turn to the work of William Hafner Cornog, the codirector of the Central Committee that produced the School and College Study. In Cornog, Chalmers found an intellectual and political sympathizer who condemned unthinking industrialization and insisted that humanistic study was relevant, and could fortify the nation's students against otherwise imminent decline. Cornog, executive director of the School and College Study, began his career as a medievalist, translating the works of Alain de Lille to fulfill his dissertation requirements. Cornog published a history of Philadelphia's Central High School, where he was principal until 1954. In the book's forward, he wrote, "We have inherited the task of realizing in our forms, institutions, and structures of government if not the ideal and perfect state, then the means by which the ideals of freedom, justice, and equality, may be more nearly approached." For Cornog, democracy was premised on the notion "that men possess or in time shall possess the qualities of mind and heart to share with equal dutifulness and skill the basic obligations of democratic citizenship."[73] In his view, public education was essential to cultivating the human potential that such a civilization required. Given mutual commitments to education for democratic aims and proclivities for shuttling back and forth between historical idioms in search of poetry, it is unsurprising that he shared many of Chalmers's views, not least of all a commitment to a humanistic view of education. Cornog's concern about the quality of education led to wariness about developing a program that was more performative than substantive. He wrote, "When the intensive courses were first being discussed by high school faculties, a number of teachers gained the impression that this was an invitation to pile on the work, to require large amounts of reading, to require long, long hours of homework. This is certainly not the spirit of the Study, and it is educationally unsound."[74] In multiple ways, Cornog was more interested in quality than in quantity, and he understood the conflation of the two as a mistake.

Like Chalmers, Cornog's vision was for a small, distinctive program. He expected the experiment to be costly and justified the program's implementation costs by appealing to recent reforms for "minority populations" and pushing for inclusion of "gifted students" in this group. For Cornog, an acceptance of inequality was baked into American education. His vision for education was Jeffersonian, inasmuch as he understood it as the birthright of each student in a democracy to receive the most challenging possible level of education.[75] Cornog wrote, "The time has long since come . . . to give our gifted students their counterpart of educational opportunity on the same terms as we have sought to give opportunity to the backward, the handicapped, and all minorities in public education."[76] In a 1980 *College Board Review* assessment of the program, he wrote, "Special education, extraordinary provision for the ablest students was as justifiable as for the disabled, on the plain principle of democracy. This argument was always called the dirtiest word in educational debating, 'elitist.'" In principle, he believed that public schools should push all students to their unique, personal limits, though "this is not to say that everyone expending honest effort will achieve the same reward."[77]

Although Cornog was unabashed about who he believed should have access to Advanced Placement courses (the first line of the first course description in the *Bulletin* stipulates that students should only be encouraged to enroll if "their native abilities are great"), he believed in broad access to the enrichment and quality of life he envisioned for "able students." He hoped that this program for gifted students would inspire high academic standards for all students: "I am unpersuaded that the majority of our students are fit only to be taught to earn a living, salute the flag, make orderly exits from burning buildings. . . . To base education in any large scope on the assumption that common men cannot be touched by greatness or uplifted by genius is to conspire with degradation and embrace despair."[78] For all students, Cornog rejected arguments for a utilitarian educational scheme that he took to deny the sanctity of the individual.

Part of the explanation for this interest in the expansion of the liberal arts is that, like Chalmers, Cornog believed this form of education to be aligned with the project of democracy. "My thesis is that poetry is more important to our salvation than rocketry," he wrote by the mid-1960s.[79] Also like Chalmers, he hoped that schools could become breeding grounds for a unifying "public philosophy."[80] Cornog took several moral propositions to be underlying the School and College Study, the first of which was an understanding that "democracy is a fluid, restless, dynamic, and thoughtful society in which men by taking thought can under their established rights of freedom of thought and expression constantly improve their lives. . . . It is organic."[81] An education that would prepare students for such a society must share in those characteristics, and so rigidity had no place in the vision he promoted. "The mature citizen" Cornog imagined "pursues the good life for its own rewards and cherishes virtue because he has seen it effective in the lives of men living and dead. And he does none of these things instinctively, out of innate goodness of heart, but because his education has taught him the force of right reason and natural law and the sanctions of a great culture."[82]

The benefits of such a system for Cornog, as for Chalmers, were not transactional. He insisted, "The school must approach an experiment in intensive college Freshman level work with the clear conviction that the aim of the experiment is not to accelerate the bright, not to coach or to tutor the bright students to jump through higher hoops, but is to provide a kind of teaching which shall, by its depth as well as its breadth, truly challenge the kind and the character of the student and the best resources and imagination of the teachers." Like Kirk and Chalmers, Cornog distinguished between education and vocational training—individual development was an end in its own right. He expected the experiment to be costly: "The teaching load for teachers of these small special groups must be lighter than ordinary." He continued, "The emphasis in all these courses should properly not be on quantity but on quality."[83]

Cornog was interested in cultivating autonomous citizens. For Cornog, the point was never to create a cost-effective slate of liberal arts courses but to provide education for the public good. In 1964, he wrote, "There is no more to be learned about the arts of war. Perfection has been achieved. Indeed with grotesque illogic it can be said that the ultimate has been surpassed; the military establishment has acquired the capacity to overkill. The hardware is ready and the delivery schedules have been plotted on both sides. So be it. School still keeps."[84] In order to prepare students for adult participation in democratic institutions, both Chalmers and Cornog understood firm grounding in letters as a defense against collectivism's soullessness.

CONCLUSION

On May 26, 1955, the *Kenyon Collegian* reported, "Kenyon's fight against the machine-made education has begun to gain followers. The first signs of this can be seen in the 'School and College Study for Advanced Standing.'"[85] To the undergraduates at Kenyon, and to Chalmers and Cornog, the Advanced Placement program represented an effort to restore integrity to secondary education by adapting it not only to the needs of liberal arts colleges but also to students' aptitudes and interests. And, in so doing, Chalmers and Cornog understood themselves to be upholding political commitments to classical liberalism and deliberative democracy. To understand education as a humanistic, rather than mechanistic, enterprise aligned with notions of the American political tradition in which citizens rely on each other's humanity in a system of self-governance. Chalmers framed this commitment as part of a conservative agenda, but, as I discuss in the next three chapters, left-leaning thinkers have championed liberal arts education for similar reasons.

Chalmers warned against education programs that were "training of those to be governed, not the education of governors. This means the education of slaves, not of free men."[86] Today, the issues of mechanistic education and recognizing the educational enterprise as humanistic are still ones of power and subjugation. In *Between the World and Me*, Ta-Nehisi Coates testified to his experience of "education rendered as rote discipline" in Baltimore's public schools. "To be educated in my Baltimore public school mostly meant always packing an extra number 2 pencil and working quietly. . . . Algebra, Biology, and English were not subjects so much as opportunities to better discipline the body, to practice writing between the lines, copying the directions legibly, memorizing theorems extracted from the world they were created to represent."[87] The lack of immediacy and personal investment Coates experienced speaks to the kind of education that Chalmers and Cornog argued could not prepare students for deliberative democracy. Now, as the Advanced Placement program grows, it is doing the opposite of what it was designed to do. Chalmers's faith in the ability of a small group of people to set national standards has led to exams that valorize unthinking compliance instead of the thoughtfulness he wrote about fostering. He recognized that the program's administration would determine its impact. The second part of this book examines its current shape.

PART II
Accountability

CHAPTER 4

Copy Paste Classroom

The College Board's marketing materials maintain that the Advanced Placement program "offers college-level courses and exams that you can take in high school."[1] Despite claiming to eradicate the line between high school and college, the College Board actually reinforces that boundary through their new digital platform, AP Classroom. Ostensibly, this service was designed to help teachers "give you assignments using resources that help you learn AP content and skills and demonstrate your knowledge and capabilities."[2] In reality, it curtails teachers' autonomy and highlights the differences between their roles and those of college instructors, as well as the nature of the instruction students receive. In this chapter, I examine recent innovations in Advanced Placement US History that threaten to transform the teaching of college-level American history—which should be an expression of care for students and for the subject matter—into a perversely dehumanized transaction.

THE NEW PLATFORM: AP CLASSROOM
AND THE "COURSE FRAMEWORK"

In 2019, current College Board CEO David Coleman appointed a former McKinsey colleague, Jeremy Singer, as the new president of the College Board. In a celebratory interview posted to the company's website, Singer said that he had originally expected his career "would involve leading a large for-profit education company" but then explained that he signed on with the nonprofit College Board because he was impressed with its "reach" and its successful efforts at expansion. He expected that in the next few years, he would work to "leverage new technology so our programs are easier to navigate for students and educators."[3] This twinned commitment to dominance and automation is evident in the company's new platform, AP Classroom.

AP Classroom is "powered by" a product called Elevate, developed by ed tech start-up Finetune.[4] On LinkedIn, Finetune advertises Elevate as "a digital assessment platform that helps instructors improve student performance in dozens of different subject areas." The company claims, "It enables a fast, virtuous cycle of formative assessments and feedback" that helps students "improve their performance for their high-stakes summative exam." A linked video advertises more specific benefits, including "an innovative workflow," "a library of thousands of questions so teachers can focus on specific skills and topics," "auto-scoring of assessments," "browser lockdown," "live status reports to the teacher," and a "credentialing engine that allows teachers to earn certification on their own pace."[5] In other words, Elevate is a surveillance and standardization machine.

In 2012, Finetune's founder, Ogden Morse, explained that he had developed a pedagogy rooted in "knowing in quantifiable fashion how each student is performing" and found that his tools "aligned seamlessly" with the Common Core standards.[6] This approach to instruction—quantification of skills, describing what students do as "performing"—differs drastically from my own, and, as we will see in the next section of this chapter, from that of the AP program's original founders. Morse admitted that many of his colleagues were resistant to "any sort of substantive change" in their own practices. But now the company's partnership with the College Board means that, according to an interview with Finetune's CEO Steve Shapiro, "Finetune's pedagogical approach will be used in all 36 AP Exams," regardless of the range of teachers and diversity of course content involved.[7]

Descriptions of AP Classroom geared toward investors indicate that the platform uses software to compensate for human teachers' perceived limitations. The College Board may technically be a "mission-driven non-profit," but Finetune has no such pretensions. Sovereignty is the goal, even if the weight of "Finetune's pedagogical approach" threatens to crush the vitality that gives coursework meaning.

Elevate powers AP Classroom, an online portal for students who are either enrolled in AP courses or planning to take AP exams. The College Board's public, if oblique, explanation to parents for the existence of this new service reads, "AP Classroom is an online resource that can be used by AP teachers and students." A list of features includes "topic questions," "personal progress checks," and a "progress dashboard." Descriptions of these elements are student-centered: "students can answer the Topic Questions after each class and get feedback," "students can complete the Personal Progress Check at the end of each unit," and "students can see how their skills are developing across units."[8] Per the description, teachers may use the platform, but as the list of features makes clear, teachers' involvement seems unnecessary for students to benefit from it. According to the College Board website, as long as a student pays his or her exam fees, they can access the site, even if not enrolled in a course.[9]

"Classroom," the name of the College Board's "resource," demands reckoning with which aspects of a physical classroom the site upholds and which it destroys. Picture a high school history classroom. Its technologies facilitate multidimensional relationships: between teacher and students, among students, between students and material. In a tacit acknowledgment that students sometimes stare at the wall, a poster offers food for thought from Frederick Douglass: "Find out just what any people will quietly submit to and you have found out the exact measure of injustice and wrong which will be imposed upon them." Thirty-five student chairs with attached tablet desks are arranged in pods of five, to facilitate both whole-class discussions and more intimate debates. On the windowsill, there's a bottle of cleaner and a roll of paper towels for wiping away the notes students scribble to each other on these surfaces: "happy wednesday" in small, penciled script. Printouts of student research papers with scrawled teacher comments on the back bulletin board display evidence of attention paid: "avoid passive voice," "awk," "strong work." In the corner of the whiteboard, the teacher lets stand a tiny haiku from someone in third period to someone in sixth. On the teacher's desk, stacks of freshly copied newspaper articles relevant to the day's topic await distribution. A bookcase holds source material, dictionaries, and thesauruses for when no one, including the teacher, knows the answer. In the case of American history especially, a classroom is a site for students to engage with, agree upon, argue over, and become part of public memory. Material conditions shape possibilities for communication and meaning.

AP Classroom is a cheaper version of the real thing, and the quality of education it offers is likewise impoverished. The presentation of information on AP Classroom is clean, sterile, and static. When students log in, they see columns and rows in a black and serene blue colorscape. A header allows students to toggle between the courses in which they are enrolled. There are links to separate pages for assessments and a "progress dashboard" that lists assignments and outcomes for both multiple-choice and free-response questions. Below the header is a welcome banner, and below that, each course offers the same grid: across the top, a list of units from 1 to 9. Click on Unit 4, and you see a list of "skill categories," skill codes, and aligned, numbered daily videos. At the bottom of each unit page, there is a "personal progress check" with links to both multiple-choice and free-response questions. Teachers can view any student's page at any time to check on their progress. The website is contingent on a definition of education without mutual learning and discovery, inert in terms of both the distribution and creation of content, and baldly transactional. In physical classrooms, teaching is a changing set of social and cultural practices. AP Classroom's rigidity shapes relationships.

In the quest to streamline, code, replicate, and expand, AP Classroom also distorts the subject matter. A document called the "Course Framework" attempts to fix US history into a set of stable ideas and skills that are compatible with AP Classroom's organizational scheme. The manual for US History teachers is simultaneously dizzying and reductive. Everything is quantifiable: there are nine units and roughly fifteen instructional periods per unit. Each day has an associated "skill" from a list of six, a "reasoning process" from a list of three, and a "theme" from a list of eight. Each skill, reasoning process, and theme has a code. So, for instance, in Unit 4, a day devoted to "The Rise of Political Parties and the Era of Jefferson" aligns with "Theme 5: Politics and Power (PCE)," skill 2.A, "Identify a source's point of view, purpose, historical situation, and/or audience," and the "causation" reasoning process. One wonders, Why not discuss Jefferson and party formation in alignment with "Theme 8: Social Structures (SOC)," skill 1.B, "Explain a historical concept, development, or process," and the "change and continuity" reasoning process? Or with "Theme 1: American and National Identity (NAT)," skill 4.A, "Identify and describe a historical context for a specific historical development or process," and the "comparison" reasoning process?[10] Who knows? And, one suspects, who cares? What's clear is that the insistence on systematizing desiccates the course's meaning.

In place of a narrative description of the course's version of US history, a chart shows how the themes "spiral" through each unit. Each theme is not present in each unit. For instance, according to the chart, "migration and settlement (MIG)" is neither a major feature of Unit 4, the period 1800–1844, nor of Unit 5, from 1844 to 1877. Is the takeaway, then, that waves of Chinese immigration or the formation of the Know-Nothing party are not relevant to today's students' understanding of the history of migration and settlement in the United States? I am not a historian by training. But it came as a surprise to me that "American national identity (NAT)" was not a main concern from 1890 to 1945, nor has it been one from 1980 to the present. It has certainly felt like one of the country's defining contests in my lifetime. The lens of "Geography and the Environment (GEO)" is pertinent to understanding the years 1491–1607, 1607–1754, 1800–1848, 1844–1877, 1890–1945, 1945–1980, but not 1754–1800, 1865–1898, or 1980–present. Why do the years for some of these units overlap? Why doesn't the course account for emerging research in colonial or contemporary environmental history? Don't worry about it.

As developers of the framework struggle to explain what the document is, they demonstrate awareness of the notion of overreach. There is a disclaimer in the preface: "Experienced AP teachers who are satisfied with their current course organization and exam results" may choose not to use the new suggestions. "As history teachers know well," the guide says in acknowledgment of its audience, "the material in this framework cannot be taught without careful attention to the individuals, events, and documents of American history; however, to ensure teachers have flexibility to teach specific content that is valued locally and individually, the course avoids prescribing details that would require all teachers to teach the same historical examples."[11] Although this disclaimer is designed to quell fears about top-down content prescription, for me it has the opposite effect. First, we need to bear in mind that today's "inexperienced AP teachers" are tomorrow's experienced AP teachers. And because of the myriad demands on a teacher's time and attention, it is difficult to radically alter established teaching habits. So even if AP Classroom does not instill uniformity in course content upon implementation, it almost certainly will over time. Second, the choice of the word "avoids" is disturbing because it signals awareness that enforced uniformity is an option, even if magnanimously avoided for the moment. The statement is an admission that the program is in control of the degree to which teachers maintain the flexibility to exercise value judgments. And since the College Board sets the final exam, it also prescribes preparation. The threat of total control may not be immediate, but it is genuine—and even more vivid now that the College Board dictates the readings for AP US Government, as I discuss in chapter 6.

Concerns about standardization of the APUSH curriculum predate the rollout of AP Classroom. In 2014, the first year an APUSH "framework" was released, backlash from conservatives resulted in an attempt to clarify that such a document is distinct from a curriculum. Ben Carson warned that the framework was so anti-American it would inspire students to "go sign up for ISIS."[12] The Republican National Committee called it "radically revisionist."[13] David Coleman published a letter commending right-wing critics as "patriots who care deeply about what students learn" and reassuring skeptics that students would need to study white men like Benjamin Franklin, George Washington, and Franklin Delano Roosevelt to succeed on the exam. "It is just a framework," Coleman insisted, as if this nonexplanation made any sense.[14] When I heard the conservatives' complaints, I rolled my eyes in response to their paranoid hyperbole. I still do. Unlike Carson and the RNC, my concern is not with the course's political argument. I like the program's inclusion of social history, its insistence on beginning in 1492, and the time devoted to the history of slavery. It pains me to think that critiquing the program's infrastructure carries with it the risk of losing commitment or access to this content. But all records—even lists of facts—have arguments and internal logics, and implicit in the APUSH "framework" are the values and commitments of its scribes, and not necessarily of its users.

In response to the RNC's concerns that the framework was composed of "requirements," the writers of the APUSH exam explained in a separate letter that by sidestepping the assignment of specific people, places, and events, teachers "could populate the course with material that is meaningful to them." If, as even the College Board's materials suggest, history relies on developing narratives based on evidence, it seems counterintuitive to offer a timeline and then charge teachers with finding evidence to support it. If teachers are expected to give the course substance, it's unclear what kind of a document the "framework" even is. Put another way, what is "the material in this framework" if not what the preface's disclaimer referred to as the "individuals, events, and documents of American history"? What is the substance of this timeline? At the college level, events, ideas, and people gain or lose historical significance through argumentation, but for AP teachers and students the calendar of topics is fixed. By dictating elements like breakneck speed through chronology, the document makes arguments about how students and teachers ought to approach the discipline. It aligns more closely with AP Classroom than with any theoretically cogent view of history.

Historian Hayden White theorized that a work of history is a narrative "that purports to be a model, or icon, of past structures and processes in the interest of explaining what they were by representing them."[15] But in the absence of a narrative, the course framework and AP Classroom make value judgments and then obscure them with codes and charts, replacing what White calls "verbal structures" with bureaucratic ones. The high-stakes exam then demands submission to this mold.

Meanwhile, undergraduate American history courses with preeminent scholars emphasize other habits of mind. At Yale, "Climate and Environment in America, 1500–1870" provides "a foundation for understanding modern American and global climate and environmental issues." "The Age of Hamilton and Jefferson" organizes information biographically, "using the lives, ideas, and writings of Thomas Jefferson and Alexander Hamilton as a starting point."[16] At Johns Hopkins University, "Black Baltimore Archives—From Frederick

Douglass to Billie Holiday" offers "an intense exploration (and excavation) of local African American history and narrative." Students "explore questions connected to creating the historical record" by visiting the "*Afro-American Newspaper* archives, the Maryland Center for History and Culture, the Maryland State Archives, and Morgan State University special collections, among other key archival repositories. Students will participate in a national conference and a local jazz event."[17] At Georgetown University, students can enroll in "The US in the World to 1945," in which students "analyze U.S. foreign relations, a broader category than simply foreign policy by examining the political, military, economic, religious, and cultural influence of the U.S. The course begins with the Declaration of Independence and ends with World War II."[18] None of these schools offer credit or placement for AP US History exams. Nor does Williams College, home of Advanced Placement's first director, Charles Keller. There, the department policy is that "all first-year students are welcome to take any of the first-year seminars or tutorials (100-level courses) or any of the broad surveys (200-level courses), and can also take advanced electives (300-level courses) with the instructor's permission."[19]

THE FOUNDERS' EMPHASIS ON
TEACHER AUTONOMY

As is true now, in the 1950s, some politicians and parents sought to control teachers' speech, and their history instruction in particular.[20] The program's architects specifically warned about the kinds of threats to teachers and students that AP Classroom poses. For these men, educational institutions held the promise of training citizens in the skills necessary for peaceful self-governance. The AP program's founders argued that the key to stimulating genuine intellectual exploration and development was creativity and flexibility for teachers—something enjoyed in the college classroom that they expected AP classes would also manifest.

In *General Education in a Free Society*, Conant's committee singled out the teaching of American history as one of the secondary school's greatest academic responsibilities. Because the group's vision for liberal education was rooted in the transmission of "a common heritage and a common citizenship," their recommendations for both form and content of American history instruction were careful. While offering a scheme for national reform, the group urged maintenance of some degree of disorder, particularly in the teaching of history. They wrote, "Intellectual orderliness can, when misplaced, be fatal to either order or justice in the changing society that is our heritage and our responsibility. What we can hope for in the teaching of the social studies is not a mathematical or logical precision, but rather an understanding based upon careful, even rigorous, study of some of the stubborn facts which have gone into the making of our social order, as well as a consideration of the theories and principles implicit in it." The group hoped that well-trained teachers could model democratic citizenship by "[carrying] on in the classroom the spirit and practice of inquiry and discussion." Warning against the imposition of external influence on classroom teachers, the committee wrote, "These limitations or compulsions come ordinarily from those who believe, or profess to believe, that they are expressing the true principles of Americanism. They too often forget that the basic doctrine of that faith is freedom of thought and speech." Even though the committee was resolute about the importance of teaching adolescents American history, they allowed that if a school was lucky enough to employ a teacher excited about ancient Greece, that teacher should teach courses in that field because the school's most important task was modeling intellectual engagement.

Similar attitudes remained constant throughout the teaching careers of committee members more directly involved in developing the program. Henry Bragdon, a member of the Blackmer Committee, wrote in 1968, "Tests too often encourage bad pedagogy" because they "dictate method and content." Before he worked on the problem of advanced coursework, he had served on the College Board's Commit-tee on Examinations in history. In explicitly political terms, Bragdon argued, "Teachers should emancipate themselves from the tyranny of testing-cum-grades and try to evolve a variety of intellectual exercises in which grading is subordinated to training in reading, writing, dis-course, methods of inquiry, and critical thought."[21] Bragdon enjoyed a prestigious position at Exeter and had built a wider reputation on his own scholarship on Woodrow Wilson and his popular textbook for other teachers. Self-possession and a sense of his own individual worth were critical to his success as an educator.

Bragdon was singular but far from anomalous. Resistance to stan-dardized courses and examinations and the mechanization of ped-agogy they inevitably demand was commonplace among historians involved in the AP program as it got off the ground. Charles Keller, Williams College historian who served as chairman of the College Board's Examination Committee in history, initially "feared that the institution of an examination might work against the coming together of school and college people by encouraging schools to teach for the tests."[22] Keller recalled that at the first meetings of history teach-ers and professors intended to facilitate communication between schools and colleges, the group "talked freely" and "bred consid-erable respect."[23] He found that the resulting fellowship and ability to articulate the benefits of particular curricular choices were the main benefits of these meetings. In a demonstration of the sort of forecasting that historical thinking can afford, the report that came out of that meeting declared, "We believe that an examination will curb student and teacher initiative and experimentation, will invite cramming, freeze the content of the course, and impede the school and college cooperation which this Study aims to promote."[24]

There were no standardized history courses or examinations in the first few years of the program—students in history earned credit (or didn't) based on teacher and school recommendations and college departments' judgments of those records. Keller's eventual submission to the examination scheme is resigned, if cheerful: "I thought things over, decided that since, no matter what, there was going to be a history examination, I might just as well be on hand to help work it out."[25] He explained that he hoped exams would inspire collaborative conversation about progression through a sequence in social studies in the same way they had in math and science. Still, warning against standardization remained even after there was an exam in place. In 1958, the course description began, "There is no desire to standardize advanced school courses in American history; American history courses vary from college to college, and teachers in schools should feel free to show initiative and to experiment in planning their courses."[26] Through at least 1964, teachers submitted a "School Report" in addition to exams, describing both the course and the student when a student had qualified for credit for the exam, and college departments would review course descriptions when determining whether to grant credit. Granting teachers professional autonomy was an important part of the program's initial plans for strengthening secondary school liberal arts education.

In a special issue of the *College Board Review* dedicated to celebrating the program's twenty-fifth anniversary, then director of Advanced Placement and former Harvard administrator of Advanced Standing Harlan Hanson reiterated one of the core principles of the program's founding: "Teachers, like students, should not be treated like interchangeable mass-produced parts." Speaking for himself as well as his colleagues, he wrote, "When we seek teachers for the gifted, we seek people who are themselves bright and who place less emphasis on conformity and more on the unusual in learning."[27] Creativity and freedom of expression should not be the preserve of the "gifted," that messy category of student the program was designed to accommodate. But we've taken the wrong turn, making education designed for privileged students more like the system it was supposed to replace rather than making the rest of the system more like a program designed with highest hopes for nurturing students' unique abilities.

AN EARLIER ATTEMPT AT
MASS DISSEMINATION OF APUSH

In the spirit of one of the College Board's designated historical "reasoning processes," "change and continuity," it is worth noting that AP Classroom is a novelty, but it's not a disjuncture. As part of the same push to innovate and improve on lackluster education that led to funding the AP program in the first place, the Ford and Carnegie Foundations also supported forays into televised instruction at both the high school and college levels. With a spirit of experimentation, the *College Board Review* reported on an effort to conduct Advanced Placement courses via television as a means of enrichment in the summer of 1963.[28]

Columbia's James Shenton offered an eight-week American history course over WNDT-CD called The Rise of the American Nation. Instead of attempting to systematize and replicate Shenton's method by forcing other teachers to impersonate his "dramatic inflection" and refusal to use notes, television held the promise of giving broader access to the passion and command of material that made him an award-winning, life-changing presence in the classroom.[29] Toward the end of his career, Shenton reflected, "For me . . . teaching is in some ways an act of love."[30] Even as the *New York Times* television critic celebrated Shenton's effectiveness at conveying his commitment to the material on television, Shenton told the *Columbia Spectator* that he would not undertake another similar course—it was exhausting to field questions from viewers numbering in the six figures, and he missed the "live, vibrating classroom."[31] Shenton's comments on the experience reflect historian Jonathan Zimmerman's conclusion that, by the end of the 1960s, the prevalent belief on college campuses was that "for the most part, teaching was considered too ineffable and idiosyncratic—indeed, too personal—to be systematized at all."[32]

BACK TO THE PRESENT

From the start, the Advanced Placement program has had the power to both reflect and shape the teaching profession to suit its mission. Initially, it promised high school teachers some of the privileges afforded to college professors—freedom to innovate, space for depth, and release from rote instruction. Contemporary guides for classroom teaching at the high school and college levels offer some overlapping techniques—in-person practices might look similar in each kind of classroom today. Guides like *Teach Like a Champion* and *The Missing Course*, for example, both advocate "student-centered" approaches. But AP Classroom, with its canned content and automated grading, highlights and reinforces the growing divergence between the professions. The current oversupply of humanities PhDs translates into more workers qualified to teach college-level courses.[33] But the AP program's anti-intellectual approach—expecting teachers to prioritize a corporation's authority, reductive curriculum, and mediated relationships with students—contradicts much of academic training.

In traditional school settings, the digital platform intervenes in the relationship between AP teacher and student. As a de facto social network, AP Classroom codifies teachers' and students' roles as franchisee and consumer, respectively. Teachers choose only whether to "unlock" canned videos, readings, and quizzes. Students who are concerned with college costs and proving their academic merit in an increasingly competitive college admissions race feel pressure to play along. Rather than enriching and deepening curriculum tailored to particular communities, AP Classroom redefines both good teaching and good learning in terms of compliance.

AP Classroom is driven by the College Board's particular financial interests, but it arises from and contributes to a broader cultural context. As media historian Lisa Gitelman writes in *Always Already New*, new forms of media are "the results of social and economic forces, so that any technological logic they possess is only apparently intrinsic."[34] In 2007, the Seventh Circuit decided to uphold a decision on the legality of firing a teacher because she had admitted in her classroom to protesting the Iraq War. The decision declares, "Children . . . ought not be subject to teachers' idiosyncratic perspectives."[35] It also clarifies the terms of the profession: "Expression is a teacher's stock in trade, the commodity she sells to her employer in exchange for a salary."[36] By divorcing instructor from curriculum, the court made an implicit argument about authority. While the First Amendment rights of university instructors are of special concern because of their sometimes dual roles as experts and researchers, and the university's raison d'etre as a space for free thinking, schoolteachers are not expected to generate knowledge. The decision indicated that a high school teacher's taking ownership of curriculum was a liability rather than an expectation.[37]

This conceptualization of a teacher as distinct from what they teach is an example of the "unbundling" of public education described by Jack Schneider and Jennifer Berkshire in *A Wolf at the Schoolhouse Door*: it becomes possible to control the curriculum while devaluing the person whose knowledge and enthusiasm should be an asset in the classroom.[38] Increased standardization and narrow focus on testing runs the risk of rewarding compliance rather than encouraging teachers, and, in turn, their students, to take their own minds seriously. By minimizing the need for a discerning, knowledgeable teacher, AP Classroom expands access to test prep. And as a corporate investment, it is, after all, a means to generate profit and to increase the number of potential consumers. Sidestepping the messy issue of qualified instructors opens possibilities for expansion. Instead of signaling investment in local teachers as capable of rationality and benevolence and students as developing citizens worthy of both trust and responsibility, an emphasis on exams and the means to enforce adherence indicates an orientation toward submission to depersonalized, infallible authority. The College Board, as a private company, has an incentive to exploit mistrust in public schools.[39]

Some level of systematization is necessary—the end goal is democracy, not anarchy. But how much, and to what ends? James Fraser and Lauren Lefty's *Teaching Teachers*, a history of teacher education, clarifies the components of preparation they believe necessary to success on the job: knowledge of academic content, adolescent psychology, pedagogical strategies, and the theories underpinning those strategies. Fraser and Lefty propose that teachers' love of their subjects and of learning itself are key to their effectiveness, as is the ability to understand and relate to the members of the communities in which their schools are situated.[40] It is possible to imagine a system that rewards teachers for addressing the specific curricular needs of their communities.

Troublingly, the College Board sells AP Classroom as a product to increase "access" to AP courses. Over the past few decades, the College Board has articulated a new commitment to "bridging the gap" for a group the company refers to in various contexts as "have-nots," "low-income, first-generation, and underrepresented students," and "those who may not have a college-going tradition in their families."[41] In this scheme, AP Classroom makes "college-level" courses accessible to students who otherwise would not enroll in the program, but calling this a solution to the problem of disparate resources might do more harm than good by papering over the underlying issues. In 2012, Mary Beard, classicist and advocate for distance learning, warned in an interview with the BBC about massive open online courses, that despite her general enthusiasm for technology, "there's a danger that what we'll do is create a new division between the privileged few who actually get to meet their professors, who listen to their lectures, who argue with them, who have their exams marked by their professors—and on the other hand the unprivileged mass who just see some star professor on the internet, have an internet chat room to go to and have a computer marked assignment at the end." She continued, "I think we're in danger of confusing here really the transmission of knowledge . . . and education. Education is about eyeball and interaction."[42] By selling a low-quality product to underprivileged communities, the College Board runs the risk of reproducing inequities while pretending to ameliorate them. Civically responsible liberal arts education requires an emphasis on meaningful interactions among teachers and students, even, and perhaps especially, in communities that are under-resourced.

Teaching American history—helping students understand their place along a common narrative, resist vilifying and lionizing historical actors, and navigate notions like truth and credibility—is fundamentally a human endeavor. It's delicate work. For reasons with long roots, entrusting teachers with messiness and complexity can be risky.[43] But outsourcing the organization and transmission of a national narrative to a corporation through a platform like AP Classroom is at least equally worrisome. Teachers are not unimpeachable, but the program reproduces a form of pedagogy that is far from innovative. We know that the "course framework" is not canard. But it lacks dynamism. Corralling both students and teachers through three centuries at a uniform, rapid-fire pace impedes the possibilities for exploring what the Organization of American Historians has recently called "the relevance of multiple narratives and evolving historical interpretations" at the center of the discipline.[44] The College Board's economic power challenges—even undermines—academic authority, endangering the social relationships at the heart of education. Making individual voices obsolete stifles conversation as it deepens the divide between high school and college instructors.

CHAPTER 5

Artificial Intelligence

In 2019, Chester Finn and Andrew Scanlan, researchers at the right-wing Thomas B. Fordham Institute, published a book-length cele-bration of the Advanced Placement program, titled *Learning in the Fast Lane*. They remarked that "a degree in English may actually do [students] greater good in the modern job market than a major in culinary services or law enforcement." They call the AP program a "bulwark of liberal education," citing as evidence the program's navi-gation of recent controversy over and improvements to history course content discussed in this book's previous chapter. They framed the program as a champion of "traditional" liberal arts course content in the midst of ever-rougher culture wars. But what they called the program's "rekindled commitment to liberal learning" under Col-lege Board CEO David Coleman deserves greater scrutiny.[1] From the outset, the AP program was not intended to be preparation for college but something like college itself. Now, the College Board's influence over student perception of the liberal arts is arguably greater than any single institution's. For this reason, and for others I discuss in this chapter, its current insistence on writing as a mechanical process is a disaster.

THE NEW RUBRICS

As of 2021, Advanced Placement English exams comprised the program's largest number of administered tests. With 518,548 test takers, AP English Language was the most popular exam on offer, and 321,029 students sat for an exam in AP English Literature. Taken together, these two subjects represent only a twentieth of the program's courses but nearly 19 percent of exams.[2] That year, 299,413 and 140,853 students earned scores of three or higher in AP English Language and AP English Literature, respectively. More colleges granted credit for AP English Literature than for any other subject. Their popularity might appear to indicate wide agreement about their value.

But surveying credit-granting policies among institutions reveals ambivalence—at best—about the Advanced Placement English exams' current worth. Half of the Ivies—Brown, Dartmouth, Princeton, and the University of Pennsylvania—offer neither credit nor placement for the English exams, regardless of score. Harvard no longer grants credit for any Advanced Placement course, and the English department does not have a placement policy. Cornell's College of Arts and Sciences awards placement out of one freshman writing course, which is distinct from an English course, and three credits. At Yale and Columbia, APs count toward neither the English major nor the college's distribution requirements, though scores of 5 can qualify students for elective credit. Among liberal arts colleges, neither Williams College nor Swarthmore College acknowledge AP English Language results, but they offer placement for a 5 on AP English Literature.[3] The placement counts toward the major. At Oberlin College, a score of 5 on the AP English Literature exam garners credit, but it does not count toward the major. Amherst College grants no credit for AP. At state schools beholden to the College Board, AP English credits help University of Florida students place out of surveys of American and world literature, while at UC Berkeley they fulfill the college's "Reading and Composition" requirement. By the time this book is published, these policies are likely to have changed.

This lack of agreement about the exams' academic merit makes sense given their misalignment with contemporary college English courses. Vassar College does not count Advanced Placement credit toward the English major. The English Department handbook explains its philosophy, which has remained constant since I was an undergraduate there:

> An English course is a conversation. . . . The placement of a grade on the paper puts an end to this part of the conversation. A student paper is not an exam but is rather an opportunity for the student to speak on a particular subject. The instructor's response is not a grade, but it is an informed response to what the student has said.[4]

Stanford, which also does not grant AP credit for English courses, insists:

> Literary study necessarily confronts us with the richness of human experiences, helping us to appreciate common values and the differences between those experiences across cultures, places, and times. . . . The study of literary texts nourishes our critical minds and our imaginations.[5]

In each of these descriptions, the emphasis is on personal growth, intellectual satisfaction, and empowered communication.

Across the two AP English exams, there are, on the surface, six different essay types, but they all use the same rubric and reward the same type of writing. Starting in 2019, for both exams, the College Board pivoted away from holistic grading toward a mechanical rubric. The new English rubrics for all six essay types attach the same point values to components: one point for the mere presence of an arguable claim, of any quality, anywhere in a piece of writing, and up to four points for evidence and "commentary." Cogent analysis is unnecessary. Credit is possible without introductions, conclusions, topic sentences, or meaningful transitions between thoughts. The only reward for coherence or style comes in the form of a single "sophistication" bonus point. In practice, these rubrics risk rewarding disturbingly simplistic, formulaic thinking.[6]

The College Board's recent merging of rubrics for the six essay types across two English exams reflects this impulse to constrict possibilities for writing and, in turn, for meaningful opportunities for students to explore their own and others' subjective experiences. Course descriptions for both AP English Literature and AP English Language admit that teachers may prefer to organize courses according to "thematic investigations," and they offer the same examples for each—"Humanity and Nature, Industry and Technology, Family and Community." "Skills" from the course guides for Language and Literature are near-exact copies. For example, Skill 5.B from AP Lang, "How does the writer achieve coherence at different levels of their argument: clause, sentence, paragraph, section, etc.?" mirrors Skill 3.C from AP Lit, "How does a text's organization and arrangement of ideas and details in lines, stanzas, sentences, paragraphs, chapters, or other sections of text contribute to a text's structure?" According to the course websites, in AP Language, students will "read closely, analyze, and interpret a piece of writing." In AP Literature, students "read a text closely and draw conclusions from details." The variance in wording here should not obscure the point that both exams test close reading. According to the College Board's course descriptions, the major distinction is that AP Language focuses on "nonfiction texts" while AP Literature explores "imaginative literature," but the methodologies the program endorses make this already dubious generic distinction irrelevant. In AP Language, students "analyze rhetorical elements and their effects in nonfiction texts—including images as forms of text— from a range of disciplines and historical periods." In AP Literature, "As they read, students consider a work's structure, style, and themes, as well as its use of figurative language, imagery, and symbolism." Again, the language varies, but the distinctions between "rhetorical elements" and "figurative language" are not immediately clear. As the identical rubrics for each essay type make clear, these courses are intended to produce the same results: evidence-based arguments, often rooted in close reading.[7]

According to the official course descriptions, today's Advanced Placement English Language course aims to "cultivate the reading and writing skills that students need for college success and for intellectually responsible civic engagement" while English Literature offers entrée into the kind of "careful reading and critical analysis" that theoretically allows students "to develop an appreciation of ways literature reflects and comments on a range of experiences, institutions, and social structures." These goals sound humanistic enough. But in practice, both course descriptions command adherence to regimented "scaffolded skill progressions" detailed in each of nine prepackaged units. Each unit represents an attempt to break down reading and writing into a series of detached, mechanical steps, represented on a chart by color-coded "skill categories." Across courses, these units are all explicitly designed with the culminating exam in mind—"personal progress checks" preloaded onto AP Classroom encourage students to think of reading and writing as processes unconnected to other contexts.

More than ever, AP essays measure a basic ability to conform and regurgitate, not the cultivation of subjectivity nor a meaningful understanding of the writing process. Importantly, the new rubrics also restrict graders from making subjective qualitative judgments that require knowledge and trust. The drive toward mechanical thinking in combination with the program's presence in over 70 percent of American public schools takes away too much power and judgment from students and teachers. Instead of empowering both parties to exercise discretion, they are rewarded for compliance to an enormously wealthy centralized authority's increasingly schematic expectations.

FINETUNE AND ARTIFICIAL INTELLIGENCE

One partial explanation for the change in grading is that the substance of the courses is secondary to their compatibility with the products from which Finetune—the subcontractor for the College Board I discussed in the last chapter—can profit. Behind the scenes, the plans are literally soulless. On May 14, 2019, Sal Daher, an angel investor based in Boston, gave a "plug for [his] investment syndicate" on a podcast. He explained that Finetune, a company he supports, was building a product so that "3.6 million high schoolers who are going to take the College Board's AP exam will have their essays scored on Finetune's software platform. . . . And the amazing thing about this is that it's available not just for scoring tests, but also for use in the classroom." Daher expressed belief in the company's mission, spelling out that the program was designed to save teachers time and allow them to give more assignments. Daher was so optimistic about this vision that he ended his plug with a rhetorical question: "And what do you think that will do to kids learning how to write?"[8] To Daher, the answer to this question must have seemed obviously positive. But to my mind, the risks and pitfalls of this approach to writing instruction are starkly dystopian.

The company's approach to writing instruction is shortsighted, utilitarian, and shallow. In 2020, Finetune won a "Shark-Tank style" contest for "fresh ideas" in education sponsored by the Fordham Institute. Finetune pitched software called Writing Hero, a "conversational agent" designed to help students draft essays because writing conferences with teachers are useful, but they "don't scale."[9] Scaling up writing conferences is possible without the interference of technology, of course. But Finetune promised a program designed to bring the process "into the future," cutting costs along the way. Writing Hero would help students brainstorm by prompting them with questions. The proposal does not mention plans for implementation with the AP program or the College Board, but it does provide insight into the company's philosophy. It explains, "The writing of an essay and the manufacturing of a product may not, on the surface, seem to have much in common, but the metaphor fits: one's ideas are the raw materials; the outline is the blueprint; the rough draft is the prototype; the final draft is the finished product." In the case of both an essay and a product, cumulative effort turns substance of questionable value into something suitable for public consumption. This idea loosely mimics book historian Robert Darnton's illustration of a "communications circuit," the network behind a publication that includes not only authors and readers but suppliers and booksellers. In the middle of Darnton's model, pressing outward on participants, are more nebulous forces like "intellectual influences and publicity," "economic and social conjuncture," and "political and legal sanctions."[10] Finetune's sense for the way an author produces text fails to account for the ways such social forces shape possibilities and meanings. The proposal imagines writing for school as a sort of "practice," detached from forms that arise from genuine concerns and have real impacts on readers. But writing always derives meaning from context.

Finetune is insistent on bloodless reading and writing. The proposal continues, "Up until now, the 'intellectual manufacturing' of writing has been inefficient—involving antiquated practices, outdated tools, and a lot of manual labor. Writing Hero will streamline this entire process, automating much of it." The notion that technology can replace teachers and, in so doing, make good academic arguments easier for students to form, is absurdly hubristic and misguided. In much of academic reading and writing, inefficiency is part of the process. Results of liberal arts education that seem serendipitous are hard to capture in an exam or rubric, but they have real value. Words like "streamlining" and "automating" are dehumanizing, and they signal contraction of intellectual possibilities rather than the expansion that AP English courses were originally designed to promote.

This mechanical, reductive approach to teaching reading and writing are apparent in Finetune's approach to grading essays. In addition to Writing Hero, as Daher suggested, Finetune has developed a scoring system called Converge to "calibrate teacher evaluations of student writing based on a universal set of criteria." Among supposed "advantages" of this innovation are "objective and consistent results, thereby increasing the efficiency of student learning." The problem, according to Finetune, is that "teachers themselves come from diverse training backgrounds and experiences."[11] Converge is based on grading with a single rubric, aligned with Common Core standards, that requires teachers to think of essays in terms of five separate categories: thinking, content, organization, diction/syntax, and mechanics. Finetune advertises that its approach also "increases the efficiency of the scoring and evaluation process."[12] Converge is already being used by Summit Learning, a "personalized learning" platform sponsored by the for-profit Chan-Zuckerberg Initiative, which in turn offers Advanced Placement courses. In English courses, Summit Learning uses Common Core Standards and AP Frameworks to build "playlists" of activities and assessments for students to work through at their own pace. Tracing the flow of influence becomes difficult: Are AP courses being designed for compatibility with the software, or vice versa? Either way, a promotional video explains that Converge "provides data to potentially create an AI scoring system."[13]

This approach to writing instruction is hostile to both students and teachers. Instead of helping students understand themselves as conversant with other readers and writers or pursuing cultivation of their own interiority, the current rubrics and exam structure encourage uniformity. Quantifying writing in this way demands a level of simplification that violates the potential for essay writing to help students organize experience—their own and others'.

AP AND THE COMMON CORE

The current AP course descriptions signal compliance with the Common Core standards for English / Language Arts, a feature Fine-tune advertises as a benefit.[14] To appreciate the change in focus of AP English courses, it is useful to have some background on the Common Core philosophy of reading and writing and to understand College Board president David Coleman's role in the standards movement.[15] Widely panned as a failure by politicians and critics on both sides of the aisle, in 2018, Betsy DeVos declared, "At the U.S. Department of Education, Common Core is dead." Some states have implemented thinly veiled versions of the same standards, or even have left the standards intact and simply renamed them.[16] In "Cultivating Wonder," Coleman's 2013 booklet celebrating these standards, he called for "a rigorous, deductive approach to reading that challenges students to draw as much as possible from the text itself."[17] In 2011, Coleman had appeared at a conference and explained his insistence on a turn from reading imaginative literature and writing personal essay to reading and writing "expository texts": "As you grow up in this world you realize people really don't give a shit about what you feel or what you think." The current AP English essay rubrics align closely with this philosophy.

Evidence-based arguments reliant on close reading are not inherently bad, and the concept of disinterested academic critique certainly occupies an important place in American thought. But educators have expressed major concerns about this narrow vision for teaching reading and writing at the secondary level. In the *Washington Post*, English teacher D'Lee Pollock-Moore wrote that the Common Core "fails to understand that one of the fundamentals of teaching literature involves character education."[18] Daniel Katz, education professor at Seton Hall University, echoed Pollock-Moore's unease about a lack of regard for less immediately measurable forms of growth when he wrote in a blog post that Common Core

appears entirely uninformed by any framework of reading as a process that includes the reader in any capacity other than as faithful
seeker of the text's internally constructed meaning. Readers who
want to understand society and history via the text? Readers who
want to explore their own humanity across space and time with
characters who live and breathe after centuries? Readers who want
to enjoy the feelings of a work of art without picking it apart into its
component parts?[19]

Doubtless, there are other valuable reasons for and modes of reading.
Much contemporary scholarship in English departments historicizes
cultural systems, describes and critiques power dynamics, and questions the value judgments implicit in earlier critics' aesthetics. And
according to English professor Jonathan Kramnick's recent defense of
disciplinarity in the context of these developments, close reading also
has an ethical dimension.[20] Part of the problem is that the Common
Core standards make a reader's unique perspective unimportant.
As Nicholas Tampio writes, "Common Core close reading teaches
children to place their own interests and concerns in a separate com-
partment of their mind than the one completing the assignment."[21]
The goal for exams—like the AP—aligned with Coleman's vision was
not the measurement of maturation or sophistication, intellectual or
otherwise, but a performance of meeting quantifiable benchmarks.

Coleman was appointed head of the College Board in 2012. In
2013, *Politico* reported on the expansion of Advanced Placement:
"For decades, the AP division had been a drain on the organization,
losing money because the tests are so pricey to grade. But surging
volume has changed that; revenues from AP tests now exceed ex-
penses by $20 million to $30 million a year." The story included an
anecdote about a Texas charter school English teacher who, under
pressure to produce high scores, felt compelled to "write a model
essay and urge his weaker students to copy it, sentence by sentence,
swapping out his phrases for their own wherever possible."[22] Now,

templates like the one given in this book's introduction are common. As AP expands and Finetune researches cost-cutting scoring systems, the College Board is reinventing what constitutes "good writing" for hundreds of thousands of high school students who should be learning to find their voices.

THE HUMANISTIC VISION FOR AP ENGLISH

The current AP English curriculum sounds like it might preserve and make accessible the liberal arts tradition, but the program is a wolf in sheep's clothing. From the start, there was tension between articulating universal performance standards and resisting reductive approaches to reading and writing. In 1955, McGeorge Bundy, who had majored in math, was a professor of government without a doctorate in the field, and, at 34, had become the youngest dean appointed at Harvard, told an audience of College Board members that regarding English composition, "out of a most limited experience . . . our very failures are some measure of our opportunity here, because here at least there is widespread agreement about the importance of the topic. What we have to deal with mainly is our own sloppy reluctance to insist upon real standards of performance."[23] The AP English courses in both language and literature were the cornerstones of the original plans for the program. Alan Blackmer, Gordon Keith Chalmers, and William Hafner Cornog all had experience teaching English and wrote about the discipline's centrality in helping individuals grapple with a common life. As I have shown in earlier chapters, for these men, notions like shaping subjectivities, developing aesthetic judgments, building imaginative worlds, and making meaning were not "soft skills." Their specific political commitments varied, but they were part of a postwar push to help students achieve self-determination.

The program's planners expected English courses to be especially expensive because small classes were central to their vision for democratic writing instruction. Cornog, himself an English PhD, argued that these smaller classes—capped at twenty or twenty-five— were a necessary investment in the nation's future. Various reports on the program's progress throughout the 1950s cite examples of schools that had managed to reduce class sizes. One such report explained, "To read and mark weekly themes . . . is an obligation that cannot be shifted to the shoulders of aids or assistants, nor shirked by neglect, nor avoided by mechanical expedients; it is the English teacher's essential professional skill and the foundation of his professional competence."[24] Some of the project's early advisors recommended that in addition to giving feedback, competent teachers needed time to read and write on their own in order to help their students understand themselves as "thinking individuals." The committee report on composition warned that if the course is taught "by means of time-saving devices . . . the pupil is almost entirely neglected as an individual and as a potentially constructive thinker."[25]

Commitments to students' individual growth shaped the committees' plans. Teaching students to read and write with greater sensitivity were meaningful goals because instructors agreed that students were, as the Blackmer Report put it, "ends in themselves." At one conference hosting a discussion on advanced placement, there was "unanimous agreement that there is no reason to base programs upon an anticipation of where the student may end up vocationally," even as teachers and professors disagreed on virtually everything else.[26] The course in language was designed to help students navigate "the art by which man exercises an order over facts and ideas, makes them his own, and puts them to ethical uses," and "to extend pupils' minds to their full capacities." The committee drafting plans for the examination understood "writing not as a means to an end but as an intrinsically valuable process of mental self-exploration and orientation." Repeatedly, the literature committee emphasized enjoyment of books because, to them, pleasure and comprehension were yoked. All of their recommendations stemmed from a commitment to the value of studying literature, "the single greatest criticism of life," because of its potential to help students organize their own experiences and to enrich their understanding of others'. "We must reiterate that there is nothing mechanical about the full reading of a piece of literature," they insisted.[27]

Attention to individuals was not at the expense of concern for socialization—to the contrary, it was part of a broader commitment to facilitating meaningful conversation. Far from a disembodied set of principles, the Kenyon Plan's committee explained, "The writer whom we wish to promote has ideas, brings both judgment and imagination to his treatment of them, and feels the difference between sincerity and pretentiousness," and "he looks up from his work often to see what he and his reader have in common."[28] The program's English committees shared an understanding of reading and writing as part of liberal democracy's social structure. One member, Scott Elledge, had helped found the Salzburg Seminars, bringing together an international group of humanists to restore postwar communication across political and ideological boundaries. Another, Louis Zahner, developed a five-phase writing activity for students to read and comment on each other's work, giving them an opportunity to develop their own criteria for writing to an audience of peers. One of the benefits was that by thinking through concerns about audience and acknowledging the necessity of revision in the safety of a relatively intimate group, students "underwent a certain amount of social growth by participating in a democratic social function."[29] Process was central to the original plans, and committee members warned, "No testing of the proficiency described here can be successful unless the examiner brings to the task his own share of judgment and imagination." In planning composition courses, they warned against textbooks that "solve all a teacher's problems by organizing the subject matter into 'daily assignments'!" They sneered, "We of course deride such prefabrication." Ridiculing the appeal of canned curriculum for overworked, undertrained teachers undercuts the point that tailoring readings and lesson plans based on discretion and relationships need not be an aristocratic practice—it should be a democratic one.

The impulse to cultivate agency and autonomy has a place in contemporary American life. The debate over the style of education that best suits the American public is long, and we should take much more seriously its implications for the concepts of equity and access. In 1903, W. E. B. Du Bois questioned Booker T. Washington's insistence on trade schooling when he asked, "Shall we teach them trades, or train them in liberal arts? Neither and both." Recognizing that no one type of education could fulfill the needs of all individuals, Du Bois insisted that "the final product of our training must be neither a psychologist nor a brickmason, but a man. And to make men, we must have ideals, broad, pure, and inspiring ends of living,—not sordid money-getting, not apples of gold." He lamented the American tendency, "born of slavery and quickened to renewed life by the crazy imperialism of the day, to regard human beings as among the material resources of a land to be trained with an eye single to future dividends."[30] It is undeniable and distressing that Chalmers's vision for the Advanced Placement program failed to account for the broad access to the humanities that DuBois imagined when he defended Shakespeare as a nonjudgmental intellectual companion. But the mutual concern for cultivating self-determination and citizenship through humanistic study taps into a vital current of thought.

THE LIBERAL ARTS NOW

The current English exams offer an impoverished vision of "equity." Private schools and wealthier public schools have moved away from AP exams, instead offering English courses intended to sharpen political acumen, broaden horizons, enchant students, and enrich experience. Why should everyone else settle for flatter experience?

Andrew Delbanco suggests in *College: What It Was, Is, and Should Be* that the value of the liberal arts is a mind set ablaze in contemplation of what's possible.[31] Freedom demands this type of agency. A turn away from liberal arts training is dangerously aligned with a turn away from civic engagement. If "equity and access" are the true aims of American education in this moment, it makes sense for a broader swath of citizens to participate in the liberal arts tradition, understood since ancient Greece as the proper training for self-governance. Even as the AP program has changed form, America has not lost its need for students who are able to step outside of themselves, to understand power structures in terms of the individuals responsible for creating them, to situate themselves in time and space, and to more fully realize their own humanity by becoming conversant with people beyond their immediate experience. It is hard to imagine how a standardized test might account for success in courses designed with these concepts in mind. It is dangerous for colleges to continue granting credit for courses that place the needs of a testing company above the humanity of students and, in turn, the needs of the country.

"Liberal education" and humanistic study are not synonymous, but they're related in their concern with values and sustained attention to narrative. While reports of the humanities' decline have been in circulation for more than half a century, a more recent and precipitous drop in English and history majors has indicated to history professor Benjamin Schmidt that "in the wake of the 2008 financial crisis, students seem to have shifted their view of what they *should* be studying—in a largely misguided effort to enhance their chances on the job market. And something essential is being lost in the process."[32] Schmidt's article is one of a spate of essays bemoaning the accelerated death of the humanities since 2008. The pandemic has made matters worse. Brian Rosenberg, outgoing president of Macalester College, said in June 2020 that the pandemic toll of liberal arts colleges' closures was devastating because "a society without a grounding in ethics, self-reflection, empathy and beauty is one that has lost its way."[33] Schmidt, Rosenberg, and many others have cited the political danger inherent in the collapse of an educational model prioritizing thoughtful communication. Most of the reports on this topic, by college presidents, professors, pundits, and cultural commentators, lament statistics about declining college English and history majors and narrowing job opportunities in the professoriate. Given the authors' backgrounds, it makes sense that so few of these essays recognize that the problem starts in high school. Too many undergraduates show up to campus with an impoverished sense of the purposes and possibilities of humanistic study.

Over the past decade, champions of the liberal arts have emerged from across the political spectrum. Fareed Zakaria's *In Defense of a Liberal Education* warns, "The irrelevance of a liberal education is an idea that has achieved that rare status in Washington: bipartisan agreement."[34] A shared commitment to skills-based learning has also found detractors from both major parties. Christopher Scalia pleads, "Yes, college is too expensive. Of course, we need to find ways to control tuition and to ensure that graduates don't find themselves chained by debt. But conservatives won't solve these problems by scorning the liberal arts. Instead, they will deprive students of our great intellectual heritage and leave them less capable of governing themselves—and that would be profoundly unconservative."[35] Wesleyan University president Michael Roth's defense is born of a commitment to a left-leaning reimagination of Deweyan pragmatism that, in fact, sounds very much like Chalmers: "Liberal education matters because by challenging the forces of conformity, it promises to be relevant to our professional, personal, and political lives."[36] If democracy is the goal, encouraging a broader, more representative swath of Americans to participate in enriching and pleasurable reading and writing makes sense; orienting public education toward accreditation and quantification for the sake of private profit does not.

CHAPTER 6

Better Citizens

The newly revised AP US Government course seems like a celebration of classical liberalism, but the structure of the AP program undermines the content's emphasis on the validity of multiple viewpoints. The College Board promises that the course offers a nonpartisan introduction to public life, but education policy shapes the program. Whereas the current course is prescriptive, midcentury education reformers insisted on the doctrine of local control. When political scientists developed the first AP US Government exam in 1986, scholars in the field debated whether the course could bridge the gap between high school civics and college-level government. Now, in claiming to do both by fixing the content and structure of the curriculum, the AP program fails to give students the experience of a college-level course in political science as it threatens the liberalism it purports to protect.

THE NEW COURSE

In 2019, Pulitzer Prize–winning *New York Times* journalist Thomas Friedman wrote an ode to College Board president David Coleman and Stephanie Sanford, the company's chief of global policy and external relations, who "happen to be people I've long enjoyed batting around ideas with." Reflecting on the role of AP US Government in

American education from their perches at the College Board, "Coleman and Sanford concluded that it was essential that every student entering college actually have command of the First Amendment."[1] This goal, which Friedman paints as his friends' brave, magnanimous response to what he categorizes as a "radical" question about what it might mean to helm a testing company with responsibility to the millions of American schoolchildren subject to its decisions, is so uncontroversial as to be almost banal. Who would argue in favor of denying young citizens knowledge of their freedoms? Friedman's unwitting reveal is about how much power Coleman and Sanford have to set an agenda that continues to affect millions of students, their families, and their schools.

Readers' comments on the piece are damning. Someone claiming to be high school senior Sabrina C. made a comment that became the most popular "reader's pick," with 1,734 reader recommendations. She wrote, "I dislike how AP classes prompt students to prioritize passing a test over being intellectually engaged with the course material. . . . The College Board knowingly feeds students into a system where they feel pressured to take AP classes rather than a class that truly piques their interest." Connie L., claiming to be a "parent of 2 college graduates and 1 high school senior," earned 702 reader endorsements: "I've not spoken with one parent over these years who doesn't see the entire College Board hold on college admission for what it is: a racket. They have created a market for their tests and wreaked havoc on what education is supposed to be, with far-reaching consequences."[2] Especially in the context of these skeptical replies, Friedman's celebratory assessment of the initiative seems tone-deaf to the concerns of people subject to Coleman's and Sanford's decisions.

Sanford justified the College Board's efforts with an obtuse companion statement on deliberative democracy. She wrote in a platitudinous essay published to Medium, "We can't entrust our future to a few specialists who know how to code or the small caste that knows how to legislate and lobby. The operating system of the modern world must be open to all." I agree with Sanford, but, as I will demonstrate in this chapter, the AP Government framework is self-defeating if the goal is truly to help students understand the nation as, in her words, "a mature community of conversation and ideas—built on the right and even obligation to speak up and, when needed, to protest, but not to interrupt and prevent others from speaking."[3] Sanford's writing appears to celebrate inclusive democratic conversations, but we will see in this chapter, the structure of the current AP is overtly domineering.

Friedman's write-up was an advertisement for a course redesign. In 2018, the College Board "revamped" AP US Government. In 2009, for the previous update, the course guide for AP US Government and Politics was eighty-six pages long. In addition to sample exam questions, it offered teachers suggestions for syllabi, activities, and materials. But in the course description, the document's authors were adamant that "there is no single approach that an AP US Gov and Politics course must follow." A breakdown of approximate weight given to a set of topics carries a disclaimer: "The outline is a guide and is by no means an exhaustive list of topics or the preferred order of topics."[4] Introducing the course guide, political scientist Kathleen Bratton gave an overview of the field, explaining how changes to the course reflected shifts in professors' foci.

In 2019, the course guide ballooned to 199 pages. An overview of the academic field was gone, as were sample syllabi. Instead, there were unit guides like the ones for APUSH, prescribing a daily schedule. Importantly, this course also dictates a canon of readings. The AP US Gov course redesign requires teachers to adhere to a fixed set of texts. The nine primary documents are:

1. The Declaration of Independence
2. The Articles of Confederation
3. The Constitution of the United States
4. *Federalist*, no. 10
5. Brutus No. 1

6. *Federalist,* no. 51

7. *Federalist,* no. 70

8. *Federalist,* no. 78

9. Letter from Birmingham Jail

The fifteen Supreme Court cases are as follows:

1. *Marbury v. Madison* (1803)

2. *McCulloch v. Maryland* (1819)

3. *Schenck v. United States* (1919)

4. *Brown v. Board of Education of Topeka* (1954)

5. *Baker v. Carr* (1961)

6. *Engel v. Vitale* (1962)

7. *Gideon v. Wainwright* (1963)

8. *Tinker v. Des Moines Independent Community School District* (1969)

9. *New York Times Company v. United States* (1971)

10. *Wisconsin v. Yoder* (1972)

11. *Roe v. Wade* (1973)

12. *Shaw v. Reno* (1993)

13. *United States v. Lopez* (1995)

14. *McDonald v. Chicago* (2010)

15. *Citizens United v. Federal Election Commission* (2010)[5]

In 2019, the College Board insisted on a single, mandatory sequence of units. Since then, the company has softened this requirement and now offers four sample syllabi with semantic changes to unit names, different orders for the same cookie-cutter units, and an expanded set of options for assessments. Whether these texts are worth reading is not the point—of course they are. And the prescribed sequences make sense. A parent, teacher, or professor glancing at these materials—from anywhere along our political spectrum—might find the course description admirable. But a required reading list this agreeable deflects conversation about a structure that undermines possibilities for civic engagement.

The College Board's March 2022 statement on "What AP Stands For" illustrates the power the company wields and the danger in allowing it to mandate course content. Beginning in late 2021, state legislatures across the country considered and sometimes passed censorship laws pertaining especially to the teaching of culture and civics. Under public pressure to respond to this attack on free speech, the College Board issued what American Enterprise Institute fellow Rick Hess called a "refreshing" list of "principles." The third item reads:

> AP opposes censorship. AP is animated by a deep respect for the intellectual freedom of teachers and students alike. If a school bans required topics from their AP courses, the AP Program removes the AP designation from that course and its inclusion in the AP Course Ledger provided to colleges and universities. For example, the concepts of evolution are at the heart of college biology, and a course that neglects such concepts does not pass muster as AP Biology.[6]

Replace "biology" with "government" and "evolution" with "our list of required readings," and it becomes clear that the College Board is poised to punish teachers who deviate from its narrow vision for civics education despite wide variance in what "passes muster" for college-level introductory government. As I've discussed in previous chapters, AP English and history courses do not require specific texts, so this statement offered no protection against book banning, as media coverage seemed to indicate it would.[7] Instead of maintaining space for genuine pluralism and civic engagement, the College Board is requiring adherence to its own strictures. The statement protects the company's brand, not students' interests or teachers' autonomy.

Civics education at high schools not beholden to the College Board for civics instruction makes plain the company's dangerously anemic vision. Four New York schools—Dalton, one of the nation's oldest private schools; Beacon, a selective public school committed to performance-based assessments; Scarsdale, a public school in one of the country's richest towns; and Democracy Prep, a charter aimed at empowering low-income students—offer twelfth graders vibrant introductions to public life. Recent senior-level social studies course titles include Inequality in America, New York City in Crisis, Climate Policy, You Are What You Eat: Food Production, Consumption, and Justice, The Black Radical Tradition, American Conservatism, and Gender and Legal History. Democracy Prep requires students to draft publications, presentations, and policy briefs in addition to mentoring, volunteering, and canvassing. In another community altogether, North Carolina's Laurinburg Institute, the oldest historically Black prep school in the country, offers its own scheme. In alignment with Booker T. Washington's philosophy—on which the school was founded—civics is taught in ninth grade. The course promises that "the roles of student in family, school, and the economy are investigated with emphasis on their rights and responsibilities." In eleventh or twelfth grades, students take Current Affairs, which focuses "on contemporary issues that are affecting North Carolina citizens for the most part. It is an open-ended course with the emphasis on acquiring information from a variety of sources, analyzing, and hypothesizing about the direction of North Carolina's future."[8] Teaching full comprehension of a complex problem and modes for understanding and remediating it is distinct from partisan activism that aims to indoctrinate. Autonomous teachers and institutions that are allowed the latitude to be passionate about particular aspects of and inroads to public life can awaken students to the benefits of civic engagement by modeling it.

Looking to the rich variety in what college-level courses in American government challenge students to do also presents a stark foil to the College Board's mandates. At Princeton, an introduction to American politics covers historical ground like "the Puritan heritage,

the Constitutional founding, the Hamiltonian, Jeffersonian, Jacksonian, and Whig visions, the slavery conflict, Populism, Progressiv-
ism, feminism, New Deal/Great Society liberalism, the Civil Rights,
Black Power, and student revolts of the 1960s, and the conservative
ascendency of the 1980s."[9] At Austin Community College, the present comes into focus: "Because our subject matter includes issues
and events that are unfolding as we discuss them the lecture may
become modified."[10] At Yale, an introduction to American politics
relies on a textbook that "frames the course in terms of understanding collective action problems."[11] At California State University, Long
Beach, a course in American government offers "special attention
to the unique features of California's political system."[12] The variety
in college-level introductions to American government reflects how
instructors modify syllabi to reflect both their own knowledge and
what they believe it will be useful for students to know. Sensitivity to
local students' and educators' concerns plays a role in determining
the course material.

In *Learning in the Fast Lane*, Finn and Scanlan admit that there
is not necessarily true equivalency between AP US Government and
Politics and college coursework in political science. They explain that
while the Advanced Placement course is designed to fulfill states'
civics requirements for high school students, "few US college students are required to take civics, and those who wish to may or may
not find a survey-style course."[13] Even though the course does not
match a collegiate introduction to political science, the authors laud
Coleman's "powerful and lofty" declaration of goals for the course.
Presenting as evidence Coleman's comments without any own analysis or commentary, Finn and Scanlan declared that Coleman's vision
is "off to a smooth start." But it's not clear that the course is even an
adequate introduction to civic life.

At first blush, the changes to the course may not seem like a problem. The newly mandatory readings are not ideologically rigid. There
is broad agreement that texts like the Declaration of Independence

and the Constitution, and Supreme Court cases like *Brown v. Board of Education* have broad influence and invite multiple interpretations. As in other courses, sets of "disciplinary practices" and "big ideas" spiral through units. Skills and notions from these lists, like "data analysis," "argumentation," "civic participation in a representative democracy," and "constitutionalism" seem like important foci.[14] And promotional materials, readings, and assessments for AP Gov make explicit attempts to avoid overt partisan bias. A note on "maintaining political balance" in the course bulletin notifies readers that "AP U.S. Government and Politics is a nonpartisan course and has been endorsed by the National Constitution Center as well as a range of conservative and liberal scholars for its political balance." The writers of the Advanced Placement US Government Course Framework take pains to seem politically neutral and to maintain classically liberal norms about keeping space for divergent opinions. For instance, writing assignments require students to engage with opposing viewpoints, even if only superficially. Rubrics for free-response questions require that students "respond to an opposing or alternate perspective using refutation, concession, or rebuttal."[15] And as of 2020, the College Board's friends at *US News and World Report* explain, "All students enrolled in AP U.S. Government and Politics must complete an applied civics or political science research project. This student-led project should link course content to a real-word issue," even though "the applied civics or political science research project does not count toward the final AP exam grade."[16] On its face, the course does appear to encourage students to engage in reasoned, informed conversations about controversial issues with people who might disagree with them. In short, the course is not a bad one.

But implicit in the new prescription of both form and content are political arguments. The course description and a prefatory letter penned by Coleman promise a "timeless," "nonpartisan" introduction to participation in public life. But such a thing is chimerical. "Right," "left," "progressive," and "conservative" are not the only categories that matter. By positioning itself as the standard-bearing provider of civics education in 9,542 high schools, the College Board is imposing a top-down uniformity at odds with democratic participation. And as Justice Robert Jackson explained in his *West Virginia v. Barnette* decision (not a College Board–required Supreme Court case reading!), attempts to impose uniformity in public education threaten to alienate citizens from the shared enterprise because, in the event of power contests, "each party or denomination must seek to control, or failing that, to weaken the influence of the educational system."[17] Any one group that has the power to determine and impose curriculum on a broad scale endangers what Jackson—and so many others—have imagined as a collaborative enterprise. But dominance is at the heart of the Advanced Placement program's ethos. The Fordham Institute's Robert Pondiscio has suggested that AP Government, "the most commonly taken civics course in the country," which by 2016 had doubled its reach since 2011, had "more than ample room for that number to double and redouble again."[18] Other advocates for the Advanced Placement program, like Finn and Scanlan, celebrate the course as a "choice" for "those—including ourselves—who see the country (and particularly its neediest students) benefiting from a high-quality national high school curriculum and from uniform standards by which to gauge student learning in relation to that curriculum."[19] Setting aside, for a moment, the gross paternalism on display here, the uniformity of the national curriculum they envision threatens to dull the very liberalism that the course readings and framework aim to promote. By wresting ownership of civics education from local authorities, the College Board infantilizes citizens while pretending to empower them, flattening the course's meaning in the process. But, as I discussed in the introduction and will explain more fully in the conclusion, the company's takeover of American high school classrooms is as structural as it is curricular. Does this system represent an introduction to the best of the American political tradition?

BUILDING COMMUNITIES

James Conant, whose advocacy for both testing and liberal arts education laid the groundwork for the program, was concerned about
the extent to and ways in which American education should be well
organized.[20] As discussed in chapter 1, Conant understood himself to have been "raked from the rubbish," and he understood the
public education system as part and parcel with the democracy he
sought to protect. Addressing the American Association of School
Administrators in April 1952, Conant outlined his understanding of
the school's role in fostering simultaneous "unity in our national life"
and "the diversity that comes from freedom of action and expression" in their local communities. With these twinned aims in mind,
Conant explained, "We look with disfavor on any monolithic type of
educational structure; we shrink from any idea of regimentation, of
uniformity as to the details of many phases of secondary education."
Schools could be sites for communities to unify "irrespective of family
fortune or cultural background." He argued that diversity "is assured
by our insistence on the doctrine of local control." "Indeed, to an outsider I should think our diversity would look like educational chaos,"
he admitted. "But this is a characteristic of our flexible decentralized
concept of democracy."[21] For Conant, developing a public-spirited,
stable electorate was not at odds with the notion of local control:
to the contrary, an empowered citizenry—both the adults planning
and executing a vision and the children in their care—would best
understand the benefits of democracy by practicing it in schools.
Conant's political philosophy aligned roughly with Jefferson's most
idealistic—or, considering his investment in protecting slavery, most
sinister—calls for a vital, dynamic democracy reliant on the formation of local communities.[22] *Brown v. Board of Education* would challenge the simplicity of Conant's, and many other people's, thinking
on this point.[23] But not before AP launched.

The tension between Conant's commitments to standards and his sense for how to best preserve the health of citizens' relationships extended to Advanced Placement's architects. In 1952, the *College Board Review* offered updates on each acceleration scheme underwritten by the Fund for the Advancement of Education. Alan Blackmer wrote, "We make no secret of our belief that there is a hierarchy of knowledge, that some things are more important for the ablest minds to know than others."[24] Meanwhile, Gordon Keith Chalmers understood a central task to be "how to define and describe a central core of required knowledge."[25] These committees agreed that moving forward, educators from grades 11 through 14 should share not only a common purpose but also broad agreement about their definitions of "quality," both in terms of course materials and student work. If the program had been governed by collaborative schools and colleges, perhaps it would have been less susceptible to seizure of opaque control by a central institution.

In 1956, the *College Board Review* celebrated Advanced Placement's success at Newton High School in Massachusetts. The article reported, "High on the list of professional benefits stands the tremendous cooperative attainment of college and secondary school subject specialists who have been able to reassess, reorganize, and revitalize subject matter." The piece concluded, "Today's schoolhouse has a greater measure of academic freedom and power than it has ever known."[26] The AP committees had extended the privilege of experimentation to a small number of other schools and teachers: between the first and second years, the number of participating schools had doubled from 104 to 212. There were glimmers of hope for the promotion of intellectual autonomy as an academic norm: it was the same year the Warren Court rebuked McCarthyism in its decisions on *Slochower v. Board of Education* and *Cole v. Young*, protecting teachers' speech rights. But it was also the same year that the *Journal of Negro Education* reported that one result of integration efforts was to "make the position of the Negro teacher more insecure than that of the white teacher, especially in rural areas where desegregation meant abandonment of the Negro school, or in states where teacher tenure laws are weak or non-existent."[27] The AP program was far from remediating widespread hostility to diverse viewpoints at scale. Still, "academic freedom and power" in schools was a stated Advanced Placement ideal.

Thirty years later, in 1986, Boston College political scientist Kay Schlozman apprised her colleagues of work toward developing an Advanced Placement course in government. She explained that the College Board had commissioned a task force of political scientists to explore what such an offering might look like, given a survey of introductory college-level courses in the field and secondary school teachers' interests and aptitudes. The course proved popular among pilot high schools. By 1991, an article cited the popular program as "an important part of political science" based on its potential to prime ambitious students for continued college work in the discipline.

Several professors worried that the program would muddy the boundary between civics and more formal, academic study of American government.[28] Schlozman responded to public critiques of the Advanced Placement program in a roundtable discussion in the pages of *The Political Science Teacher*. She addressed her colleagues' concerns about the distinction between high school- and college-level instruction in American politics: "With good reason, political scientists have long been skeptical about what passes for instruction about American politics in the high schools. State-required courses in American government—for which AP courses are now serving as a more intellectually demanding substitute—are notorious for their emphasis on civic-minded platitudes and an absence of teaching about politics."[29] The hope was to build relationships and invigorate secondary school teaching.

Collaborators approached this new opportunity with a spirit of experimentation. In the summer of 1987, a group of professors offered a ten-week institute on American government for high school teachers. They stated a commitment to viewing teachers as "our professional colleagues, rather than our students," and aimed to shape the institute as "an exploration of disciplinary subjects of common interest, rather than a transmission of knowledge from initiates to novices. We came to this exploration with different backgrounds and different kinds of expertise, but we assumed that everyone had something to contribute."[30] Inherent in this insistence on mutual respect is the hope that teachers would not merely impersonate professors, but would enrich their own practices. In response to concerns about teachers' preparedness to teach college-level courses, AP teacher Ann Serow explained that more useful than didactic curriculum was "an on-going reliable relationship between a high school AP teacher and a college professor who is familiar with the introductory American government course."[31] These plans evince possibilities for the kinds of thoughtful, democratic relationships Conant imagined.

It is perhaps unsurprising that in the course of developing new patterns, political scientists would think about navigating notions of equality and power imbalances. In 1971, the American Political Science Association's formal statement on the organization recommended going beyond the transmission of academic knowledge and imparting to students "an understanding of the sociopsychological sources and historical-cultural origins of their own political attitudes and values, as well as the capacity to critically analyze alternative values," and "an understanding of the skills needed to effectively participate in a democratic society."[32] The field demands awareness about the structures that define public life, and internal debates over Advanced Placement indicate thoughtfulness about how the program might work. The summer institute facilitated the development of multiple units on a variety of topics.

By 1986, the privatization of public education was an incipient development. That year, Spelman president and political scientist Donald M. Stewart was newly installed as the head of the College Board. Stewart was "convinced that government couldn't do it all, that there had to be a market mechanism at work to make efficient decisions," but he espoused this belief in the name of "individuality and individual creativity."[33] In an interview with the *College Board Review*, he explained, "I don't like heavy-handed government or other forms of centralization." He cited Jefferson as one of his main influences and quoted Bertrand de Jouvenel: "A society of sheep must in time beget a government of wolves."[34] According to the *New York Times*, Stewart's was a "high-quality conservatism." *A Nation At Risk* had spurred serious debate about the best path forward for American education, and Stewart believed that private industry held the potential to innovate. By then, Ronald Reagan's education secretary William Bennett had indicated commitment to higher standards for "reading, writing, and 'rithmetic." In 1988, Gregory Anrig, then president of the Educational Testing Service, told the *New York Times*, "The growth in testing over this decade has been remarkable, and I don't think it's healthy."[35] But still, George H. W. Bush's America 2000 plan for accountability—the kernel at the center of "school choice" and later legislation including No Child Left Behind, Race to the Top, and Every Student Succeeds—would not be communicated to the public until 1991. In 1986, the Advanced Placement exam in Government was not yet part of a testing regime. It was possible to imagine that codifying standards could stimulate "greater involvement by university faculty in pre-college education" and provide an occasion for a collaborative summer institute.[36]

By 2001, a report by Richard G. Niemi and Julia Smith indicated that despite the AP, there was still a gulf between the teaching of American politics at the high school and college levels. Whereas high schools usually teach "civics," professors usually teach "government." They explained, "Civics better conveys the idea of broad citizenship training, and it has a relatively non-partisan, non-ideological connotation. But the term civics is to a large extent discredited among political scientists; it conveys uncritical, low-level subject matter that is not at all descriptive of what most of us teach at the college level." Niemi and Smith warned that even if political scientists understood

their discipline as distinct from the field of "civics," abdicating responsibility for the teaching of politics "means turning this aspect of education over to others who may not share our interests or, one vainly
hopes, our level of knowledge. It is hard to see how this will help
turn out better citizens or better students for our entering classes."[37]
A 2015 update on the status of civics education told professors, "We
still need you! Increased national emphasis on STEM-related fields
in both K–12 education and teacher education programs has placed
civics education at a crossroads. If the quality of students' K–12 civics
education is an important factor for future civic participation and
engagement, then it is critical that all stakeholders work together and
take steps to improve the visibility and quality of civics education in
the United States."[38]

In 2011, the *New York Times*'s Christopher Drew reported that the
College Board was "rethinking" the AP program. After citing teachers'
and students' frustrations with the state of the program and their endorsements of its new direction, the article's penultimate paragraph
explains, "In many ways, the changes will complete a broad turn for
the College Board, from its origins as a purveyor of tests to a much
more deliberate arbiter of what the nation's top students will study."
In the preceding years, College Board president Gaston Caperton
had committed to expanding access to the program's offerings. When
David Coleman took the helm in 2012, fresh from his experience as
architect of the Common Core standards, he built on Caperton's work
extending the program's reach and understood his new role as an
opportunity to continue his Common Core work by other means. He
tapped into the narrative of No Child Left Behind when he told the
New York Times, "We have a crisis in education, and over the next
few years, the main thing on the College Board's agenda is to deliver
its social mission. . . . The College Board is not just about measuring
and testing, but designing high-quality curriculum."[39] Never mind
the evolving particulars of this social mission and why, suddenly,
designing and meting out curriculum was part of it.

PRIVATIZING CIVIC EDUCATION

Today, Newton North High School, located in one of the country's wealthiest districts, does not offer AP US Government. Instead, the school's Center for Civic Engagement and Service develops curriculum, forms partnerships within and beyond the institution, and invites community members to apply for grants "to improve or change something," or to "plan something related to civics for your classroom or group." At Andover, which also no longer offers AP, courses in American government and politics include North American Borders; US Immigration History: Inclusion and Exclusion in the Making of Law, Policy, and Nation; House Divided: Political Polarization, Nixon to Obama; Critical Race Theory: The American Dream Deferred; Urban Crisis; and Schooling in America. There is clear immediacy and agency in these approaches. Even as the College Board promises "equity and excellence," today's AP program extends only a simulation of the freedoms enjoyed by some of the nation's best-funded institutions.

There are many potential paths to preparing students as citizens. Beyond the United States, as the National Center for the Study of Privatization in Education's Samuel Abrams argues, Finnish schools are centers for nation building. National core curriculum is balanced with local curriculum. Inspiration from the business sector takes the form of "enfranchising employees with significant opportunities for professional advancement" and emphasis on "leadership over scrutiny." Of course, Finland has a population of only 5.55 million—there are more people in New York City alone.

Democracy relies on people who have not only the knowledge but also the will to carry forward the balance of autonomy and compromise that makes self-governance possible. Standardization and the obeisance it requires can breed disempowerment or, worse, cynicism. Self-determination can emancipate. Consider Noliwe Rooks's account of segrenomics in *Cutting School*. She argues, "In the past,

Black teachers who successfully educated generations of Black children to and through college were able to do so when they worked with Black community members and parents, and when they also creatively controlled the instructional strategies, curriculum, disciplinary methods, ideologies, and assessment strategies."[40] Historically, ordinary citizens' engagement in education has been not only possible but successful.

Schools hold the potential to institutionalize an ethos of political cooperation across difference by teaching democratic skills and habits. This mandate aligns with a model of participatory, rather than elite, democracy, in which citizens are empowered agents. In *Federalist* no. 70, one of the AP US Government course readings, Alexander Hamilton lamented, "Men often oppose a thing, merely because they have no agency in planning it."[41] In some realms, perhaps this alienation is an unavoidable price for progress. In education, it is not.

CONCLUSION

Opportunity and Transparency

In 1956, Bronx High School of Science principal Morris Meister published a hopeful report on Advanced Placement. One of the program's initial champions and a member of Chalmers's committee, Meister rearticulated its promise. He wrote, "What we seek is a good junction point in a living organism. We know that a living joint functions properly not when mere friction is eliminated, but when muscle tone, blood supply, and healthy nerve action are also present."[1] He expected that the program could keep education vital if teachers and professors worked together to strengthen it. Meister was not alone in his optimism after the program's first year. Oberlin College German professor Joseph R. Reichard wrote, "The effect upon these cooperating institutions was not long in making itself felt, for the unusual exchange of educational experiences among representatives of colleges and secondary schools at conferences and committee meetings brought extraordinary results. . . . Each group soon acquired increasing understanding, appreciation, and respect for the problems and accomplishments of the other."[2] He beseeched colleagues to "let us take maximum advantage of the opportunities which it affords"—energetic, purposeful collaboration. Optimizing the scheme's

155

potential has taken on a different meaning. In 2016, David Coleman told the *Washington Post* that he was in "the anxiety field," with special reference to students' concerns about the SAT and college admissions. But the College Board's role in negotiating fear runs deeper.

In 2006, the *Chronicle of Higher Education*'s Eric Hoover reported that Gaston Caperton, then president of the College Board, had turned the entity into "a service organization with a corporate ethos."[3] Caperton had convinced Bill Clinton's secretary of education Richard Riley that every high school in the United States should offer ten AP courses.[4] Caperton left the organization in 2011. On October 24, 2012, incoming College Board president David Coleman gave his first public talk at the organization's annual conference, titled "Achieving the Social Mission of the College Board." Coleman began the talk by celebrating Caperton's successful expansion of Advanced Placement. "Something has happened in America," he said. "A program that was seen as elite has broken through."[5]

Here is one version of the story: like Thomas Jefferson, James Bryant Conant hoped for a school system that would rank students in a pyramidical education scheme to secure the nation's economic future. Today, Advanced Placement does this on a scale unforeseen. Millions of students are being measured against each other by the same academic standards, and those standards are transparent to anyone looking for them. Teachers and administrators who deviate from the program make life harder for students who need credentials for the sake of social mobility. The College Board makes college credit more affordable and easier to obtain. If access to the program is uneven, this is a reason to expand it. If students need more help passing exams, the College Board should provide extra services, like a Pre-AP program. If the tests expose disparities between demographic groups, those groups need even more resources from the College Board. With all of the additional support, the exams give a truer picture of those students deserving of college credit. Partnerships with major businesses secure students' job prospects.

Here is another version of the story: like Jefferson, Conant hoped for a school system that would protect self-governance by apportioning scarce resources to the students most likely to defend the nation from predation while preparing the rest for other meaningful forms of citizenship. Today, Advanced Placement is a business that exploits government, children, families, and universities as it benefits from the astronomical cost of college tuition and perceived scarcity of spots at "good colleges." As our country's definition of "success" narrows, racial tensions rise and economic inequality deepens, the College Board profits from mistrust between and among the students, parents, teachers, professors, administrators, and politicians under immense pressure to improve their own and others' conditions through higher education. Instead of facilitating meaningful communication about multiple possible missions and purposes and allowing for a panoply of empowered communities to proliferate, the College Board obfuscates its definition of "excellence" with metrics and seeks adherence to this scheme from all but the best-funded high schools and colleges. Corporate partnerships represent a dangerous conflation of economic, academic, and political power. The main beneficiaries of AP are College Board executives. The money both is and is not the point: the structure is authoritarian, and the profit motive exacerbates the problem.

Per the latest available 990, in 2019, Coleman made more than $1.6 million. In the country of Facebook and Purdue, this is a pittance for an alum of Yale and McKinsey. One year, at the Monsanto-funded Aspen Institute, Coleman said, "We are building an iron wall of inequality" and that the solution was to put "every kid, particularly if they are poor, if they are Black, if they are Latino," into AP.[6] A high school student in the audience challenged him: "Many of my peers feel like they're learning things in this nebulous arms race. . . . They get burnt out from that model of what education is for. What can you, or our government, or we do to foster a meaningful intellectual experience?" Coleman responded, "There's a certain amount of competition. . . . I can't end that." At one point during the talk, he joked about the SAT-ACT rivalry: "It's fun to do Coke-Pepsi stuff."[7] He is one of our nation's most influential arbiters of educational quality, equity, and justice.[8] In 2019, the College Board collected $48,637,176 from investments alone.[9] Some researchers question how much else went unreported.

State governments pay the College Board subsidies for students' exam costs. The sticker price is $96 per exam. Schools get a $9 rebate on every test they sell, to cover "administrative costs." The College Board discounts exams by $34 for low-income students. State governments step in to cover the rest. Policies have slight variations—North Dakota covers the remaining cost of all students' first English, math, science, and computer science exams, and up to four exams in each field for low-income students, while Massachusetts covers the full cost of all low-income students' STEM exams, contingent on enrollment in virtual AP courses, and pays $38 of exam costs in all other subjects for low-income students.[10] Kentucky covers the majority of the cost—$77 each—per exam, in any field, even for "standard-fee" students in public schools. The state covers the full cost—$87—of AP Computer Science and Computer Science Principles exams.[11] State governments also spend money promoting the program. In 2014, North Carolina established the NC Advanced Placement Partnership to "broaden access."[12] Other states have similar initiatives, with similar names: "AP for All" is the slogan in New York, for example, while in Tennessee, it's "AP Access for All."[13]

Despite economists' research raising questions about AP's academic value, states also spend money incentivizing the program by paying schools, administrators, teachers, and students for participation.[14] To encourage adherence to the company's standards, in Missouri, the state pays students who "achieve two grades of three or higher on Advanced Placement exams in the fields of math and/or science while attending a Missouri public high school" a $500 "Advanced Placement Incentive Grant."[15] Until February 2022, San Francisco paid public schools $600 for each student taking an exam.[16] At least through 2017, Alaskan teachers earned $100 per passing score in their classes.[17] To provide "support," the College Board charges for teacher training—summer institutes, workshops, webinars, and online modules, including some that share how teachers can "help to recruit" students—that teachers can pay for out of pocket, or that schools can subsidize. "Member institutions" that pay the College Board an annual fee incur reduced costs for these services. Cancellation less than twenty-one days from an in-person training costs $50, and cancellation less than fourteen days from one online costs $30.

Meanwhile, the College Board recruits public school students and teachers to lobby state legislatures for more funding. "AP Alumni" are invited to share stories with policymakers about how "AP prepared them for success, saved them time and money, and helped them secure meaningful careers." AP Advocates—a program that "creates a cadre of AP teachers to make the case for protecting and expanding AP"—is a multipronged campaign that offers teachers the opportunity to write op-eds, speak with policy makers, and make presentations about the benefits of the College Board's professional development offerings, and to "share personal, compelling messages about the power of AP to change lives." In New York, on "AP Day," at the state legislature, "At circular tables, each seat came with a navy blue fleece scarf embroidered with The College Board's logo. Julie Harris-Lawrence, senior director at the College Board and host of AP Day, urged teachers and students alike to wear the scarves all day long." Students were advised not to stop smiling until they didn't "see any more cameras."[18] Because there is no central, public database detailing all educational policy and budgets from the national to the district level, it is impossible to gauge the extent to which taxpayers support the company's activities.

At the same time, families pay exam fees. In 2019 alone, the College Board made $1,049,403,797 in "program service revenue." Many students pay the full $96—outside of the United States, $126—per

AP exam. Exams for AP Seminar and AP Research, new programs promising to facilitate college-level scholarly work, are $144. Late registration and cancellation each cost $40 per exam. The SAT costs $52 without the essay section and $68 with the essay section, and $30 for late registration. Revenue from that exam pales in comparison to income from AP.

The College Board also profits from collecting and sharing student data. No Child Left Behind required that public schools produce score reports aggregated by sex, race, ethnicity, and economic status in order to qualify for funding. The purpose of this legislation seems distinct from current practices. With the advent of AP Classroom and the company's policy demanding that all students enroll in it, the College Board has the capacity to amass huge amounts of data about minors. In 2020, *Consumer Reports* explained, "When you create an account on collegeboard.org to register for the SAT, sign up for an AP test, or research colleges and scholarships, the College Board sends details about your activity to at least seven tech companies that profit from advertising. The list includes Adobe, Facebook, Google, Microsoft, Snapchat, Yahoo, and an advertising network called AdMedia."[19]

Because AP's value—its "deliverable," in the language of business consulting—is purportedly college credit, the College Board works with state legislatures to mandate that public universities grant credit for scores of 3 or higher. As is true in the case of subsidies, policies follow a template, even if there are slight variations. Here is Ohio's language:

1. A score of 3 or higher will provide credit at any public institution of higher education (PIOHE) in Ohio. The credit must count towards graduation and will meet a general education requirement if the course to which the AP credit is equivalent fulfills a requirement at the receiving institution.
2. When it clearly enhances the opportunity for student success, an institution should strongly advise that an AP score

of at least a 4 is needed for a student to be successful in a second course in a highly dependent sequence of courses in a STEM area. For example, an advisor should strongly recommend that an AP score of at least 4 is needed on the AP Chemistry.

3. A score of 3 or higher on an AP exam in a foreign language area will provide credit for at least the first year of foreign language at any PIOHE.

4. Each PIOHE in Ohio will provide information on awarding AP credits, which should include the number of credits awarded and the course equivalents earned for scores of 3 or higher.

5. Credits earned via AP exams are transferable within PIOHE in Ohio according to the state's transfer module and transfer policy.

State colleges and universities must grant credit for AP courses, and this credit must count toward requirements. Public university professors' thoughts about the academic value of the courses and exams are irrelevant—just like in schools, the state determines the proper intellectual orientation toward the College Board. As is true in Oregon, Tennessee, and many other states, the law uses the language of "consistency and clarity" to justify this policy.[20]

For admission at the most competitive colleges and universities, students and their families are convinced that AP is necessary for transcripts. In policies explaining the decision to drop AP at the most privileged private schools, like Sidwell Friends, parents are told, "We surveyed a large number of colleges and universities that our students attend and have been assured this change will not result in any negative repercussions. Admissions officers have explained that they judge students on the strength of the courses they have taken relative to the rigor of all courses offered at the school."[21] The University of Chicago tries to encourage prospective applicants, "When making curriculum choices, seek out courses that will enrich and challenge you, rather than worry about how they will look to a college application reader. Every college looks at applications differently, so it's difficult to predict what will look 'good' to every college." But for students applying from beyond Sidwell, this is a reminder of precarity: at least AP is identifiable across the nation, even if other courses are more substantial. The College Board has long had tiers of AP awards for students—AP Scholars for passing scores on 3 or more exams, AP Scholars with Honors for passing scores on 4 or more, AP Scholars with Distinction for passing scores on 5 or more, and an AP International Diploma. The company promises the last on the list is an "internationally recognized certificate."

What does the certificate itself recognize? By what dark magic do small, private committees of educators and psychometricians distill the essential meanings and purposes of fields like English, history, and political science, as well as the best ways to measure whatever it is they determine high school and undergraduate students should know? In June 2021, the *Jackson Free Press* celebrated the replacement of one English professor from Mississippi College with another as chief reader for AP English Literature. The paper reported, "The selection of two national chief readers from the same geographical area is very rare. The selection of one just down the hall from the other is unheard of." The outgoing reader said, "If [students] receive a score on the English Literature exam, colleges understand that that score is not local. It's not subjective. It's objective."[22]

The previous year, the College Board used one of my students' essays as a national model for excellence, despite a factual error. The student—one of the most nuanced, deliberate, brilliant readers I've ever had the pleasure to know—had rushed through the essays and focused more on rhetorical flourish than on substance. He got a 5. Another student, who had worked all year to reimagine herself as a writer, with levels of soul and determination that made going to work worthwhile, showed up at my classroom after the exam, distraught about having made me "look bad." She was so nervous during the test that she'd misread the prompt and written an essay in the wrong format. I told her the exam wasn't a measure of her worth or mine. Her relief was palpable. She got a 5. A third student hadn't read a single book all year. He had, however, plagiarized a major essay. He got a 5, too. Two of the three got college credit. Does it matter at which institutions? All of this was before the pandemic exacerbated inequalities in families' access to resources like reliable internet. Whether AP scores are "objective" is debatable. Whether they're meaningful is another issue. I have serious doubts about both. So do a lot of students.

As insecure students, families, governments, universities, schools, and educators bow to the College Board in the name of transparency and fairness, it is impossible to penetrate the opacity of the organization's financial relationships to subsidiaries and partners, including "nonprofits" like the Educational Testing Service and for-profits like Finetune. Additional revenue comes from licensing the AP brand name. In 2021, textbook publishers implored teachers to spend federal Elementary and Secondary School Emergency Relief (ESSER) funds on AP-aligned textbooks.[23] And in 2019, the company received $10,380,203 in contributions and grants. Over the past two decades, the Bill and Melinda Gates Foundation has made eleven major contributions to the company. Amazon is bankrolling the development and implementation of AP Computer Science Principles as part of its "childhood to career" public school curriculum.[24] From 2003 to 2017, the George Lucas Educational Foundation supported development of project-based learning for AP US Government, AP Physics, and AP Environmental Studies.[25] "Partner" "nonprofit" test prep website Khan Academy, which offers study guides for AP exams, made $46,244,725 according to its last 990, filed in 2019.

On May 22 of that year, in the midst of the Varsity Blues scandal, the *Atlantic* published an Ideas essay by Coleman, "There's More To College Than Getting Into College." It began, "The crazed pursuit of college admissions helps no one thrive."[26] A majority share of that

magazine is owned by the Emerson Collective, a for-profit "philan-
throcapitalist" organization founded by Laurene Jobs. When eight
elite private schools published an open letter in the *Washington Post* in
2018 explaining their decision to drop Advanced Placement, reporter
Jay Mathews said their stance "flunked the smell test."[27] Maybe the
schools were acting out of self-interest, distancing themselves from the
unwashed hordes, and not firing a public warning shot about the program's quality. But Mathews has published multiple articles celebrating AP, including a glowing profile of College Board vice president of
Advanced Placement Trevor Packer.[28] In his rankings of high schools,
he uses participation and success rates in AP as criteria. Why? In the
acknowledgments to *Learning in the Fast Lane*, Finn and Scanlan
thanked Mathews for "beaucoup encouragement." They also wrote, "As
we embarked on fieldwork around the United States, we leaned hard
on—and took inexcusable advantage of—many, many people." Is this a
joke? I don't get it. They explained that their book would not have been
possible without the long-standing support of the Thomas B. Fordham
Institute, a think tank and philanthropy that advances the interests of
the "charter sector," including the development of assessments and
teacher accountability measures.[29] In the process of writing this book,
I was a runner-up for the one fellowship I had time to apply for while
teaching full time. The apologetic rejection email explained I'd been
up against "a particularly competitive pool." No kidding.

The College Board's opaque empire is far from complete. In late
2021, the College Board established the College Board Foundation.
According to *The Elective*, the company's "brand journalism" blog,
the foundation is "a new capability aimed at forging partnerships to
address some of the most urgent issues in education."[30] As the Biden
administration supports vocational credentialing in high schools and
community colleges, it's clear that the College Board has plans to
expand its influence. Coleman has touted taking "broader responsibility for outcomes." Who is asking him to do this? Not voters. In 2021,
talking about students whose SAT scores indicated they "weren't

yet ready for college," Coleman said, "What we've done so far is not enough, they've been betrayed to harm, and it's the majority of students."[31] Who is "we"? Why is his eye on the majority of students? In defense of this pivot, Coleman said, "The power of being seen is so fundamental." I agree. But in this model, the eyes belong to a company that profits from data collection.[32] The responsibility to see and protect our most vulnerable citizens is not the College Board's—it is the entire nation's. Already, the company is expanding other academic programs: in partnership with TNTP (The New Teacher Project), "Pre-AP" courses promise to "deliver grade-level appropriate instruction through focused course frameworks, engaging instructional resources, and learning checkpoints," and "Springboard," "driven by its mission to help students in college and beyond," is a math and English curriculum that "integrates instruction, assessment, and professional learning to clear the path to student success."[33] Who knows what this means? Not me. What's clear is that a disproportionate and unrepresentative minority are writing the rules of the game.

In 2022, the company hosted a conference for historically Black colleges and universities called "A Dream Deferred™." When I first saw the name of this event, I stared at my computer for several minutes: Was the company trying to communicate that they had trademarked and now owned Langston Hughes's poem and its sentiment—that there is personal and collective danger in forestalling and frustrating Black Americans' hope? The College Board does not, cannot, should not, must not own this country's promise, its failures, its history, or its future. The company is awash in money. Students test out of required college courses with mangled or hollow understandings of the country's culture, history, and politics—and, if Harvard, Stanford, and MIT are to be believed, calculus—as schools and colleges abandon other meaningful purposes in the quest for "excellence." Higher education faculty have decreased time to teach other habits of mind. Students who go from Andover to Harvard are, as ever, insulated from the whole system. Even if the College Board's finances were transparent and irreproachable, we should still dispense with the AP program before it extinguishes the skills and interest in American culture, history, and government necessary for a broad citizenry to criticize it.

The AP's origin story is about the complexity of interpreting and implementing American ideals. The elite educators who started the AP behind closed doors and with private money had some valid concerns about the fragility of self-governance, but they designated themselves standards bearers with gross self-assurance. Their plans were marked by a facile grasp on the pernicious and enduring effects of slavery and by noblesse oblige that allowed for acknowledging social problems from on high while maintaining distance from them. Best understood as part of the midcentury "façade of consensus," the program promised individualistic cohesion, but only for a narrow sliver of students.[34] At least the committees' elitism meant the program's influence was relatively small. Proclamations about freedom and diversity of ideas came up against financial and institutional limitations, and a lot of thoughtful people and a lot of money built a structure with serious vulnerabilities, including a pride in exclusion that the College Board is now perverting to spread a kind of education diametrically opposed to the one in which the educators placed their sincerest hopes for democracy. But running through their work was an idea worth perpetuating: a government founded on a constitution that is transparent, legible, and accessible and a system of education that aligns with the responsibilities attendant to such a form of authority.[35]

A chasm exists between what the AP program is and what many people perceive it to be. For better or worse, many parents think it's the same as it was five, ten, twenty, or even seventy years ago. By the time this book goes to press, in less than a year, it will be different even from what I've described. The history of liberal education outlined here is, of course, part of a much longer narrative about who has access to books and to big ideas in this country. The program took shape as part of a culture obsessed with how to best forge American consensus. Now, it profits from deep divisions. The social status of the rich white men at the center of the history no longer confers the authority to justify their vision (it never really did), but some of their ideas are worth revisiting, if only in contrast to the current totalitarian structure that affects millions of Americans. The original architects may have been elitist, but the program's authority now rests on much murkier substance, even as it shapes hundreds of thousands of minds, careers, and institutions. We have been desperate to grant "access" to this one thing. But there is so much more to do.

Today, Advanced Placement distorts the meaning and purpose of higher education—it both literally and figuratively cheapens the experience. Andrew Delbanco's *College* and Johann Neem's *The Purpose of College* each explain how the word "college" can mean different things at different institutions, but they agree that campuses should be spaces set apart for reflection and building community.[36] Advanced Placement offers neither of those benefits. Continual efforts to refine the mission of higher education by scholars with distinct perspectives indicate that equating high school education with "college" would entail levels of dynamism that AP Classroom and a static set of exams fail to capture.[37] The program destroys divergent thinking and innovation in the name of fairness. Even if the editors of the US News rankings pretend otherwise, schools have distinct missions and cultures. The diversity of attitudes toward education across institutions makes college life vibrant. There is no such thing as a school, curriculum, or teacher that satisfies every curiosity, aspiration, and need. As the preceding chapters and the epilogue make clear, I believe in liberal education. But it's not for everyone. And even within that approach, as the Kenyon group's resistance to a core curriculum demonstrates, there are multiple ways to frame reading the same books.

In schools, Advanced Placement often creates more problems than it solves. It is the target of criticism about perpetuating inequities.[38] Even the most ambitious, academically inclined students are unduly anxious. When Advanced Placement offers real solutions— like awakening students to the notion that they are, in fact, college material, or providing teachers a sense of community—there must be alternatives that would be more genuinely empowering. The same is true for determining curriculum. In *The Big Test*, Nicholas Lemann proposed that the nation turn away from the SAT as a measure of academic aptitude. While critiquing Conant's faith in technocratic solutions, he argued that in order to achieve meritocracy, the nation ought to consolidate curriculum and hold students accountable to universal standards. With idealism and hedging adverbs, Lemann wrote, "The process of nationally determining [a core body of knowledge and a set of basic skills] would be a contentious but ultimately healthy one—hardly impossibly difficult or inescapably ideological."[39] By the time *The Big Test* was published in 1999, a national curriculum had been in quiet development for decades. Several years prior, in 1995, as momentum grew for sweeping education reforms, Scarsdale High School history teacher Eric Rothschild published an article in the *College Board Review* praising the AP program. He summed up current events: "Both sides in the struggle over national standards have called for a fair and scholarly curriculum. It's here. It's AP." Scarsdale, like many other wealthy public schools, no longer participates in AP.[40] This "national" curriculum, determined by a private company, has perverse interests. It wrests control over schools from local communities and authorities, and in so doing, consolidates economic power. Whether some other process might have produced better results is debatable—some researchers point to Finland's nationalized system as a model, even as they acknowledge that American culture, history, and politics complicate the notion of unified, public agreement on what students need to know.

The AP program founders' values are not necessarily compatible with today's educators' values. But as the second part of this book shows, its current guardians' principles might not be, either. The AP program is far from executing the best of the original vision. Instead of facilitating conversation about the meaning, purpose, and methods for offering liberal arts courses among teachers and professors, it is exploiting insecurities for profit. Dual Enrollment, Running Start, Concurrent Enrollment, the International Baccalaureate, and the Bard Sequence offer acceleration alternatives to AP. But as long as college costs keep rising and admissions remain cutthroat, families will prioritize the promise of efficiency over other forms of meaning, even if we are wasting students' time rather than enriching it. The bipartisan technocratic coalition built over the past three decades is starting to crumble.[41] Republican activist and Hillsdale College president Larry Arnn is promoting a chain of "classical education" charters featuring reactionary curriculum as an escape from "tangled layers of testing and oversight from multi-level bureaucracies."[42] Why should this be our country's most visible version of "liberal education" that is free to families? Some homeschoolers and other charter founders who feel alienated from district schools are staking space for various forms of the liberal arts. For all the chatter about "reimagining" education in the wake of the pandemic, the public school system is missing a huge opportunity to reconsider definitions of "equity" and "access." Going back in time is neither possible nor desirable. The current scheme is the best answer American education has so far to redressing various forms of inequality that breed resentment and division. So where do we go from here?

Education is, as Meister put it, a living thing. Or at least, it should be. If we want to cultivate a national atmosphere of reasoned discussion and civic engagement, in addition to preparing students to make life-changing scientific advances and do other forms of meaningful work, many of the outstanding questions about how to do it are humanistic ones. What do we want schools to do? Why? What does any of it have to do with American identity?

A dangerous conglomeration of nonsynonymous factors contribute to an academic program's "elite" reputation—exclusion, visibility, prestige, high quality, money. Discussing the word's simultaneous appeal and repulsiveness might help us figure out how to move forward. The original AP program relied on a shallow reading of

Jefferson's philosophy. It was a precarious foundation. Reevaluating that framework is helpful for understanding alternatives' ramifications. We need straighter lines between schools and universities. We would benefit from deeper, more honest discussions of our current definitions of equal opportunity and democratic citizenship. The college admissions process needs an overhaul. I don't know what the right balance might be between public and private funding in education, though I know we haven't struck it. And someone ought to look into the College Board's latest vision for the meaning and purpose of STEM education.[43]

The AP program's architects made recommendations that are worth revisiting. Some of them are straightforward and concrete, if expensive. Limiting class size and facilitating exchange among teachers and professors about materials, mission, and pedagogy could help promote the kind of discussion about values that democracy requires. More debate and communication about the meaning and purpose of liberal education across secondary and higher education should lead to policy that is respectful of students' growth and teachers' intellectual autonomy. It is imperative to ground secondary education in means and ends beyond the rigid standardized tests that fail to incentivize nuanced writing and the kind of ongoing learning for teachers that makes their presence most meaningful. Universities—public and private—could help.

I expect to be panned for failing to offer a clear path out of this mess. A plan to recapture the hope and sense of agency that gave life to the original vision for Advanced Placement needs to involve collaboration, conversations about values, and consideration of the multiple educational philosophies aligned with giving all students a full sense of belonging and ownership over the nation's future. As it stands, Advanced Placement displaces that process. I can't fix it alone. That's the whole point.

Formative Assessments

Todd had started teaching history in a public school after finishing a doctorate, with a dissertation on American culture in the age of Eisenhower. A year after I started working in a classroom one floor below his, we decided to experiment with an interdisciplinary American Studies course for juniors. We advertised our project as an "alignment of AP English Language and AP US History" so that administrators would let us offer it and transcript-conscious students would enroll in it. We made a public display of disagreeing over or converging on interpretations of primary sources, histories, and theories. We went on tirades about the dangers of the passive voice. Writing assignments drew on historical modes and overlapping readings. Students asked us to clarify what was going to be on the tests. In the age of AP, collaborating and innovating at the school level is a liability, not an asset.

My section was a chronological survey of American literature culminating in a reading of Ralph Ellison's *Invisible Man*. In writing the curriculum, I designed every assignment to equip students with the ability to think more deeply about the themes and techniques they'd encounter in the novel. In class, Todd and I were both adamant about the value of reading across disciplinary lines to achieve deep understanding. As we moved chronologically through surveys of American culture and history, we kept asking students to revisit the same questions: What is an American? How do you know? Planning was fun—we tossed books, poems, and articles back and forth. We weren't paid (by whom?) for most of the work. At least we weren't fired (by whom?) for it.

One year, we started reading Ellison just as AP exam review was supposed to kick into high gear. In an interview published in the *Paris Review* in the spring of 1955, Ellison said, "If the Negro, or any other writer, is going to do what is expected of him, he's lost the battle before he takes the field. I suspect that all the agony that goes into writing is borne precisely because the writer longs for acceptance—but it must be acceptance on his own terms."[1] In class, we discussed the perils of conformity and unthinking acquiescence. At the beginning of the year, in response to an onslaught of identical essays that had left me anxious about my students' abilities to form independent thoughts about such things as elections, I had tried to design academic writing assignments that would function like pool cues breaking a rack. By April, I'd given up. Parents, students, and administrators were anxious about the tests, so we'd been drilling forty-minute, five-paragraph essays for months.

Within a few days of starting *Invisible Man*, a student with excellent citywide standardized English Language Arts test scores sent me an email: "Hey Dr. Abrams! Hope you had a great weekend. I just wanted to email you about some problems I had about reading. So I've never *read* read a book like I've read a couple paragraphs and gotten the gist, but I've never read a book front to back but I actually want to read this book because it sounds so interesting." I met with him after school and told him to go at his own pace. I asked him to keep checking in with me. He did, giving me a thumbs-up and holding up a book full of Post-it Notes when I'd make eye contact at the beginning of class. Still, I was skeptical when he followed up a month later, as students were requesting college recommendation letters: "Hey Dr. Abrams! Hope you're having a good evening. So after finishing *Invisible Man*, I kind of enjoy reading when I have nothing else to do and everything else gets boring. Do you have any other book recommendations for me?" Was he angling for something? But then, two months later, after the transactional part of school had ended, recommendation letters were filed, and grades entered, he sent another note: "Hey Dr. Abrams! Hope you have a very eventful and relaxing summer! I was just on the train and saw an ad for News 4 New York that catches you up on 'real life in 2 minutes' and it reminded me about our class conversation about how social media limits our thoughts into a small text bubble. Kind of a nerdy moment but I thought you'd like to hear that I'm applying our class conversation in real life." Expansive books shape people's imaginations. So do standardized exams.

My summer was neither relaxing nor eventful. I spent most of it reeling, reflecting on the distance between my job and the work I wanted to do. When I submitted my tenure application that fall, my principal threw away the curricular materials and students' testimonials I'd prepared, explaining, "I think they're very nice, but your students' AP scores are enough for the superintendent." I was livid, then despondent. I understand now. AP scores determine school and administrator evaluations and rankings, a proxy for quality and achievement.[2] My principal was doing her job.

I've struggled with the weight and scope of this book, and with its implications for my own place in the three systems the program was supposed to integrate: K–12 education, college education, and democracy. As I've explained, the AP program relies on a tractable workforce. Every incentive promotes acquiescence, in direct contradiction to my graduate school training to develop questions and research answers. College Board's YouTube channel has turned off comments on videos. The College Board archives in Princeton seem to have disappeared. I sent an email to the reference department asking about Henry Dyer. An automated reply informed me:

"Recipient address rejected: Access denied." I've spoken with multiple AP teachers from districts across the continent who have asked for our conversations to be off the record, fearing professional repercussions for nonconformity. The whole apparatus is forbidding. Instead of grappling with difficult questions about our nation's identity and its future, we've entrusted them to a private company that benefits from opacity, compliance, and erosion of trust in public institutions. All are anathema to democracy.

This book is about who brokers truth and common understanding, and to what ends. My deepest concern is that the AP's current form represents a strain of cynicism that threatens the possibility of self-governance. A metal regime of profitable standardized tests disproportionately affecting public school students attending public universities cannot be the only way to navigate the devastating economic inequalities and very real racism and hatred that plague this country. If we can't build exchange and solidarity around other philosophies of education, what hope is there for a creedal nation that espouses freedom as a core value?[3] Some of the services the AP provides teachers are valuable—training, community, extra pay, a sense of purpose. There are other ways to offer such things. Invitations to use tools like AP Classroom to streamline our practices—to save labor instead of expending it—are tempting. But it's dangerous to outsource the work of thinking and knowing.

The AP depreciates the value of those skills as it pretends to celebrate them. This, at least, is consistent with institutions of higher education more generally. By the time I had finished my dissertation in 2016, teaching nineteenth-century American literature at the college level had all but ceased to be a full-time job for which one could apply. Friends from graduate school were either leaving academia or taking a string of temporary positions. Instead of subjecting myself to a capricious job market, I decided to try public school teaching. Between sessions at an academic conference that spring, one graduate school colleague wrinkled her nose: "Why would you do that?"

At least I'd have a salary, health insurance, maternity leave. The certification process was excruciating, but I love teaching. A room full of people thinking about a poem is the most fun, regardless of what kind of credit they're getting for the exercise.

It appears that the number of such spaces is shrinking across the nation. A recent spate of defenses of liberal education have articulated concern for intellectual life on college campuses. One such book, Roosevelt Montás's *Rescuing Socrates*, retaliates against accusations that the great books are outdated and elitist, and argues in favor of liberal education at scale. Montas is reflective about public school's place in his own intellectual autobiography: he reminisces about a favorite teacher who kindled his interest in Plato, and he finds meaning in sharing works of political philosophy with high school students during summer institutes at Columbia. Following a comment on the university's potential for equalizing opportunity, there's a footnote: "Perhaps the obvious also needs to be said here: that pre-K–12 education is a far more important and critical tool for addressing social stratification. As a society, we should be ashamed of the failing of our public school system to live up to the values of equal opportunity and fairness that we claim to stand for."[4] If, as Montás warns, we are "facing a return to a time when liberal education was the exclusive province of the social elite," could public schools also have a place in holding space for a humanistic approach to democratic life?[5]

High-minded considerations of the imperfect institutional contexts for the liberal arts from the professoriate—recent examples include Montás's, Chad Wellmon's and Paul Reitter's *Permanent Crisis*, and Zena Hitz's *Lost in Thought*—are necessary. But they don't ask specific policy questions about why so many undergraduates arrive on campus predisposed to devaluing humanistic inquiry. Biden's campaign promises included orienting the public school system toward vocational education and computer science. Of course, these goals are not incompatible with offering robust humanities education at the secondary level—workers are multidimensional, and designers of worlds should have rich imaginations. But time and money are both scarce, and corporate-minded reforms like the AP continue to hollow out the possibilities for teaching kids to love reading and history. It's no wonder that students who never read for pleasure in high school don't major in English at 18. Even less surprising—and more alarming—is that they don't understand how this tendency relates to citizenship.

The question of who goes on to major in the humanities is an important one, but there are also direct implications for the ways high schools treat these fields. Most students won't specialize in them. It's a misuse of everyone's time if tests are the only context that give high school writing meaning. Academic writing can be mind-altering. Having spent weeks revising a paper about Ralph Waldo Emerson, one student said, "My uncertainty over ideas of my own, the ones that existed as stream-of-consciousness scribbles throughout the pages of my notes, tempted me to adopt established viewpoints for the sake of relief. I learned what being accountable for my own words meant. Writing empowered me to work through the discomfort to find my voice, one that is specific, candid, and considerate to my readers." She's a computer science major. I don't think her experience was a waste.

History teaches that other kinds of writing can be worthwhile too. On Fridays during the spring term, American Studies classes repeated a three-lesson cycle. We'd pause whatever else we were doing to think about the news. Week 1, we'd read two conflicting op-eds, break down elements of style and structure for each, and discuss which was more convincing. Week 2, Thursday's homework was to "care about something and research it." The next day, students spent half the class talking about norms, conventions, and rules—what did they expect of their own and their classmates' writing in this context, and why? Then they began writing op-eds in class, with breaks to talk about style and purpose. Week 3, I redistributed class sets in different periods and students commented on each other's work in the same way they had with professional writers.' I never graded this work—just a check for completion, to make sure everyone was in the mix. In the absence of pressure to write to me or to the College Board, most students took advantage of the opportunity to invest in their work. One student, now double majoring in economics and history, said, "The consequence of writing a formulaic paragraph is the loss of a personal connection with the audience. I learned to see each paragraph or essay I wrote this year as an opportunity to change the way someone perceived the world, rather than showcase my ability to blithely follow rules." Students left class thinking that writing is a valuable skill. I hope that's not a lie.

Participatory democracy requires contemplative, empathetic people in conversation with each other. In my classroom, I banned the phrase "the text states." There's no heartbeat in it. My wry, exhausted colleague says that giving feedback on essays feels like plowing the sea. Still, he does not desist. In some ways, it is a hugely inefficient exercise. But direct, quantifiable outcomes do not measure the value of engaging with students' thoughts. I agree with the AP program's founders—one antidote to forces that seek to dominate and control is taking seriously each student as an independent thinker. In a year-end reflection, one student, now majoring in biomedical engineering, wrote something that I've thought about throughout this project: "It is worth contributing ideas one cares about at the risk of feeling exposed. This emotion can be scary, but not caring is much more detrimental."

Adolescents need cushioning as they navigate what to care about and how to act on their distress. Surreality—a level of remove from "real life"—is elemental to high school. It's important to be able to dismiss some of what goes on day to day as educators help guide students through the disorientation that accompanies growth. That vulnerability shouldn't be exploited. We are constructing a reality in which students and their families are marks and neither teachers nor researchers matter.

The story of Advanced Placement is part of a broader cultural and political reckoning over mission facing every American institution and communication platform. In this case, the language of education policy can detach us from what's at stake, which is the texture and meaning of students' lives. People who care about students and who think qualitatively and with long-term vision—teachers, administrators, parents, scholars in humanities departments, and experts in education schools—need to bridge the divides that hinder serious discussions about the values and purposes underpinning public education. There is so much hope in students. We are squandering it. And as we fail to invest in the nation's future, a private company is making a killing.

Acknowledgments

At its core, this book is about collaboration. It's something I value.

Without an institutional affiliation, access to information can be tricky. JSTOR's policy for independent researchers, the New York Public Library, the Internet Archive, and alumni privileges at New York University's Bobst Library were crucial. I'd have been lost without the archivists and librarians at Brown University's John Hay Library, Haverford College's Quaker and Special Collections, the Middlebury College Archives, the Williams College Archives, the Swarthmore College Archives, Harvard's Houghton Library, the Baker Library at Harvard Business School, the Kenyon College Archives, the Phillips Andover Academy Archives, the John F. Kennedy Memorial Library, and the Ford Foundation's Rockefeller Archives. With grace and generosity, dozens of academics responded to research queries and challenged my thinking. Jonathan Zimmerman offered provocative comments on chapter drafts. Special thanks to Allen Ballard for a check-in about his teachers, Dr. Chalmers and Dr. Cornog.

I've lucked into occasions for writing. Emily Cooke, Carly Goodman, Gregg Levine, Katie McDonough, Brian Rosenwald, Anna Schechtman, and John Warner edited essays and articles that informed chapters. The History of Education Working Group critiqued chapter 1 and chapter 3. Reviewers at the *Journal of American Studies* helped sharpen the latter. Presenting material from the introduction to a higher education seminar at Columbia helped clarify AP's role in college admissions. I'm grateful to the incisive, humane Greg Britton for taking a chance on me, and to the rest of the team at Johns Hopkins University Press for their guidance and support. Anonymous reviewers provided valuable suggestions for revision.

Many teachers and professors have shaped my thinking, in ways both subtle and overt. Without the four I mention here, there would be no book. As principal of Brooklyn's Edward R. Murrow High School, Saul Bruckner invited generations of students (including me) to consider the dangerous notion that public education might have something to do with freedom. With humor and patience, Andrew Bush has helped me to understand and practice complicated traditions like reading, writing, learning, teaching, friendship, and America. Pat Crain's work on early American literacy has defamiliarized contemporary public schooling, clarified its stakes, and illuminated other possibilities. For years, her acumen has humbled me. Nick Tampio's support for this project has been unflagging and essential. For his many acts of kindness, I'm grateful beyond words.

At Lehman College, Tiffany Dejaynes, Monica Brooker, and a cohort of new public school teachers including Eva Arapian and Masoud House made teacher certification a hopeful experience.

At Bronx Science, I've been inspired by colleagues both within and beyond the English Department. They have helped me to understand the many things a school can be. Alex Seoh's multiple forms of encouragement (birthday pie, making clear to students that physics teachers read novels) have buoyed me. As I hope is clear from this book's epilogue, Todd Davis's care for the structure of this country, the structure of our course, and the structure of this sentence is a constant source of motivation. Conversations with teachers at other schools have broadened my perspective.

Students have pushed me to reevaluate my commitments. Those reading should note that I've tried to use the correct number of sentences per paragraph. I've tried to do right by them in other ways, too.

Through an unreal year, and many other kinds of years, too, Heidi Bender, Abby Deutsch, Josh Glick, Lindsey Gurin, Sandy and Zak Haviland, Leigh Johnson, Allison Kean, Jo Livingstone, Rajiv Menon, Eli Spindel, Blevin Shelnutt, Colin Snow, Katya Waitzkin, and Jenna Weinberg have oriented me and fed me babka.

Norma, Stewart, and the whole Schwab mob have at turns shared my outrage, disagreed with vehemence, supplied books, and ranted about law, education, and America.

My father, Marc Abrams, who dropped out of high school to join the navy, was the most voracious reader I've ever known. He taught me to love learning, to be thoughtful about authority, and to value understanding. My mother, Francine Abrams, was a public high school teacher for more than thirty years. She taught me that institutions can be good and she laughed when my tenth-grade English teacher called home to complain that I asked too many questions. She has long nourished my curiosity with candor and unconditional love.

Whitney Jack Schwab, who has read so many drafts, makes me laugh on impossible days. Marlowe's extraordinary drive to learn and to grow is a continual source of delight. I love you both to the moon and back.

Errors and misinterpretations are mine alone. This book is imperfect. Thank you for reading.

Notes

INTRODUCTION

1. "AP Literature Study Tips and How to Get a 5?" reddit, accessed October 29, 2020, https://www.reddit.com/r/APStudents/comments/bc8fer/ap _literature_study_tips_and_how_to_get_a_5/.
2. "AP Literature Transition Words Flashcards," Quizlet, accessed May 24, 2022, https://quizlet.com/111977408/ap-literature-transition-words -flash-cards/.
3. Garden of English, "The Only Thesis Template You'll Ever Need for Ap Lit!" posted October 31, 2021, YouTube video, https://www.youtube.com /watch?v=Y1eQjJcflu0.
4. CliffsNotes, "AP English: Pacing Your Exam Essays," accessed May 24, 2022, https://www.cliffsnotes.com/test-prep/high-school/ap-exams /articles/ap-english-pacing-your-exam-essays.
5. See the US News and World Report's data on school rankings to explain increased pressure to provide AP courses: "Find the Best Public High Schools," accessed November 25, 2021, https://www.usnews.com /education/best-high-schools.
6. Robert Morse and Eric Brooks, "How US News Calculated the 2022 Best High Schools Rankings," *US News and World Report,* April 25, 2022, https://www.usnews.com/education/best-high-schools/articles/how-us -news-calculated-the-rankings. The text of No Child Left Behind (2002) and the Every Student Succeeds Act (2015) make clear that federal funding is tied to Advanced Placement. One bill under consideration building on this legislation "to increase enrollment and performance of under-represented students in advanced courses and programs" was sponsored by Cory Booker, Sherrod Brown, Tina Smith, and Chris Van Hollen in 2021 (https://www.congress.gov/bill/117th-congress/house-bill/2765?s =1&r=3). Also under consideration is the Fast Track to and through College Act, cosponsored by Margaret Wood Hassan and Todd Young, which relies on "nationally recognized high school academic assessment of high school students' knowledge and skills" in exchange for funding (https:// www.congress.gov/bill/117th-congress/senate-bill/1719).
7. The Albert Team, "AP English Literature Score Calculator," last updated on March 1, 2022, https://www.albert.io/blog/ap-english-literature-score -calculator/.
8. The Albert Team, "The Ultimate AP English Literature Reading List," last updated on March 1, 2022, https://www.albert.io/blog/ultimate-ap -english-literature-reading-list/.

9. Shmoop Editorial Team, "Invisible Man Writing Style," accessed May 24, 2022, https://www.shmoop.com/study-guides/literature/invisible-man-wells/analysis/writing-style.

10. "2019 AP English Literature and Composition Free-Response Questions, Question 3," accessed July 11, 2022, https://apcentral.collegeboard.org/pdf/ap19-frq-english-literature.pdf.

11. "The Only Thesis Template You'll Ever Need for Ap Lit!"

12. Ralph Ellison, *Invisible Man* (New York: Random House, 1952), 447.

13. See, for example, policies at Boston College (https://www.bc.edu/bc-web/admission/sites/advanced-placement.html), Stony Brook University (https://www.stonybrook.edu/sb/bulletin/current/policiesandregulations/admissions/apcredit.php), Azusa Pacific University (http://catalog.apu.edu/admissions/undergraduate-policies/credit-examination/credit-advanced-placement-ap-exams/), and Western Washington University (https://admissions.wwu.edu/apply/ap-ib-cic). For policies on English exams at Ivies, see chapter 5.

14. For an overview of the increasing urgency behind arguments about the endangerment of the liberal arts, see Benjamin Schmidt, "The Humanities Are in Crisis," *The Atlantic*, September 4, 2018, https://www.theatlantic.com/ideas/archive/2018/08/the-humanities-face-a-crisisof-confidence/567565/. It is worth noting that these defenses do not only take the form of essays and polemics. A 2019 study directly refutes claims about the "uselessness" of liberal arts degrees by politicians like Marco Rubio. See Catherine B. Hill and Elizabeth Davidson Pisacreta, "The Economic Benefits and Costs of a Liberal Arts Education," Mellon Foundation, January 2019, https://mellon.org/news-blog/articles/economic-benefits-and-costs-liberal-arts-education/.

15. College Board, "AP English Language: Scoring Rubrics," accessed May 24, 2022, https://apcentral.collegeboard.org/pdf/ap-english-language-and-composition-frqs-1-2-3-scoring-rubrics.pdf.

16. Cynthia Howell, "Advanced Placement Test Scores Rise for State Students," *Arkansas Democrat-Gazette*, February 8, 2020, https://www.arkansasonline.com/news/2020/feb/08/advanced-placement-test-scores-rise-for/.

17. Oklahoma State Department of Education, "Oklahoma State Department of Education Advanced Placement Program Rules," accessed May 24, 2022, https://sde.ok.gov/sites/ok.gov.sde/files/AP-Rules.pdf.

18. "Oklahoma HB3400: 2020: Regular Session," LegiScan, accessed May 24, 2022, https://legiscan.com/OK/bill/HB3400/2020.

19. For background on and a critique of the Common Core movement, see Nicholas Tampio, *Common Core: National Education Standards and the Threat to Democracy* (Baltimore: Johns Hopkins University Press, 2018).

20. Catherine Gewertz, "Illinois Law Requires College Credit for AP Scores of

3 or Higher," EducationWeek, August 18, 2015, https://www.edweek.org /teaching-learning/illinois-law-requires-college-credit-for-ap-scores-of-3 -or-higher/2015/08; Matthew Watkins, "Law Allows More College Credits for High Schoolers," *Texas Tribune,* June 19, 2015, https://www.texastribune .org/2015/06/19/new-law-could-make-it-easier-high-schools-get-ap-c/.

21. "An Act Relative to Advanced Placement Examinations and College Credit," Bill H.1349, https://malegislature.gov/Bills/192/H1349.

22. "AP Cohort Data Report—College Board," accessed June 21, 2022, https:// reports.collegeboard.org/pdf/2020-ap-cohort-data-report.pdf.

23. Titus Wu, "Missouri Could Join 31 Other States in Uniform AP Policy," *Columbian Missourian,* March 2, 2020, https://www.columbiamissourian .com/news/state_news/missouri-could-join-31-other-states-in-uniform -ap-exam-credit-policy/article_93a89056-4da8-11ea-a56a-ef44e8028ec3 .html.

24. University of Missouri, "Mizzou Admissions," accessed July 6, 2022, https://admissions.missouri.edu/apply-freshmen/college-credits/.

25. Tanner Spearman, "Memorial Teachers Helping Create Statewide AP Courses," *Edmond Way,* March 10, 2021, https://www.theedmondway .com/news-newsletters/memorial-teachers-helping-create-statewide -ap-courses. For more on how virtual schooling is distorting education in Oklahoma, see Sean Murphy, "Audit of Oklahoma Virtual School Reveals Numerous Problems," *AP News,* October 1, 2020, https://apnews.com /article/oklahoma-archive-charter-schools-144e85f8b5ba6d8ba6c55df5e da70e90, and "Pandemic Spurs Enrollment at Oklahoma Virtual Charter School," *AP News,* July 23, 2020, https://apnews.com/article/charter -schools-oklahoma-city-oklahoma-pandemics-virus-outbreak-2b1600ae 9484757a8e70f74a560fdcd6.

26. Dan Fisher, "Oklahoma HB2374: 2021: Regular Session," accessed June 21, 2022, http://webserver1.lsb.state.ok.us/cf_pdf/2015-16%20INT/hB/HB1380 %20INT.PDF.

27. World's Editorial Writers, "Effort to Ban AP History in Oklahoma Is Ignorant," *Tulsa World,* February 19, 2015, https://tulsaworld.com/archive /tulsa-world-editorial-effort-to-ban-ap-history-in-oklahoma-is-ignorant /article_43581b08-7c3f-5e01-85ee-167d7a0cc26d.html.

28. Alli Hill, "Column: Oklahoma Education Reaches a New Level of Embarrassment," *The O'Colly,* February 25, 2015, https://www.ocolly.com /opinion/column-oklahoma-education-reaches-a-new-level-of -embarrassment/article_53eb0e74-bd72-11e4-8c7d-8f509321bf39.html.

29. Catherine Sweeney, "Potential Ban on AP Classes Would Cost Students," *The O'Colly,* February 26, 2015, https://www.ocolly.com/news/potential -ban-on-ap-classes-would-cost-students/article_8020d954-be14-11e4 -9117-1fbd5bac9ed9.html.

30. Rick Green and Tim Willert, "Oklahoma Lawmaker Reworking Advanced Placement Bill Says He Supports Program," *The Oklahoman*, February 18, 2015, https://www.oklahoman.com/story/news/politics/2015/02/18 /oklahoma-lawmaker-reworking-advanced-placement-bill-says-he -supports-program/60764975007/.

31. For scholarly discussions of the perils of culture wars in schools, see Andrew Hartman, *A War for the Soul of America: A History of the Culture Wars* (Chicago: University of Chicago Press, 2015); Adam Laats, *Fundamentalism and Education in the Scopes Era: God, Darwin, and the Roots of America's Culture Wars* (New York: Palgrave Macmillan, 2010); Jonathan Zimmerman, *Whose America? Culture Wars in the Public Schools* (Cambridge, MA: Harvard University Press, 2002).

32. Catherine Gewertz, "College Board Accused of Using Parkland Shootings for Self-Promotion," EdWeek, February 22, 2018, https://www.edweek.org /education/college-board-accused-of-using-parkland-shootings-for -self-promotion/2018/02.

33. David Coleman, "New Excellence, New Opportunity," streamed live on October 23, 2018, YouTube video, https://www.youtube.com/watch?v =Dap7HmKbYTQ. See also Eric Hoover, "College Board President's Letter, Prompted by School Shooting, Sparks Criticism," *Chronicle of Higher Education*, February 21, 2018, https://www.chronicle.com/article/college -board-presidents-letter-prompted-by-school-shooting-sparks-criticism/.

34. This book builds on work by humanists including Lisa Gitelman (*Always Already New: Media, History, and the Data of Culture*), Jill Lepore (*If Then: How the Simulmatics Corporation Invented the Future*), Alan Liu (*Friending the Past: The Sense of History in the Digital Age*), and Audrey Watters (*Teaching Machines: The History of Personalized Learning*).

35. College Board, "Introducing the AP Alumni Network," College Board Blog, April 29, 2021, https://blog.collegeboard.org/introducing-ap-alumni -network.

36. NYC Department of Education, "Equity and Excellence," accessed October 27, 2020, https://web.archive.org/web/20220107233922/https://www .schools.nyc.gov/about-us/vision-and-mission/equity-and-excellence.

37. "Moving On Up," Office of Equity and Access, June 20, 2018, https:// oea.nyc/2018/06/20/moving-on-up/.

38. Eight Heads of Washington-Area Private Schools, "Opinion | Our Schools Will Get Rid of AP Courses. Here's Why," June 18, 2018, https://www .washingtonpost.com/opinions/our-schools-got-rid-of-ap-courses-heres -why/2018/06/18/24018654-7316-11e8-9780-b1dd6a09b549_story.html.

39. See Jay Mathews on Jaime Escalante, hero of Stand and Deliver: "Lessons for a Lifetime," *Los Angeles Times*, April 4, 2010, https://www.latimes.com /archives/la-xpm-2010-apr-04-la-oe-mathews4-2010apr04-story.html.

40. "Mayor De Blasio and Chancellor Carranza Announce Record-High 55,011 Students Taking Advanced Placement Exams," NYC, February 26, 2019, https://www1.nyc.gov/office-of-the-mayor/news/113-19/mayor-de-blasio -chancellor-carranza-record-high-55-011-students-taking-advanced#/0.

41. "Transcript: Mayor De Blasio and Chancellor Fariña Announce Highest-Ever Number of NYC Students Taking and Passing Advanced Placement Exams," NYC, January 17, 2017, https://www1.nyc.gov/office-of-the-mayor /news/28-17/transcript-mayor-de-blasio-chancellor-fari-a-highest-ever -number-nyc-students.

42. Matt Stevens, "Joe Biden Says 'Poor Kids' Are Just as Bright as 'White Kids,'" *New York Times*, August 9, 2019, https://www.nytimes.com/2019/08/09/us /politics/joe-biden-poor-kids.html.

43. Jacqueline Rabe Thomas and Adria Watson, "Miguel Cardona's Ideas about Education Were Forged in Meriden, CT. Now He Will Bring Them to Washington, D.C.," *CT Mirror*, January 19, 2021, https://ctmirror.org/2021/01/19 /miguel-cardonas-ideas-about-education-were-forged-in-meriden-ct -now-he-will-bring-them-to-washington-d-c/.

44. Paul Weinstein, "How Biden Can Cut the Cost of College," *Forbes*, December 14, 2020, https://www.forbes.com/sites/paulweinstein/2020/12/14 /how-biden-can-cut-the-cost-of-college/.

45. Chester E. Finn Jr. and Andrew Scanlan, "The Role of Advanced Placement in Bridging Excellence Gaps," Thomas B. Fordham Institute, February 11, 2020, https://fordhaminstitute.org/national/research/role-advanced -placement-bridging-excellence-gaps.

46. "Executive Order on White House Initiative on Advancing Educational Equity, Excellence, and Economic Opportunity for Black Americans," The White House, October 19, 2021, https://www.whitehouse.gov/briefing -room/presidential-actions/2021/10/19/executive-order-on-white-house -initiative-on-advancing-educational-equity-excellence-and-economic -opportunity-for-black-americans/.

47. Morehouse College, "General Education: Program Structure," accessed May 24, 2022, https://morehouse.edu/academics/general-education /program-structure/.

48. College Board, "AP English Language and Composition Development Committee," AP Central, accessed May 24, 2022, https://apcentral .collegeboard.org/courses/ap-english-literature-and-composition /course/development-committee.

49. Merve Emre, *The Personality Brokers: The Strange History of Myers-Briggs and the Birth of Personality Testing* (New York: Doubleday, 2018), 2.

50. "Advanced Placement," *College Board Review*, no. 28 (Winter 1956): 2.

51. Eric Rothschild, "Four Decades of the Advanced Placement Program," *History Teacher* 32, no. 2 (1999): 175–206; Jack Schneider, "Privilege,

Equity, and the Advanced Placement Program," *Journal of Curriculum Studies* 41, no. 6 (2009): 813–31; Tim Lacy, "Examining AP: Access, Rigor, and Revenue in the History of the Advanced Placement Program," in *AP: A Critical Examination of the Advanced Placement Program*, ed. Philip M. Sadler, Robert H. Tai, Kristin Klopfenstein, and Gerhard Sonnert (Cambridge, MA: Harvard Education Press, 2010), 17–50; Frank Bowles, *The Refounding of the College Board, 1948–1963* (New York: College Entrance Examination Board, 1967); John Valentine, *The College Board and School Curriculum, 1900–1980* (New York: College Entrance Examination Board, 1987); and Michael Johanek, *A Faithful Mirror: Reflections on the College Board and Education in America* (New York: College Entrance Examination Board, 2001).

52. I began this project in 2017: College Board, "Program Summary Report," https://secure-media.collegeboard.org/digitalServices/pdf/research/2017/Program-Summary-Report-2017.pdf. The last available data is from 2021: College Board, "Program Summary Report," https://reports.collegeboard.org/media/pdf/2021-ap-program-summary-report_1.pdf.

53. Brown v. Board of Education, https://www.law.cornell.edu/supremecourt/text/347/483%26gt.

CHAPTER 1. RATIONAL REFORM

1. Conant would repeat this phrase at Irwin Stewart's inauguration as president of West Virginia University and in an article titled "The University and the State," both in 1947, and then again in *Education in a Divided World*.

2. On Conant and antisemitism, see Stephen Norwood, "Legitimating Nazism: Harvard University and the Hitler Regime, 1933–1937," *American Jewish History* 92, no. 2 (2004): 189–223.

3. Faye Levine, "Conant's 'Shaping Educational Policy,'" *Harvard Crimson*, December 8, 1964, https://www.thecrimson.com/article/1964/12/8/conants-shaping-educational-policy-pone-of/.

4. Jennet Conant, *Man of the Hour: James B. Conant, Warrior Scientist* (New York: Simon and Schuster, 2018), 15.

5. Michael Halberstam, "James Bryant Conant: The Right Man," *Harvard Crimson*, June 19, 1952, https://www.thecrimson.com/article/1952/6/19/james-bryant-conant-the-right-man/.

6. James Bryant Conant, *My Several Lives: Memoirs of a Social Inventor* (New York: Harper and Row, 1970), 19.

7. Conant, *My Several Lives*, 24.

8. James Bryant Conant, *Slums and Suburbs: A Commentary on Schools in Metropolitan Areas* (New York: McGraw-Hill, 1961), 7.

9. David Labaree has argued that, in policy and pedagogy, we should con-

sider the influence of social efficiency reformers like David Snedden. See David Labaree, "How Dewey Lost," in *Pragmatism and Modernities*, ed. Daniel Trohler, Thomas Schlag, and Fritz Osterwalder (Leiden: Brill, 2010), 163–88.

10. James Bryant Conant, *The Child, the Parent, and the State* (Cambridge, MA: Harvard University Press, 1959), 107.

11. For reasons of space and scope, this is an extremely broad brushstroke. For an argument about distinctions between Dewey and Conant, see Kelly Ritter, *Reframing the Subject* (Pittsburgh: University of Pittsburgh Press, 2015). Accounts of their views on science education, in particular, are available in John Rudolph, *How We Teach Science: What's Changed and Why It Matters* (Cambridge, MA: Harvard University Press, 2019).

12. John Dewey, *Democracy and Education*, Project Gutenberg, 2015, https://www.gutenberg.org/files/852/852-h/852-h.htm.

13. Dewey, *Democracy and Education*.

14. Dewey, *Democracy and Education*.

15. Conant, *The Child, the Parent, and the State*.

16. Fred Hechinger, "John Dewey's Philosophy of Education and the Issues of the Day," *New York Times*, October 18, 1959, https://www.nytimes.com/1959/10/18/archives/education-in-review-john-deweys-philosophy-of-education-and-the.html?searchResultPosition=1.

17. In a 1950 *Foreign Affairs* article titled "Science and Politics in the Twentieth Century," Conant asked, "Can there ever be genuine scientific freedom in a society where all philosophical opinions must conform to the official interpretation of party dogma?" https://www.foreignaffairs.com/articles/1950-01-01/science-and-politics-twentieth-century. For a discussion of Conant's views on Communism and the study of genetics, see James Bryant Conant, *Science and Common Sense* (London: G. Cumberlege, 1951), 367.

18. This chapter builds on work about Cold War public school education reform including Andrew Hartman, *Education and the Cold War: The Battle for the American School* (New York: Palgrave Macmillan, 2011); Adam Laats, *The Other School Reformers: Conservative Activism in American Education* (Cambridge, MA: Harvard University Press, 2015); Diana D'Amico Pawlewicz, *Blaming Teachers* (New Brunswick, NJ: Rutgers University Press, 2020); Thomas D. Fallace, *In the Shadow of Authoritarianism: American Education in the Twentieth Century* (New York: Teachers College Press, 2018); and Marjorie Heins, *Priests of Our Democracy: The Supreme Court, Academic Freedom, and the Anti-Communist Purge* (New York: New York University Press, 2016).

19. Conant's advocacy for liberal education as an alternative to dogma was part of a broader postwar movement by university professors. See Ethan

Schrum, "Establishing a Democratic Religion: Metaphysics and Democracy in the Debates over the President's Commission on Higher Education," *History of Education Quarterly* (Cambridge University Press, February 24, 2017), https://www.cambridge.org/core/journals/history-of-education-quarterly/article/abs/establishing-a-democratic-religion-metaphysics-and-democracy-in-the-debates-over-the-presidents-commission-on-higher-education/198FF5B289F3EF7E992E1562F61B5C64.

20. William M. Tuttle, "American Higher Education and the Nazis: The Case of James B. Conant and Harvard University's 'Diplomatic Relations' with Germany," *American Studies* 20, no. 1 (1979): 49–70.

21. See Wayne J. Urban's *Scholarly Leadership in Higher Education: An Intellectual History of James Bryant Conant* (New York: Bloomsbury, 2021) for a broader overview of Conant's influences.

22. Conant, *My Several Lives*, 138.

23. Nicholas Lemann, *The Big Test: The Secret History of the American Meritocracy* (New York: Farrar, Straus and Giroux, 1999), and Michael J. Sandel, *The Tyranny of Merit: What's Become of the Common Good?* (London: Penguin Books, 2020).

24. Thomas Jefferson, "From Thomas Jefferson to William Johnson, 4 March 1823," National Archives and Records Administration, March 4, 1823, https://founders.archives.gov/documents/Jefferson/98-01-02-3373.

25. Thomas Jefferson, *Notes on the State of Virginia: Edited with an Introduction and Notes by William Peden* (Chapel Hill: University of North Carolina Press, 1955); Thomas Jefferson, "79. A Bill for the More General Diffusion of Knowledge, 18 Jun . . . ," Founders Online, National Archives and Records Administration, accessed October 28, 2020, https://founders.archives.gov/documents/Jefferson/01-02-02-0132-0004-0079; Thomas Jefferson, "Thomas Jefferson to John Adams, 28 October 1813," Founders Online, National Archives and Records Administration, https://founders.archives.gov/documents/Jefferson/03-06-02-0446.

26. "Thomas Jefferson to John Adams, 28 October 1813."

27. On Jefferson's faith in science as progress, see Annette Gordon-Reed and Peter S. Onuf, *"Most Blessed of the Patriarchs": Thomas Jefferson and the Empire of the Imagination* (New York: Liveright Publishing, 2017).

28. John Adams, "From John Adams to Thomas Jefferson, 15 November 1813," Founders Online, National Archives and Records Administration, https://founders.archives.gov/documents/Adams/99-02-02-6198.

29. Karen Fields and Barbara Fields, *Racecraft: The Soul of Inequality in American Life* (London: Verso, 2014), 98. For Jefferson's awful math, see "Thomas Jefferson to Francis C. Gray, 4 March 1815," *Founders Online*, National Archives and Records Administration, https://founders.archives.gov/documents/Jefferson/03-08-02-0245. [Original source: *The Papers*

of Thomas Jefferson, Retirement Series, vol. 8, *1 October 1814 to 31 August 1815*, ed. J. Jefferson Looney (Princeton, NJ: Princeton University Press, 2011), 310–12.

30. Jefferson, *Notes on the State of Virginia*.
31. Alan Taylor, *Thomas Jefferson's Education* (Charlottesville: University of Virginia Press, 2019), 307. See also Annette Gordon-Reed's review of Taylor's book at https://www.theatlantic.com/magazine/archive/2019/12/thomas-jefferson-alan-taylor-university-of-virginia/600793/.
32. For a more comprehensive discussion of Jefferson historiography through the 1940s, see Merrill Daniel Peterson, *The Jefferson Image in the American Mind* (New York: Oxford University Press, 1962).
33. See also Roy Honeywell, *The Educational Work of Thomas Jefferson* (Cambridge, MA: Harvard University Press, 1931); Saul K. Padover, *Jefferson* (New York: Harcourt, Brace, 1942); and John Dewey, *The Living Thoughts of Thomas Jefferson. Presented by John Dewey, with a Portrait* (Greenwich, CT: Fawcett, 1941).
34. See Brian Steele, "Consulting the Timeless Oracle," in *Thomas Jefferson's Lives: Biographers and the Battle for History*, ed. Robert McDonald, Jon Meacham, and Gordon S. Wood (Charlottesville: University of Virginia Press, 2019), 177–99.
35. Claude Bowers, *Young Jefferson, 1743–1789* (Boston, Houghton Mifflin, 1945), viii.
36. For a discussion of Conant's position on the periphery of the Harvard set, see Jerome Karabel, *The Chosen: The Hidden History of Admission and Exclusion at Harvard, Yale, and Princeton* (Boston: Houghton Mifflin Harcourt, 2014).
37. Richard Hofstadter, *The Progressive Historians* (New York: Knopf Doubleday, 1968), 350.
38. Karabel, *The Chosen*.
39. Vernon Louis Parrington, *Main Currents in American Thought*, vol. 2 (New York: Harcourt, Brace, 1954).
40. James Bryant Conant, "Education for a Classless Society: The Jeffersonian Tradition," *The Atlantic*, May 1940, https://www.theatlantic.com/past/docs/issues/95sep/ets/edcla.htm.
41. Parrington, *Main Currents in American Thought*, 1:356.
42. Conant, "Education for a Classless Society."
43. Parrington, *Main Currents in American Thought*, 1:344.
44. Conant, "Education for a Classless Society."
45. See Peterson, *Jefferson Image in the American Mind*.
46. See also Franklin D. Roosevelt, "Address at Jefferson Day Dinner in St. Paul, Minnesota," American Presidency Project, April 18, 1932, https://www.presidency.ucsb.edu/documents/address-jefferson-day-dinner-st

-paul-minnesota; Franklin D. Roosevelt, "Address at the Home of Thomas Jefferson, Monticello, Virginia," American Presidency Project, July 4, 1936, https://www.presidency.ucsb.edu/documents/address-the-home-thomas -jefferson-monticello-virginia; Franklin D. Roosevelt, "Campaign Address on Progressive Government at the Commonwealth Club in San Francisco, California," American Presidency Project, September 23, 1932, https:// www.presidency.ucsb.edu/documents/campaign-address-progressive -government-the-commonwealth-club-san-francisco-california; Franklin D. Roosevelt, "Fireside Chat," American Presidency Project, March 9, 1937, https://www.presidency.ucsb.edu/documents/fireside-chat-17.

47. When Roosevelt spoke at Harvard's tercentenary celebration during the third year of Conant's presidency, he said, "In this day of modern witch-burning, when freedom of thought has been exiled from many lands which were once its home, it is the part of Harvard and America to stand for the freedom of the human mind and to carry the torch of truth." Without reference to Jefferson, Roosevelt used Increase Mather as the touchstone for the notion that America's future was predicated on truth. As Alan Taylor and Annette Gordon-Reed have noted, Jefferson envied New England schools. There is some irony in a New Englander shoring up his vision with Jefferson's scheme.

48. Lemann, Big Test, 38.

49. James B. Conant, "Wanted: American Radicals," The Atlantic, May 1943, https://www.theatlantic.com/past/docs/issues/95sep/ets/radical.htm.

50. Conant, "Wanted."

51. Conant, "Education for a Classless Society."

52. Conant, "Education for a Classless Society."

53. Conant, "Education for a Classless Society."

54. For Conant's faith in social science, see Jamie Cohen-Cole, The Open Mind: Cold War Politics and the Sciences of Human Nature (Chicago: University of Chicago Press, 2016). For Conant's interest in promoting science as a social enterprise, see Christopher Hamlin, "The Pedagogical Roots of the History of Science: Revisiting the Vision of James Bryant Conant," Isis 107, no. 2 (2016): 282–308.

55. Education for All American Youth (Washington, DC: Educational Policies Commission, National Education Association of the United States and the American Association of School Administrators, 1944).

56. Education for All American Youth, 10.

57. Education for All American Youth, 12.

58. General Education in a Free Society: Report of the Harvard Committee (Cambridge, MA: Harvard University Press, 1945).

59. Jamie Cohen-Cole, The Open Mind: Cold War Politics and the Sciences of Human Nature (Chicago: University of Chicago Press, 2014), 27.

60. See Thomas Fallace, *In the Shadow of Authoritarianism* (New York: Teachers College Press, 2018), and Arthur G. Powell, Jeffrey Mirel, and Richard J. Murnane, "American High Schools and the Liberal Arts Tradition," *Brookings Papers on Education Policy*, no. 6 (2003): 7–53.

61. United States Bureau of Education, *Report of the Committee on Secondary School Studies* (Washington, DC: Government Printing Office, 1893). For an overview of the development of public schooling up to this point, see Johann Neem, *Democracy's Schools* (Baltimore: Johns Hopkins University Press, 2017).

62. Diane Ravitch, *Left Back: A Century of Battles over School Reform* (New York: Simon and Schuster, 2001), 44.

63. In addition to Labaree, "How Dewey Lost," see Harvey Kantor, "Work, Education, and Vocational Reform: The Ideological Origins of Vocational Education, 1890–1920," *American Journal of Education* 94, no. 4 (1986): 401–26.

64. In addition to Ravitch, see Audrey Watters on Sal Khan's irresponsible interpretation of the committee's influence in the introduction to *Teaching Machines* (Cambridge, MA: MIT Press, 2021), 1–18.

65. Jacques Barzun, *Teacher in America* (Boston: Little, Brown and Company, 1945); Sidney Hook, *Education for Modern Man* (New York: Knopf, 1946); and Walter Lippmann, "Education vs. Western Civilization," *American Scholar* 10, no. 2 (1941): 184–93. For other contemporary reports on general and liberal education, see William Nelson Lyons, "A Further Bibliography on General Education," *Journal of General Education* 4, no. 1 (1949): 72–80.

66. Robert Maynard Hutchins, *The Higher Learning* (New Haven, CT: Yale University Press, 1936).

67. See John Dewey, "President Hutchins' Proposals to Remake Higher Education," *Social Frontier* 3, no. 22 (1937): 103–4; Robert Maynard Hutchins, "Grammar, Rhetoric, and Mr. Dewey," *Social Frontier* 3, no. 23 (1937): 137–39; and John Dewey, "Was President Hutchins Serious?" *Social Frontier* 3, no. 24 (1937): 167–69. See also Mortimer Adler and Robert Maynard Hutchins, *Great Books of the Western World: The Great Conversation* (Chicago: Encyclopedia Britannica, 1952), 11–13.

68. *General Education in a Free Society*, 93.

69. See also Martha Nussbaum's account of this book's influence at https://www.nybooks.com/articles/1987/11/05/undemocratic-vistas/.

70. Richard Wright, *Black Boy* (New York: Harper Perennial Modern Classics, 2020), 227.

71. James Bryant Conant, *On Understanding Science: An Historical Approach* (New Haven: Yale University Press, 1947). This borrowed phrase from a 1643 pamphlet justifying Harvard College's existence originally signaled concern for replenishing the community's ministry.

72. James Bryant Conant to John K. Norton, January 3, 1949, "Educational Policies Commission, 1948–1949" folder, box 340.

73. For longer histories of the competing visions for schooling to establish "American" habits of mind and behaviors, see David Tyack and Larry Cuban, *Tinkering toward Utopia: A Century of Public School Reform* (Cambridge, MA: Harvard University Press, 1995), and Johann Neem, *Democracy's Schools* (Baltimore: Johns Hopkins University Press, 2017).

74. James B. Conant, *Education in a Divided World: The Function of the Public Schools in Our Unique Society* (Cambridge, MA: Harvard University Press, 1949), 99.

75. Conant, *Education in a Divided World*, 1.

76. Conant's understanding of Jefferson aligned with Gunnar Myrdal's influential analysis of the American education system's reason for existence and the promise it held for Black Americans: "Education has . . . been considered as the best way—and the way most compatible with American individualistic ideals—to improve society." See Gunnar Myrdal, *An American Dilemma*, Vol II (New York: Harper and Brothers, 1944), 882.

77. Conant, *Education in a Divided World*, 54.

78. Alain Locke, "Review: Education in a Democracy," *Journal of Negro Education* 18, no. 4 (Autumn 1949): 504–6, https://doi.org/10.2307/2966165.

79. By 1961, Fred M. Hechinger reported on Conant's outrage over disparities in suburban and underfunded urban schools—Conant issued "a grim warning to all Americans" in which "the former Harvard president and Ambassador to Germany has rejected the language of educator or diplomat." In Conant's word, "This republic was born with a congenital defect." He still believed in tests as a matter of stewardship, and also wanted tests to defer "status-seekers" from wealthy suburban schools from becoming unqualified professionals on which the nation could not rely. Conant's change of tone here underscores the extent to which his earlier choices were just that—choices.

80. James B. Conant, "Some Problems of the American High School (A Preliminary Report of the Conant Study)," *Phi Delta Kappan* 40, no. 2 (1958): 50–55.

81. Conant, "Education for a Classless Society."

82. Conant, *On Understanding Science*.

83. Conant, "Education for a Classless Society."

84. Howard J. Savage, "Toward a National Testing Agency," *Higher Education* 3, no. 8 (December 15, 1946), 8.

85. Lemann, *Big Test*, 71–77.

86. Lemann, *Big Test*, 93–95.

87. For Conant on academic standards and the GI Bill, see Glenn C. Altschuler and Stuart M. Blumin, *The GI Bill: A New Deal for Veterans*

(Oxford: Oxford University Press, 2009), and "Conant Suggests GI Bill Revision," *Harvard Crimson*, January 23, 1945, https://www.thecrimson .com/article/1945/1/23/conant-suggests-gi-bill-revision-pother/.

88. Frank Bowles, *The Refounding of the College Board, 1948–1963: An Informal Commentary and Selected Papers* (New York: College Entrance Examination Board, 1967).

89. On standardized testing as a regime, see, for example, Valerie Strauss, "Confirmed: Standardized Testing Has Taken Over Our Schools," *Washington Post*, October 24, 2015, https://www.washingtonpost.com/news /answer-sheet/wp/2015/10/24/confirmed-standardized-testing-has-taken -over-our-schools-but-whos-to-blame/. For Conant's optimistic view of the consolidation of testing agencies, see *My Several Lives*, 430–32.

90. "Distinguished Service Award Presented to Conant at 1959–1960 Convention," official report (Washington, DC: American Association of School Administrators, 1960), 147–48.

91. James Conant, *Thomas Jefferson and the Development of American Public Education* (Berkeley: University of California Press, 1962). The book was published a year after *Slums and Suburbs*, but the text was of a lecture he'd delivered at Berkeley in 1960.

92. Conant, *Slums and Suburbs*, 16.

93. "The Conant Vacancy," *New York Times*, February 14, 1978, https://www .nytimes.com/1978/02/14/archives/the-conant-vacancy.html.

94. For Harvard's history of attempts to secure its prestige, see Karabel, *The Chosen*, especially chapter 3, "Harvard and the Battle over Restriction," 77–109.

CHAPTER 2. COMMON STANDARDS AND COMMON PURPOSES

1. "Tennis Season Opens with Prospects Fair," *The Philipian*, April 9, 1930, 3. http://pdf.phillipian.net/1930/04091930.pdf.

2. "A Review of the Mirror," *The Philipian*, December 7, 1929, 2. http://pdf .phillipian.net/1929/12071929.pdf.

3. Frederick Allis, *Youth From Every Quarter* (Phillips Academy, Andover, and the UPNE, 1979), 360.

4. John Kemper, "Faculty Retirements," *Andover Bulletin*, August 1968, 6. https://archive.org/details/andoverbulletin6264phil.

5. "Alan Blackmer, 72, Educator, Is Dead," *New York Times*, November 2, 1975. https://www.nytimes.com/1975/11/02/archives/alan-blackmer-72 -educator-is-dead.html.

6. "Educators Plead for Moral Values; 20 Leaders, Including Conant and Eisenhower, Stress Big Tasks Confronting Schools," *New York Times*, February 19, 1951, https://www.nytimes.com/1951/02/19/archives/educators

-plead-for-moral-values-20-leaders-including-conant-and.html; see also James Hershberg, *Harvard to Hiroshima* (Palo Alto: Stanford University Press, 1995), 583–85.

7. Blackmer Committee, *General Education in School and College* (Cambridge, MA: Harvard University Press, 1952), viii.

8. *General Education in School and College*, x.

9. *General Education in School and College*, 3.

10. *General Education in School and College*, 41.

11. See Julian Nemeth, "The Case for Cleaning House: Sidney Hook and the Ethics of Academic Freedom during the McCarthy Era," *History of Education Quarterly* 57, no. 3 (2017): 399–426; Ellen Schrecker, *No Ivory Tower: McCarthyism and the Universities* (New York: Oxford University Press, 1986); Marjorie Heins, *Priests of Our Democracy: The Supreme Court, Academic Freedom, and the Anti-Communist Purge* (New York: New York University Press, 2016); Andrew Hartman, *Education and the Cold War: The Battle for the American School* (New York: Palgrave Macmillan, 2011).

12. "Report of the Trustees of the Ford Foundation," September 27, 1950. https://www.fordfoundation.org/media/2411/1950-annual-report.pdf, 17.

13. See Nielsen Waldemar, *The Big Foundations* (New York: Columbia University Press, 1972); Francis X. Sutton, "The Ford Foundation: The Early Years," *Daedalus* 116, no. 1 (1987): 41–91.

14. "Report of the Trustees of the Ford Foundation," 21.

15. Robert Bendiner, "Report on the Ford Foundation; in the Two Years since It Went into High Gear It Has Encouraged Many Diverse Projects, All in the Interest of Human Welfare," *New York Times*, February 1, 1953, https://www.nytimes.com/1953/02/01/archives/report-on-the-ford-foundation-in-the-two-years-since-it-went-into.html.

16. On tracing acceleration schemes from Charles Eliot, through Robert Hutchins, to Sal Khan, see Robert Hampel, *Fast and Curious: A History of Shortcuts in American Education* (Lanham, MD: Rowman and Littlefield, 2017).

17. Benjamin Fine, "Request for Help Deluge Ford Fund; $23,000,000 Grants in Year Peace Serum Proposed Requests for Help Deluge Ford Fund," *New York Times*, September 26, 1951, https://www.nytimes.com/1951/09/26/archives/request-for-help-deluge-ford-fund-23000000-grants-in-year-peace.html. It is unsurprising that under Hutchins, the foundation would support accelerating study of the liberal arts. He regularly challenged established academic structures. As president of the University of Chicago, George Dell explained, "Hutchins wanted a completely prescribed curriculum in the College because students simply could not know what a good education was until they had experienced one." In 1942, he proposed that Chicago grant a BA to students who had completed a

truncated program of humanities, natural sciences, social sciences, and writing, plus one year of philosophy and two electives. He resented the perception of a four-year degree as "fixed and immutable." Insulted, members of the faculty called the new degree "the Bastard of Arts." Hutchins defended his wartime effort to shorten the time to degree by arguing that traditional degrees conferred not quality of education but "a certain number of years in an educational institution." Despite his own lengthy academic record, he was convinced that prolonged time in school was detrimental to students' assumption of "adult responsibilities," including, but not limited to, military service. Hutchins was committed to the notion of compressed, intensive humanistic study. See also Milton Mayer, *Robert M. Hutchins, A Memoir* (Berkeley: University of California Press, 1993).

18. Alvin Eurich, "Transition from School to College," in *A Report of the Educational Conference* (New York: American Council on Education, 1953), 29.

19. Fund for the Advancement of Education, *Bridging the Gap between School and College* (New York: Fund for the Advancement of Education, 1953), 14.

20. Testimony of Robert M. Hutchins, associate director of the Ford Foundation, November 25, 1952, in Hearings before the House Select Committee to Investigate Tax-Exempt Foundations and Comparable Organizations, pursuant to H. Res. 561, 82d Cong., 2d Sess.

21. Weiman v. Updegraff, 344 US 183, 187 (1952); see also Frankfurter's dissenting opinion in Adler v. New York.

22. William R. Conklin, "Eisenhower Says Farewell to Columbia University," *New York Times*, January 17, 1953, https://www.nytimes.com/1953/01/17/archives/eisenhower-says-farewell-to-columbia-university-eisenhower-takes.html.

23. *National Security Report, NSC 68, "United States Objectives and Programs for National Security*, April 14, 1950, History and Public Policy Program Digital Archive, US National Archives, https://digitalarchive.wilsoncenter.org/document/116191.pdf?v=2699956db534c1821edefa61b8c13ffe.

24. US Congress. *United States Code: Universal Military Training and Service Act, 50a U.S.C. §§ 451–473.* 1952. https://www.loc.gov/item/uscode1952-005050a009/.

25. In the finding aid for the folder dedicated to Advanced Placement, the Ford Foundation archives list a letter from Harvard Business School dean Donald K. David to Clarence H. Faust. That letter has been lost. David was known for promoting "social responsibility" (see Christy Ford Chapin, "The Politics of Corporate Social Responsibility," *Business History Review* 90, no. 4 [2016]: 647–70) and, upon his retirement from Harvard, he joined the Ford Foundation as vice chairman of the trustees.

Some correspondence with Faust is available at Harvard Business School's Baker Library (box 20, folder 20 of Donald K. David's papers). A fuller picture of his involvement—his relationships with Ford administrators and with Blackmer Committee members, particularly Bundy, for instance—might reshape the narrative I've presented here. The Ford Foundation's account of the program's history starts with this letter, which it says introduced Kemper to Faust. Faust's involvement deserves closer attention too. He studied Jonathan Edwards, taught at the University of Chicago, and publications during his tenure as president of the Fund for the Advancement of Education include an essay titled "The Humanities in General Education," *Teachers College Record* 53, no. 9 (1952): 97–11. His *New York Times* obituary, May 22, 1975, reads, "Before he retired, Dr. Faust expressed concern that Americans were 'in danger of becoming too manpower-minded. Youngsters are being pressed,' he said, 'to decide what they want to do in later life but each child should be allowed a full flowering of his desires and talents before preparing for an occupation.'" Whether this position was lifelong commitment or an expression of regret is worth exploring. See "Clarence H. Faust Dead at 74," *New York Times*, May 22, 1975, https://www.nytimes.com/1975/05 /22/archives/clarence-h-faust-dead-at-74-teacher-and-aide-of-ford -fund.html.

26. "The School and College Study under Grant from the Ford Fund for the Advancement of Education," *Phillips Bulletin*, October 1951, 5.
27. "The School and College Study," *Phillips Bulletin*, November 1953, 7.
28. Alan Blackmer, "Shop Talk," *Phillips Bulletin*, October 1939, 25.
29. Blackmer, "Shop Talk," 25.
30. "Summary of Information on School and College Study of General Education," 5. Fund for the Advancement of Education files (FA740), Series II (Grant Files), Subseries 1, Box 29, Rockefeller Archive Center, Sleepy Hollow, NY.
31. See https://www.aspeninstitute.org/programs/executive-leadership -development/aspen-institute-seminar-history/. For background on Aspen, see James Sloan Allen's *The Romance of Commerce and Culture* (Boulder: University Press of Colorado, 2002). I was unable to find a history of the Aspen Institute's effects on higher education.
32. See Ralph M. Hower, "Is Private Enterprise Undermining Our Citizenry— and Itself?" *Harvard Business School Alumni Bulletin* XXVI, no. 4 (Winter 1950): 144.
33. Elmore Harris Harbison, *Christianity and History: Essays* (Princeton, NJ: Princeton University Press, 1964), 108.
34. For more on the group's discussion of religious values, see papers at the Ford Foundation.

35. Allis, *Youth from Every Quarter*; Henry Wilkinson Bragdon and Samuel Proctor McCutcheon, *History of a Free People* (New York: Macmillan, 1958), 671.

36. Henry Bragdon, "History Tests: Uses and Abuses," in *The Teaching of History*, ed. Joseph S. Rouček (New York: Philosophical Library, 1967), 233–45. See also Henry Wilkinson Bragdon, "The Textbook Game," *Proceedings of the Massachusetts Historical Society* 82 (1970): 82–102.

37. McGeorge Bundy, "The Issue Before the Court: Who Gets Ahead in America?" *The Atlantic*, November 1977. https://www.theatlantic.com /past/docs/politics/race/bundy.htm.

38. "Charles Seymour Jr. of Yale, 65, Authority on History of Italian Art," *New York Times*, April 9, 1977, https://www.nytimes.com/1977/04/09/archives /charles-seymour-jr-of-yale-65-authority-on-history-of-italian-art.html.

39. "Summary of Information on School and College Study of General Education," 8. Fund for the Advancement of Education files (FA740), Series II (Grant Files), Subseries 1, Box 29, Rockefeller Archive Center, Sleepy Hollow, NY.

40. "Central Committee," October 7, 1951. Fund for the Advancement of Education files (FA740), Series II (Grant Files), Subseries 1, Box 29, Rockefeller Archive Center, Sleepy Hollow, NY.

41. Alan R. Blackmer, "The Three School, Three College Plan," *College Board Review* 18 (November 1952): 300.

42. Stephen Vine, "Blackmer: An Important Influence in Education," *The Philippian*, June 7, 1968, 3.

43. "Questions for the Panel on Arts and Letters," February 22, 1952. Fund for the Advancement of Education files (FA740), Series II (Grant Files), Subseries 1, Box 29, Rockefeller Archive Center, Sleepy Hollow, NY.

44. Wendell Taylor, "The Place of Science in Grades 11–14," February 7, 1952, Fund for the Advancement of Education files (FA740), Series II (Grant Files), Subseries 1, Box 29, Rockefeller Archive Center, Sleepy Hollow, NY.

45. "The School and College Study of General Education: A Report of Progress to Date, April, 1952," Fund for the Advancement of Education files (FA740), Series II (Grant Files), Subseries 1, Box 29, Rockefeller Archive Center, Sleepy Hollow, NY.

46. "Summary of Information on School and College Study of General Education." Fund for the Advancement of Education files (FA740), Series II (Grant Files), Subseries 1, Box 29, Rockefeller Archive Center, Sleepy Hollow, NY.

47. Blackmer Committee, *General Education in School and College*.

48. Blackmer Committee, *General Education in School and College*, 100.

49. Blackmer Committee, *General Education in School and College*, 121.

50. Blackmer Committee, *General Education in School and College*, 10.

51. In *General Education for a Free Society*, Conant's committee wrote, "A truly democratic education must . . . try to equalize opportunity by counteracting impediments. . . . Democracy is not only opportunity for the able. It is equally betterment for the average, both the immediate betterment which can be gained in a single generation and the slower groundswell which works through generations" (11).

52. Blackmer Committee, *General Education in School and College*, 21.

53. Blackmer Committee, *General Education in School and College*, 102.

54. Blackmer Committee, *General Education in School and College*, 20.

55. Blackmer Committee, *General Education in School and College*, 40.

56. Blackmer Committee, *General Education in School and College*, 10.

57. "Addenda," Fund for the Advancement of Education files (FA740), Series II (Grant Files), Subseries 1, Box 29, Rockefeller Archive Center, Sleepy Hollow, NY.

58. Blackmer Committee, *General Education in School and College*, 10.

59. Alan Blackmer to McGeorge Bundy, December 26, 1953, McGeorge Bundy Personal Papers, Series 3.4. Subject Files, 1949–1960, Box 027, John F. Kennedy Presidential Library and Museum, Boston.

60. Blackmer Committee, *General Education in School and College*, ix.

61. Alfred North Whitehead, *The Aims of Education: And Other Essays* (New York: Simon and Schuster, 1964), 5.

62. Whitehead, *The Aims of Education*, v.

63. Whitehead, *Aims of Education*, 45.

64. Blackmer Committee, *General Education in School and College*, 21.

65. Ralph Ellison to Jim and Madge Randolph, September 18, 1953. In *Selected Letters of Ralph Ellison*, edited by John F. Callahan and Marc C. Conner (New York: Random House, 2019), 338.

66. For the story of a midcentury teacher-activist operating with agency and with limited resources beyond Harvard, see Michael Hines, *A Worthy Piece of Work: The Untold Story of Madeline Morgan and the Fight for Black History in Schools* (Boston: Beacon Press, 2022).

67. Blackmer Committee, *General Education in School and College*, 20.

68. Blackmer Committee, *General Education in School and College*, 24.

69. Alan Blackmer to Alvin Eurich, May 13, 1952, Fund for the Advancement of Education files (FA740), Series II (Grant Files), Subseries 1, Box 29, Rockefeller Archive Center, Sleepy Hollow, NY.

70. Alan Blackmer to Alvin Eurich, February 7, 1953, Fund for the Advancement of Education files (FA740), Series II (Grant Files), Subseries 1, Box 29, Rockefeller Archive Center, Sleepy Hollow, NY.

71. Earle G. Eley to Alan Blackmer, August 4, 1950. College Board Essay Exam folder, Box 2, Dean of Faculty (Blackmer) records, Phillips Academy Archives & Special Collections.

72. Eric Rothschild, "Aspiration, Performance, Reward: The Advanced Placement Program at 40," *College Board Review*, no. 176-77 (Summer 1995): 24-32.

73. Wolfgang Saxon, "Henry S. Dyer, 88; Test Expert Studied Role of the S.A.T.," *New York Times*, December 3, 1995, https://www.nytimes.com/1995/12 /03/nyregion/henry-s-dyer-88-test-expert-studied-role-of-the-sat.html; meeting minutes at the Ford archives list only the committee's questions at the meeting, not Dyer's responses.

74. Henry S. Dyer, "What Point of View Should Teachers Have Concerning the Role of Measurement in Education?" *Yearbook of the National Council on Measurements Used in Education*, no. 15 (1958): 11-15. http://www .jstor.org/stable/41862796.

75. Henry S. Dyer, "The Menace of Testing Reconsidered." *Educational Horizons* 43, no. 1 (1964): 3-8. http://www.jstor.org/stable/42923461.

76. Blackmer Committee, *General Education in School and College*.

77. A firm believer in quantification as a tool for progress, he capitalized on the development of wartime technology and spearheaded the use of an "IBM gadget" to grade multiple-choice exams. See "A Rank System," *Harvard Crimson*, March 26, 1949, https://www.thecrimson.com/article /1949/3/26/a-rank-system-pthe-administration-has/.

78. "Inhuman Test Corrector Has Perfect Score," *Harvard Crimson*, January 29, 1949, https://www.thecrimson.com/article/1949/1/29/inhuman-test -corrector-has-perfect-score/.

79. Claude Fuess, *The College Board* (New York: College Entrance Examination Board, 1950).

80. By 1960, then as a vice president at the Educational Testing Service, Dyer had published multiple warnings about the value of IQ testing. See, for example, "A Psychometrician Views Human Ability," *Teachers College Record* 6, no. 7 (1960): 1-8.

81. See Norbert Elliott, *On a Scale: A Social History of Writing Assessment in America* (New York: Peter Lang, 2008).

82. By 1950, Andover teacher Claude M. Fuess lamented the corporation's businesslike new direction. He celebrated a newly expanded, heterogeneous membership of colleges beyond Ivies and Seven Sisters, and even beyond the East Coast, but admitted that at meetings, "something of the homelike atmosphere has disappeared." He argued that the board's sense of purpose needed continual readjustment, as "today our lack of articulation is not a matter of detail; it is a matter of complete difference in philosophy and in understanding of the approach of education." Fuess cheerily predicted that debate between "humanists and vocationalists" would keep meetings lively, and that the conversation would remain a two-sided and valuable one. See Fuess, *College Board*.

83. Frank Bowles, *The Refounding of the College Board, 1948–1963: An Informal Commentary and Selected Papers* (New York: College Entrance Examination Board, 1967), x.

84. William Fels, "Bennington College Commencement," June 28, 1958.

85. "Research Program Started," *College Board Review*, no. 19 (February 1953): 322.

86. Alan Blackmer to McGeorge Bundy, December 6, 1952. McGeorge Bundy Personal Papers, Series 3.4. Subject Files, 1949–1960, Box 027, John F. Kennedy Presidential Library and Museum, Boston.

87. E. Harris Harbison to McGeorge Bundy, December 21, 1952. McGeorge Bundy Personal Papers, Series 3.4. Subject Files, 1949–1960, Box 027, John F. Kennedy Presidential Library and Museum, Boston.

88. Henry Bragdon to McGeorge Bundy, December 18, 1952. McGeorge Bundy Personal Papers, Series 3.4. Subject Files, 1949–1960, Box 027, John F. Kennedy Presidential Library and Museum, Boston.

89. *The Mississippi Gambler* is a 1953 film. *Harvard Crimson* reviewer Michael Finkelstein wrote of the protagonist: "His discreet gambling and Puritan manner would put a benevolent granny to shame." The movie is about a genteel gambler who toes the line between do-gooder and manipulative degenerate.

90. Alan Blackmer to Alvin Eurich, December 15, 1952. Fund for the Advancement of Education files (FA740), Series II (Grant Files), Subseries 1, Box 29, Rockefeller Archive Center, Sleepy Hollow, NY.

91. See records of Harvard's Committee on Educational Policy, January 7, 1953, and February 2, 1954, Houghton.

92. Harlan P. Hanson's role as director of Harvard's Program for Advanced Standing—a distinct, singular program grappling with similar issues—warrants more study. He supported the Advanced Placement program and championed the cause of transfer credits from high schools by urging academic departments to align their standards with the College Board's once the organization took over in 1955. From 1965 to 1989, he served as the program's director. Tracking his influence on its development is beyond the scope of this chapter. In addition to his papers at Harvard, a few early letters with Cornog and Chalmers are housed at Kenyon. See also John G. Wofford, "Hanson States Need for Uniformity," *Harvard Crimson*, December 8, 1955.

93. Stephen F. Jencks, "Sophomore Standing: The Making of a Policy," *Harvard Crimson*, June 15, 1961, https://www.thecrimson.com/article/1961/6/15/sophomore-standing-the-making-of-a/.

94. Luke Steiner to William Cornog, July 10, 1953, Archives and Special Collections, Kenyon College, Gambier, OH.

95. See LARB review of Sandel's book on meritocracy: Christopher Kutz,

"Meritocracy and Its Discontents: The View from Outside Harvard Yard," *Los Angeles Review of Books*, January 30, 2021, https://lareviewofbooks .org/article/meritocracy-and-its-discontents-the-view-from-outside -harvard-yard/.

96. David Halberstam, "Faculty Approves Advance Standing Program, Allowing Special Status for Qualified Students," *Harvard Crimson*, March 3, 1954, https://www.thecrimson.com/article/1954/3/3/faculty-approves -advance-standing-program-allowing/.

97. David Halberstam, *The Best and the Brightest* (New York: Random House, 1972).

98. McGeorge Bundy, "Panel on Values," December 15, 1951. Fund for the Advancement of Education files (FA740), Series II (Grant Files), Subseries 1, Box 29, Rockefeller Archive Center, Sleepy Hollow, NY.

99. *Bridging the Gap between School and College; a Progress Report on Four Related Projects Supported by the Fund for the Advancement of Education* (Fund for the Advancement of Education, 1953).

100. McGeorge Bundy, "Four Subjects and Four Hopes," *College Board Review*, no. 27 (Fall 1955): 17–20.

101. For a fuller discussion of the program's rapid evolution into a credentialing service, see Jack Schneider, "Privilege, Equity, and the Advanced Placement Program: Tug of War, *Journal of Curriculum Studies* 41(2009): 813–31.

102. Alan Blackmer, "Andover in the Future," *Andover Bulletin*, Spring 1962, 62. https://archive.org/details/andoverbulletin5658phil/page/n59/mode /2up?q=shrink.

CHAPTER 3. THE BLUEPRINT

1. Raymond English, "His Memory," *Kenyon Collegian*, May 25, 1956, 1–3.

2. Allan Ballard, *The Education of Black Folk* (New York: Harper, 1973), 4.

3. Tommy Johnson, "1949 Football Season Cut Short after a Stand Against Racism," *Kenyon Collegian*, February 27, 2020, https://kenyoncollegian .com/features/2020/02/1949-football-season-cut-short-after-a-stand -against-racism/.

4. Bayes M. Norton to Richard Pearson, January 5, 1960, Kenyon College Archives, Gambier, OH.

5. English, "His Memory," 142.

6. English, "His Memory," 144.

7. English, "His Memory," 338.

8. John Dewey, *Liberalism and Social Action* (New York: Putnam, 1935), 53.

9. Dewey, *Liberalism and Social Action*, 54.

10. See, for example, Walter Lippmann, *Public Opinion* (New York: Simon

and Schuster, 1922), and John Dewey, *The Public and Its Problems* (Athens, OH: Swallow Press, 1927). For background on Lippmann, see Michael Petrou, "Should Journalists Be Insiders?" *The Atlantic*, September 19, 2018, https://www.theatlantic.com/ideas/archive/2018/09/should -journalists-be-insiders/570637/.

11. Mortimer Smith, *And Madly Teach* (Chicago: Regnery, 1949), 18.

12. In 1937, he'd appointed Lippmann as one of the first committee members to select Nieman Fellows, still a yearlong program for journalists at Harvard.

13. Gordon Keith Chalmers, *The Republic and the Person: A Discussion of Necessities in Modern American Education* (Chicago: Regnery, 1952), 43.

14. Chalmers, *Republic and the Person*, 37.

15. Chalmers, *Republic and the Person*, 51.

16. Chalmers, *Republic and the Person*, 55.

17. Chalmers, *Republic and the Person*, 226.

18. Gordon Chalmers Keith, "The Academy and the 'Enquiry Squad,'" *American Scholar* 26, no. 2 (1957): 165–80.

19. Russell Kirk, "The American Conservative Character," *Georgia Review* 8, no. 3 (1954): 249–60.

20. Russell Kirk, *Confessions of a Bohemian Tory* (New York: Fleet Publishing Corporation, 1963), 137–40.

21. Peter Robert Edwin Vierick, *Conservatism: From John Adams to Churchill* (Princeton, NJ: Van Nostrand, 1956), 107.

22. George H. Nash, *The Conservative Intellectual Movement in America since 1945* (Wilmington, DE: ISI Books, 2008), 63–64.

23. Andrew Hartman, *Education and the Cold War: The Battle for the American School* (New York: Palgrave Macmillan, 2011).

24. Patrick Allitt, *The Conservatives: Ideas and Personalities throughout American History* (New Haven, CT: Yale University Press, 2010).

25. Gordon Chalmers, "Review of 'The Conservative Mind,'" *New York Times*, May 17, 1953.

26. Russell Kirk, *The Conservative Mind: From Burke to Eliot* (Gateway Editions, an imprint of Regnery Publishing, 2016), 495.

27. John Crowe Ransom, "Reconstructed but Unregenerate," in *I'll Take My Stand: The South and the Agrarian Tradition*, ed. Susan V. Donaldson (Baton Rouge: LSU Press, 2005), 1–27.

28. John Crowe Ransom, "Criticism, Inc." VQR, Autumn 1937. https://www .vqronline.org/essay/criticism-inc-0.

29. "Keyon College Bulletin 1955 Catalogue," Kenyon College Course Catalogs 1954, 137. https://digital.kenyon.edu/coursecatalogs/137.

30. Chalmers, *Republic and the Person*, 232.

31. Hartman, *Education and the Cold War*.

32. Chalmers, *Republic and the Person*, 19.

33. Lewis Mumford, "The Corruption of Liberalism," *New Republic*, April 29, 1940, https://newrepublic.com/article/119690/lewis-mumfords-corruption-liberalism.

34. Chalmers, *Republic and the Person*, 176. For a discussion of midcentury conservatives' rejection of social science in favor of history, see Jill Lepore, *If Then* (New York: W. W. Norton, 2020), 47–66.

35. Chalmers, *Republic and the Person*, 12.

36. Chalmers, *Republic and the Person*, 17.

37. For more on the import of Buckley's work, see Julian Nemeth, "The Passion of William F. Buckley: Academic Freedom, Conspiratorial Conservatism, and the Rise of the Postwar Right," *Journal of American Studies* 54, no. 2 (2020): 323–50.

38. Nemeth, "Passion of William F. Buckley," 183.

39. Chalmers, *Republic and the Person*, 184.

40. Gordon Keith Chalmers, "The Purpose of Learning," *ANNALS of the American Academy of Political and Social Science* 301, no. 1 (September 1955): 7–16.

41. Chalmers, "Purpose of Learning."

42. Chalmers, "Purpose of Learning."

43. Chalmers, "Purpose of Learning."

44. Gordon Keith Chalmers, "Black-Letter Man and the Man of Statistics," *Georgia Review* 7, no. 1 (1953): 5–17.

45. Chalmers, "Black-Letter Man and the Man of Statistics."

46. For more on the foundation's roots and political positions, see John J. Scanlon, "The Fund for the Advancement of Education," *AIBS Bulletin* 7, no. 3 (1957): 12–14, Francis X. Sutton, "The Ford Foundation: The Early Years," *Daedalus* 116, no. 1 (1987): 41–91; and Ford Foundation, *Ford Foundation Annual Report* (New York: Ford Foundation, 1951).

47. For a detailed recounting of the program's inception, see William H. Cornog, "Initiating an Educational Program for the Able Students in the Secondary School," *School Review* 65, no. 1 (1957): 49–59.

48. James Phinney Baxter to Gordon Keith Chalmers, January 16, 1952, Kenyon College Archives, Chalmers Library. Gambier, OH.

49. Gordon Keith Chalmers, "Statement II," Kenyon College Archives, Chalmers Library, Gambier, OH.

50. Colleges also had different stated reasons for participating. In a section of all-male Bowdoin College president's report titled "The Undergraduate and Military Service," Kenneth M. Sills explained, "In the past year the Draft Boards and other military authorities have been so considerate in allowing men to complete their four-year course. . . . In order to have an anchor to windward, in view of conditions that are liable to be unsettled

for some time, Bowdoin is joining with eleven other colleges . . . in a coop-erative enterprise to study the possibility and practicability of giving ad-vanced credit. . . . Such credit may enable a student to complete his work in three and a half, or in extraordinary circumstances, in three years." See Bowdoin College, *Report of the President, Bowdoin College 1951–1952*, January 1, 1952, 61. https://digitalcommons.bowdoin.edu/presidents -reports/61. At Haverford, also all-male, minutes from two meetings dis-cussing the college's involvement make no mention of conscription. Con-cerns focused instead on strengthening academic quality and attracting gifted students. See Haverford College Faculty meeting minutes and rec-ords (HCE.003.001), Quaker & Special Collections, Haverford College, Haverford, PA.

51. Gordon K. Chalmers, "Advanced Credit for the School Student," *College Board Review* no. 18 (1952): 309.

52. Gordon Keith Chalmers to John O. Hallowell, December 28, 1953, Kenyon College Archives, Chalmers Library, Gambier, OH.

53. See, for instance, his contribution to Norman Foerster and Wendell L. Willkie, *The Humanities after the War* (Freeport, NY: Books for Libraries Press, 1944), and "The Place of Letters in Liberal Education: Report of the Commission on Liberal Education of the Association of American Colleges." *Association of American Colleges Bulletin* 33, no. 4 (December 1947): 1–8.

54. *The School and College Study of Admission with Advanced Standing: A Report to the Faculties of the Twelve Participating Institutions: Bowdoin College, Brown University, Carleton College, Haverford College, Kenyon College, Massachusetts Institute of Technology, Middlebury College, Ober-lin College, Swarthmore College, Wabash College, Wesleyan University, Williams College* (Philadelphia: Office of the Executive Director, 1953), 29.

55. *Study of Admission with Advanced Standing*, 9.

56. *Study of Admission with Advanced Standing*, 9.

57. *Study of Admission with Advanced Standing*, xi.

58. *Study of Admission with Advanced Standing*, xii.

59. *Study of Admission with Advanced Standing*, 132.

60. William Cornog to Luke Steiner, July 15, 1953, Kenyon College Archives, Chalmers Library, Gambier, OH.

61. Charles Coffin to William Cornog, October 28, 1953, Kenyon College Archives, Chalmers Library, Gambier, OH.

62. *Study of Admission with Advanced Standing*.

63. William Cornog to Luke Steiner, July 15, 1953, Kenyon College Archives, Chalmers Library, Gambier, OH.

64. Bayes Norton to Morton Briggs, October 1, 1953, Kenyon College Archives, Chalmers Library, Gambier, OH.

65. William Hafner Cornog to Gordon Keith Chalmers, February 9, 1953, Kenyon College Archives, Chalmers Library, Gambier, OH.

66. Alvin Eurich to Gordon Chalmers, February 3, 1954, Kenyon College Archives, Chalmers Library, Gambier, OH.

67. Gordon Chalmers, "Third Report," Kenyon College Archives, Chalmers Library, Gambier, OH.

68. Gordon Chalmers to Alvin Eurich, May 27, 1953, Kenyon College Archives, Chalmers Library, Gambier, OH.

69. William Fels, "How Tests May Be Used to Obtain Better Articulation of the Total Educational System," in *The Refounding of the College Board*, ed. Frank Bowles (Princeton, NJ: College Entrance Examination Board, 1967), 122–27.

70. "AP College Entrance Examination Board Meeting Minutes," November 14, 1955, Kenyon College Archives, Chalmers Library, Gambier, OH.

71. Charles Keller to Gordon Chalmers, December 30, 1955, Kenyon College Archives, Chalmers Library, Gambier, OH.

72. For more on Charles Keller's vision for AP, see his papers at the Williams College Archives, especially "The Advanced Placement Program: Its Impact on American Education, 1957-12-2," Box: 8, Folder: 1. Charles R. Keller papers, MC-115. Williams College Archives and Special Collections, accessed August 31, 2021, https://archivesspace.williams.edu/repositories /2/archival_objects/114048; "The Advanced Placement Program in Jeffersonian Terms, 1957-11-1," Box: 8, Folder: 1. Charles R. Keller papers, MC-115. Williams College Archives and Special Collections, accessed August 31, 2021, https://archivesspace.williams.edu/repositories/2/archival_objects /114047; "Keeping the Colleges on Their Toes, 1958-4-25," Box: 8, Folder: 2. Charles R. Keller papers, MC-115. Williams College Archives and Special Collections, accessed August 31, 2021, https://archivesspace.williams.edu /repositories/2/archival_objects/114057; "The Advanced Placement Program Now Has a History, 1958-6-27," Box: 8, Folder: 2. Charles R. Keller papers, MC-115. Williams College Archives & Special Collections, accessed August 31, 2021, https://archivesspace.williams.edu/repositories/2/archival _objects/114060; "What Can the Advanced Placement Program Contribute to the Excellence of High School Education, 1959-12-4," Box: 8, Folder: 3. Charles R. Keller papers, MC-115. Williams College Archives and Special Collections, accessed August 31, 2021, https://archivesspace.williams.edu/ repositories/2/archival_objects/114074.

73. William Hafner Cornog, *School of the Republic* (Philadelphia: Rittenhouse Press, 1952), ii.

74. Cornog, "Initiating an Educational Program."

75. Conant advocated for a system in which the top 3 percent of students were tracked into special courses—this was part of his meritocratic vision.

See Jefferson's Bill for the Diffusion of Knowledge (1789) for a description of the mechanisms by which particularly intelligent students would have the opportunity to advance in their studies "at the public expense."

76. William Cornog, "Purposes and Scope," *Bulletin of the National Association of Secondary School Principals* 39, no. 213 (October 1955): 5–72.

77. Cornog, "Initiating an Educational Program."

78. William H. Cornog, "College Admission with Advanced Standing," in *Proceedings of the Invitational Conference on Testing Problems* (10th, New York, New York, October 30, 1954), 113–19. Princeton, NJ: Educational Testing Service. https://files.eric.ed.gov/fulltext/ED173435.pdf.

79. William H. Cornog, "Teaching Humanities in the Space Age," *School Review* 72, no. 3 (1964): 377–93.

80. Chalmers and Cornog both cite Lippman, who built on an idea of public conversation in circulation during the nation's founding. In public debates, Dewey and Lippmann argued about the most viable configurations for democratic media. While Lippmann expressed faith in a class of experts in service of a public incapable of making truly well-informed decisions in multiple fields, Dewey advocated for a more equal distribution of information and decision making. This conversation spanned books, lectures, and articles. See, for example, Walter Lippmann, *Public Opinion* (New York: Harcourt, 1922), and Dewey's review of that book in *The New Republic*.

81. Cornog, "Initiating an Educational Program."

82. Cornog, "Initiating an Educational Program."

83. William H. Cornog, "Initiating an Educational Program for the Able Students in the Secondary School." *The School Review* 65, no. 1 (1957): 49–59, http://www.jstor.org/stable/1083613.

84. Cornog, "Teaching Humanities in the Space Age."

85. "Kenyon Collegian—May 26, 1955" (1955). https://digital.kenyon.edu/collegian/2080/.

86. Gordon Keith Chalmers, "The Education of Governors," *Virginia Quarterly Review* 31, no. 3 (1955): 404–20.

87. Ta-Nehisi Coates, *Between the World and Me* (New York: Random House, 2017), 26.

CHAPTER 4. COPY PASTE CLASSROOM

1. College Board, "What Is AP?," AP Students, accessed April 2, 2021, https://apstudents.collegeboard.org/what-is-ap#:~:text=The%20AP%20Program%20offers%20college,can%20take%20in%20high%20school.

2. College Board, "January-May: Continue Using AP Classroom Resources," accessed July 11, 2022, https://apstudents.collegeboard.org/dates/use-ap-classroom-resources-spring.

3. Abby Jacobs, "David Coleman Appoints Jeremy Singer as President of the College Board," All Access, January 27, 2020, https://allaccess.college board.org/david-coleman-appoints-jeremy-singer-president-college -board.

4. "Finetune Revolutionizes Assessment Content Creation Speed, Quality, and Creativity with Finetune Generate," Finetune, June 9, 2021, https://finetunelearning.com/finetune-revolutionizes-assessment-content -creation-speed-quality-and-creativity-with-finetune-generate/. See also Finetune, "Finetune Elevate—AP Classroom," May 18, 2020, https://vimeo.com/419999653.

5. Finetune, "Elevate," June 30, 2022, https://www.linkedin.com/products /finetunelearning-finetune-elevate/.

6. Victor Rivero, "Interview: A Question of Academic Merit," EdTech Digest, January 23, 2012, https://www.edtechdigest.com/2012/01/23/interview -a-question-of-academic-merit/.

7. Steve Shapiro, "Miracle Working CEO," Angel Invest Boston, accessed June 30, 2022, https://www.angelinvestboston.com/ep-70-steve-shapiro -finetune.

8. "Parent Resource: Understanding AP," College Board Blog, September 21, 2020, https://blog.collegeboard.org/parent-resource-understanding-ap.

9. In keeping with other College Board products, AP Classroom collects students' data. Before entering or exploring it, students must create an account with the College Board for access. The terms of service warn, "Data collected from the AP Classroom system could also be shared with researchers and partners." Students (and their parents) must swallow whatever concerns about privacy this might raise, because engagement with the portal is mandatory if students want college credit for AP exams. Once signed up for the platform, students must opt out of, not into, exam registration.

10. College Board, "AP U.S. History: Course and Exam Description," https://apcentral.collegeboard.org/pdf/ap-us-history-course-and-exam -description.pdf.

11. College Board, "AP U.S. History: Course and Exam Description."

12. Valerie Strauss, "Ben Carson: New AP U.S. History Course Will Make Kids Want to 'Sign up for ISIS,'" Washington Post, September 29, 2014, https://www.washingtonpost.com/news/answer-sheet/wp/2014/09/29/ben -carson-new-ap-u-s-history-course-will-make-kids-want-to-sign-up-for -isis/.

13. RNC, "Resolution Concerning Advanced Placement U.S. History (APUSH)," RNC website, August 8, 2014, https://prod-cdn-static.gop.com/docs /resolution_concerning_advanced_placement_us_history_apush.pdf.

14. David Coleman, "A Note from David Coleman," College Board, 2014,

https://secure-media.collegeboard.org/digitalServices/pdf/ap/ap-us
-history-letter-from-david-coleman.pdf.

15. Hayden V. White, *Metahistory: The Historical Imagination in 19th-Century Europe* (Baltimore: Johns Hopkins University Press, 1987).

16. Bulletin of Yale University, Yale College Programs of Study, "History (HIST)," accessed June 30, 2022, http://catalog.yale.edu/ycps/courses /hist/.

17. Johns Hopkins Krieger School of Arts and Sciences, Department of History, "Undergraduate Courses," accessed June 30, 2022, https://history .jhu.edu/undergraduate/courses/.

18. Georgetown University, Department of History, "Undergraduate Level Courses," accessed June 30, 2022, https://history.georgetown.edu/course -descriptions/undergraduate-level-courses/.

19. Williams College, Registrar's Office, "Advanced Placement Guide," accessed June 30, 2022, https://registrar.williams.edu/course-registration /placement-information/ap-placement-guide/.

20. For a brief history, see Adam Laats, "How Picking on Teachers Became an American Tradition," *Slate*, January 28, 2022, https://slate.com/human -interest/2022/01/history-of-spying-on-teachers.html.

21. Henry Wilkinson Bragdon, "History Tests: Uses and Abuses," in *The Teaching of History*, ed. Joseph Rouček (New York: Philosophical Society, 1967), 233–45.

22. Charles Keller, "AP: Reflections of the First Director," *College Board Review* 116 (Summer 1980), 22.

23. Charles R. Keller, "The Advanced Placement Program Now Has a History," *Bulletin of the National Association of Secondary School Principals* 42, no. 242 (December 1958): 6–12. https://doi.org/10.1177/019263655804224202.

24. School and College Study of Admission with Advanced Standing. "Reports of Committees, 1952–1953" ([Philadelphia]: The Central Committee of the Study, 1953).

25. Keller, "Advanced Placement Program Now Has a History," 22.

26. Keller, "Advanced Placement Program Now Has a History," 22.

27. Harlan P. Hanson, "Recognizing the Gifted: Is Differentiation Undemocratic?" *College Board Review* 115 (Spring 1980): 6.

28. "TV Courses Succeed," *College Board Review* 51 (Fall 1963): 5.

29. Eric Wakin, "Professor James P. Shenton '49: History's Happy Warrior," Columbia College Today, accessed June 8, 2022, http://www.columbia .edu/cu/record/archives/vol22/vol22_iss3/Professor_Shenton.html; Christopher Lehmann-Haupt, "James P. Shenton, 78, Dies; History Professor at Columbia," *New York Times*, July 28, 2003, https://www.nytimes .com/2003/07/28/nyregion/james-p-shenton-78-dies-history-professor -at-columbia.html.

30. Wakin, "Professor James P. Shenton '49"; Lehmann-Haupt, "James P. Shenton, 78, Dies."

31. Mike Drosnan, "Shenton Favors Classroom Despite Summer TV Success," *Columbia Daily Spectator*, Volume CVIII, no. 7, October 3, 1963, http://spectatorarchive.library.columbia.edu/cgi-bin/columbia?a=d&d=cs19631003-01.2.4&e=-------en-20--1--txt-txIN-------.

32. Jonathan Zimmerman, *The Amateur Hour: A History of College Teaching in America* (Baltimore: Johns Hopkins University Press, 2020).

33. See the AHA jobs report here: https://www.historians.org/ahajobsreport2020.

34. Lisa Gitelman, *Always Already New* (Cambridge, MA: MIT Press, 2006), 10. For the ways technology reproduces norms and biases in education in particular, see also Audrey Watters, *Teaching Machines* (Cambridge, MA: MIT Press, 2021); and Tressie McMillan Cottom, "Black Cyberfeminism: Intersectionality, Institutions, and Digital Sociology," in *Digital Sociologies*, ed. Jessie Daniels, Karen Gregory, and Tressie McMillan Cottom (Bristol: Policy Press, 2016).

35. Mayer v. Monroe County Community School District, 2007.

36. For a fuller discussion about this decision, see Emily Robertson and Jonathan Zimmerman, *The Case for Contention: Teaching Controversial Issues in American Schools* (Chicago: University of Chicago Press, 2017).

37. See also Andrew Hartman, "How the Culture Wars Destroyed Public Education," *Washington Post*, September 5, 2017, https://www.washingtonpost.com/news/made-by-history/wp/2017/09/05/how-the-culture-wars-destroyed-public-education/.

38. Jack Schneider and Jennifer Berkshire, *A Wolf at the Schoolhouse Door* (New York: New Press, 2020).

39. Tamar Lewin, "Testing Group Ends Effort to Make Profit on Web Site," *New York Times*, January 14, 2003, https://www.nytimes.com/2003/01/14/business/testing-group-ends-effort-to-make-profit-on-web-site.html?searchResultPosition=35.

40. James W. Fraser and Lauren Lefty, *Teaching Teachers: Changing Paths and Enduring Debates* (Baltimore: Johns Hopkins University Press, 2018). See also suggestions in Dana Goldstein, *The Teacher Wars: A History of America's Most Embattled Profession* (New York: Anchor, 2015), and Kenneth Zeichner, *Struggle for the Soul of Teacher Education* (New York: Routledge, 2018).

41. College Board, "First Generation Students," accessed June 30, 2022, https://professionals.collegeboard.org/guidance/prepare/first-generation. The website explains: "First-generation students can come from families with low incomes or from middle- or higher-income families without a college-going tradition. Some have parents who support their plans for higher

education; others are under family pressure to enter the workforce right after high school." Of course, this is a false dichotomy: a family can be in dire circumstances and still value education.

42. Mary Beard, *Today* program, BBC 4, March 4, 2014.

43. For histories of Americans' resistance to trusting teachers, see Diana D'Amico Pawlewicz, *Blaming Teachers: Professionalization Policies and the Failure of Reform in American History* (New Brunswick, NJ: Rutgers University Press, 2020), and Goldstein, *Teacher Wars.*

44. "OAH Issues an Open Letter to the Biden Administration on the 1776 Report and the 'Future of the Past,'" Organization of American Historians, February 18, 2021, https://www.oah.org/insights/posts/2021/february /oah-issues-an-open-letter-to-the-biden-administration-on-the-1776 -report-and-the-future-of-the-past/.

CHAPTER 5. ARTIFICIAL INTELLIGENCE

1. Chester E. Finn and Andrew E. Scanlan, *Learning in the Fast Lane: The Past, Present, and Future of Advanced Placement* (Princeton, NJ: Princeton University Press, 2019).

2. College Board, "AP Program Participation and Performance Data 2020," October 9, 2020, https://web.archive.org/web/20201030094643/https:// research.collegeboard.org/programs/ap/data/participation/ap-2020.

3. College Board, "AP Credit Policy Search," accessed June 8, 2022, https:// apstudents.collegeboard.org/getting-credit-placement/search-policies.

4. Vassar English, "FAQ," accessed June 8, 2022, https://www.vassar.edu /english/students/faq.html.

5. Stanford Department of English, "About the Department," accessed June 8, 2022, https://english.stanford.edu/about/about-department.

6. College Board, "AP English Language: Scoring Rubrics," 2019, https:// apcentral.collegeboard.org/pdf/ap-english-language-and-composition -frqs-1-2-3-scoring-rubrics.pdf; College Board, "AP English Literature and Composition Scoring Rubrics (Effective Fall 2019)," September 2019, https://apcentral.collegeboard.org/pdf/ap-english-literature-and -composition-one-page-scoring-rubrics-2019-2020.pdf?course=ap -english-literature-and-composition.

7. College Board, "AP English Language: Scoring Rubrics"; College Board "AP English Literature and Composition Scoring Rubrics."

8. Saleh Daher, "Christian Magel, 'Venture Lane Startup Hub,'" Angel Invest Boston, accessed June 29, 2022, https://www.angelinvestboston.com /ep-88-christopher-magel/tag/Fine+Tune+Learning.

9. See Audrey Watters, *Teaching Machines: The History of Personalized Learning* (Cambridge, MA: MIT Press, 2021), and Patricia Crain, *Reading Children: Literacy, Property, and the Dilemmas of Childhood in*

Nineteenth-Century America (Philadelphia: University of Pennsylvania Press, 2018).

10. Thomas B. Fordham Institute, "A Moonshot for Kids," accessed June 8, 2022, https://fordhaminstitute.org/national/events/moonshot-for-kids.

11. Finetune, "Converge," accessed June 29, 2022, https://www.finetune learning.com/converge/.

12. Finetune, "Writing Hero," executive summary, https://fordhaminstitute .org/sites/default/files/2019-11/FineTune_Ogden%20Morse.pdf.

13. Finetune Converge, "Corporate Learning Management Systems," accessed June 29, 2022, https://www.linkedin.com/products/finetunelearning -finetune-converge.

14. Victor Rivero, "Interview: A Question of Academic Merit," EdTech Digest, January 23, 2012, https://edtechdigest.blog/2012/01/23/interview-a -question-of-academic-merit/.

15. For more comprehensive accounts, see Lyndsey Layton, "How Bill Gates Pulled Off the Swift Common Core Revolution," *Washington Post,* June 7, 2014, https://www.washingtonpost.com/politics/how-bill-gates-pulled -off-the-swift-common-core-revolution/2014/06/07/a830e32e-ec34-11e3 -9f5c-9075d5508f0a_story.html; Mercedes Schneider, *Common Core Dilemma* (New York: Teachers College Press, 2015); and Nicholas Tampio, *Common Core: National Education Standards and the Threat to Democracy* (Baltimore: Johns Hopkins University Press, 2019).

16. Nicholas Tampio, "Betsy DeVos Said Common Core Was 'Dead'—It's Not," The Conversation, March 26, 2018, https://theconversation.com/betsy -devos-said-common-core-was-dead-its-not-92800.

17. David Coleman, "Cultivating Wonder," 2013, https://simplebooklet.com /userFiles/a/4/1/0/7/6/RglFZX37Iaup7i97hzLAJw/63g92LeZ.pdf.

18. Valerie Strauss, "The 'Seven Deadly Sins' of Common Core—by an English Teacher," *Washington Post,* August 18, 2016, https://www.washingtonpost .com/news/answer-sheet/wp/2016/08/18/the-seven-deadly-sins-of -common-core-by-an-english-teacher/.

19. Daniel Katz, "Dear Common Core English Standards: Can We Talk? *Daniel Katz, Ph.D.* (blog), September 19, 2014, https://danielskatz.net /2014/09/19/dear-common-core-english-standards-can-we-talk/.

20. Jonathan Kramnick, "Criticism and Truth," *Critical Inquiry* 47, no. 2 (Winter 2021): https://doi.org/10.1086/712118.

21. Tampio, *Common Core,* 54.

22. Stephanie Simon, "Advanced Placement Classes Failing Students," *Politico,* August 21, 2013, https://www.politico.com/story/2013/08/education -advanced-placement-classes-tests-95723_Page2.html.

23. McGeorge Bundy, "Four Subjects and Four Hopes," *College Board Review,* no. 27 (Fall 1955): 18.

24. National Council of Teachers of English, "Articulation of Secondary

School and College Work," *College Composition and Communication* 9, no. 3 (1958): 192–96.

25. Gordon Keith Chalmers and William Hafner Cornog, "Reports of Committees, 1952–1953," School and College Study of Admission with Advanced Standing, 20–48.

26. National Council of Teachers of English, "Administering the Freshman Course," *College Composition and Communication* 11, no. 3 (October 1960): 166–68.

27. Gordon Keith Chalmers, *A Report to the Faculties of the Twelve Participating Institutions: Bowdoin College, Brown University, Carleton College, Haverford College, Kenyon College, Massachusetts Institute of Technology, Middlebury College, Oberlin College, Swarthmore College, Wabash College, Wesleyan University, Williams College* (Philadelphia: Office of the Executive Director, 1953).

28. Chalmers, *A Report to the Faculties of the Twelve Participating Institutions.*

29. As reported in John G. Cotter, "Paragraph Evaluation," *English Journal* 38, no. 8 (October 1949), 458–60.

30. W. E. B. Du Bois, *The Souls of Black Folk* (New York: Knopf, 2010).

31. Andrew Delbanco, *College: What It Was, Is, and Should Be* (Princeton, NJ: Princeton University Press, 2014).

32. Benjamin Schmidt, "The Humanities Are in Crisis," *The Atlantic*, September 4, 2018, https://www.theatlantic.com/ideas/archive/2018/08/the-humanities-face-a-crisisof-confidence/567565/.

33. Cited in Frank Bruni, "The End of College as We Knew It?," *New York Times*, June 4, 2020, https://www.nytimes.com/2020/06/04/opinion/sunday/coronavirus-college-humanities.html.

34. Fareed Zakaria, *In Defense of a Liberal Education* (New York: W. W. Norton, 2016).

35. Christopher J. Scalia, "Conservatives, Please Stop Trashing the Liberal Arts," Wall Street Journal, March 27, 2015, https://www.wsj.com/articles/christopher-scalia-conservatives-please-stop-trashing-the-liberal-arts-1427494073.

36. Michael S. Roth, *Beyond the University: Why Liberal Education Matters* (New Haven, CY: Yale University Press, 2015), 195.

CHAPTER 6. BETTER CITIZENS

1. Thomas L. Friedman, "The Two Codes Your Kids Need to Know," *New York Times*, February 12, 2019, https://www.nytimes.com/2019/02/12/opinion/college-board-sat-ap.html.

2. Friedman, "The Two Codes Your Kids Need to Know."

3. Stefanie Sanford, "Hacking Democracy: Two Codes for the Modern

World," *Medium*, September 26, 2019, https://medium.com/@ssanford
_77683/hacking-democracy-two-codes-for-the-modern-world
-e6561a77dc12.

4. College Board, "Government and Politics: United States Comparative
Course Description," Course Description, 2009. https://www.greeley
schools.org/cms/lib/CO01001723/Centricity/Domain/1056/AP%20course
%20description%20from%20AP%20central.pdf.

5. College Board, "AP US Government and Politics: Course and Exam
Description," accessed June 30, 2022, https://apcentral.collegeboard.org
/pdf/ap-us-government-and-politics-course-and-exam-description
.pdf?course=ap-united-states-government-and-politics.

6. College Board, "What AP Stands For," accessed June 30, 2022, https://
apcentral.collegeboard.org/about-ap/what-ap-stands-for#:~:text=AP
%20opposes%20censorship.,provided%20to%20colleges%20and%20
universities.

7. See, for example, Scott Jaschik, "Could High Schools Lose AP Programs?"
Inside Higher Education, March 21, 2022, https://www.insidehighered
.com/admissions/article/2022/03/21/college-board-reminds-high
-schools-possibility-losing-ap-program, and Scott Stump, "High Schools
Could Lose AP Classes," *Today*, March 4, 2022, https://www.today.com
/parents/parents/high-schools-lose-ap-classes-banning-required-topics
-rcna18813.

8. Laurinburg Institute, "Curriculum," accessed June 20, 2022, https://www
.laurinburginstitute.org/curriculum/.

9. Princeton University, "American Political Thought," course description,
accessed December 1, 2021, https://m.princeton.edu/default/courses
/detail?area=POL&course=005305&term=1214.

10. "American Government 2305," Austin Community College syllabus, accessed December 1, 2021, https://www.austincc.edu/vrodrigu/usgov.htm.

11. "Introduction to American Government," Yale University syllabus, Summer
2019, https://summer.yale.edu/sites/default/files/files/Syllabi/2019
/PLSC%20S113%20Introduction%20to%20American%20Government.pdf.

12. "POSC 100—Introduction to American Government," course description,
accessed December 1, 2021, http://catalog.csulb.edu/preview_course
_nopop.php?catoid=5&coid=43550.

13. Chester E. Finn and Andrew E. Scanlan, *Learning in the Fast Lane: The
Past, Present, and Future of Advanced Placement* (Princeton, NJ: Princeton University Press, 2019), 199.

14. College Board, "AP U.S. Government and Politics," accessed December 1,
2021, https://apcentral.collegeboard.org/pdf/ap-united-states-government
-and-politics-course-overview.pdf?course=ap-united-states-government
-and-politics.

15. College Board, "Government and Politics," course description, accessed December 1, 2021, https://apcentral.collegeboard.org/pdf/ap-us -government-and-politics-course-description.pdf?course=ap-united -states-government-and-politics.

16. Tiffany Sorenson, "The Test-Taker's Guide to US Government and Politics," *US News and World Report*, October 11, 2021, https://www.usnews.com /education/blogs/college-admissions-playbook/articles/the-test-takers -guide-to-ap-us-government-and-politics-course.

17. "West Virginia State Board of Education v. Barnette, 319 U.S. 624 (1943)," Justia Law, accessed December 1, 2021, https://supreme.justia.com/cases /federal/us/319/624/.

18. Robert Pondiscio, "Civics Education: Now or Never," Thomas B. Fordham Institute, November 29, 2016, https://fordhaminstitute.org/national /commentary/civics-education-now-or-never.

19. Chester Finn and Andrew Scanlan, *Learning in the Fast Lane: The Past, Present and Future of Advanced Placement* (Princeton, NJ: Princeton University Press, 2019), 149.

20. Robert L. Hampel, "Blurring the Boundary between High School and College: The Long View," *Phi Delta Kappan*, October 23, 2017, https:// kappanonline.org/hampel-blurring-boundary-high-school-college -long-view/.

21. "Conant Lauds Public School System," *Harvard Crimson*, April 10, 1952, https://www.thecrimson.com/article/1952/4/10/conant-lauds-public -school-system-pithe/.

22. Consonant with Dewey's reflections on Jefferson, 1939, in which he characterized schools as "local agencies of communication and cooperation, creating stable loyal attachments"; he worried that "economic forces" have acted "at the expense of the intimacy and directness of communal group interests and activities." From John Dewey, "Introduction," *The Living Words of Thomas Jefferson* (New York: Longmans, Green, and Company, 1940).

23. See Danielle Allen, *Talking to Strangers: Anxieties of Citizenship since Brown v. Board* (Chicago: University of Chicago Press, 2014); Ansley Erickson, *Making the Unequal Metropolis* (Chicago: University of Chicago Press, 2016); Bruce Ackerman and Jack Balkin, eds., *What Brown v. Board of Education Should Have Said* (New York: New York University Press, 2002); and James T. Patterson, *Brown v. Board of Education: A Civil Rights Milestone and Its Troubled Legacy* (New York: Oxford University Press, 2002).

24. Alan Blackmer, "The Three School, Three College Plan," *College Board Review*, no. 18 (1952): 300.

25. Gordon Keith Chalmers, "Advanced Credit for the School Student," *College Board Review*, no. 18 (1952): 310.

26. Harold B. Gores and Leo Barry, "College-Level Courses in Secondary Schools," *College Board Review* 28 (1956): 10.

27. Preston Valien, "The Status of Educational Desegregation, 1956: A Critical Summary," *Journal of Negro Education* 25, no. 3 (1956): 359–68. See also Leslie Fenwick, *Jim Crow's Pink Slip: The Untold Story of Black Principal and Teacher Leadership* (Cambridge, MA: Harvard Education Press, 2022).

28. Kay L. Schlozman, "A Reply to the Evaluation of the AP Program in Political Science," *Political Science Teacher* 2, no. 4 (October 30, 2015): https://www.cambridge.org/core/journals/political-science-teacher/article/abs/reply-to-the-evaluation-of-the-ap-program-in-political-science/C465CF78E3C8295497FD7451E9C779F6.

29. *Political Science Teacher*, Cambridge Core, accessed December 1, 2021, https://www.cambridge.org/core/journals/ps-political-science-and-politics/past-title/the-political-science-teacher/all-issues/0C26D20831BAFEE406A1D823C28634B7.

30. Gerald M. Pomper, "A Summer Institute in American Politics," *Political Science Teacher* 1, no. 1 (October 30, 2015): https://www.cambridge.org/core/journals/political-science-teacher/article/abs/summer-institute-in-american-politics/0c3b1b25daaea1def571b542636d24de.

31. Ann G. Serow, "Thoughts on the AP: A Teacher Responds," *Political Science Teacher* 3, no. 1 (1990): 23–24.

32. American Political Science Association Committee on Pre-Collegiate Education. "Political Education in the Public Schools: The Challenge for Political Science." *Political Science and Politics* 4 (1971): 431–57.

33. Paul Barry, "The New President of the College Board: Donald M. Stewart," *College Board Review* 142 (Winter 1986–87): 14.

34. Donald M. Stewart, "Leadership in a Democratic Society," *College Board Review* 149 (Fall 1988): 13.

35. Claudia H. Deutsch, "A Mania for Testing Spells Money," *New York Times*, October 16, 1988, https://www.nytimes.com/1988/10/16/business/a-mania-for-testing-spells-money.html?searchResultPosition=28.

36. Gerald M. Pomper, "A Summer Institute in American Politics," *Political Science Teacher* 1, no. 1 (1988): 20–21.

37. Richard G. Niemi and Julia Smith, "Enrollments in High School Government Classes: Are We Short-Changing Both Citizenship and Political Science Training?" *Political Science and Politics* 34 (2001): 281–87.

38. Wayne Journell, "We Still Need You! An Update on the Status of K–12 Civics Education in the United States," *Political Science and Politics* 48, no. 4 (2015): 630–34.

39. Tamar Lewin, "Backer of Common Core School Curriculum Is Chosen to Lead College Board," *New York Times*, May 16, 2012, https://www.nytimes.com/2012/05/16/education/david-coleman-to-lead-college-board.html.

40. Noliwe Rooks, *Cutting School: Privatization, Segregation, and the End of Public Education* (New York: New Press, 2017).

41. *Federalist*, no. 70, Avalon Project, Yale Law School, accessed December 1, 2021, https://avalon.law.yale.edu/18th_century/fed70.asp.

CONCLUSION

1. Morris Meister, "Co-Operation of Secondary School and Colleges in Acceleration of Gifted Students," *Journal of Educational Sociology* 29, no. 5 (1956): 220, https://doi.org/10.2307/2263967.

2. Joseph R. Reichard, "The College Board and Advanced Placement in German," *German Quarterly* 29, no. 4 (1956): 220, https://doi.org/10.2307/401493. For other evaluations of the program's initial success, see "Articulation between Secondary School and College," *College Composition and Communication* 8, no. 3 (1957): 162, https://doi.org/10.2307/355844.

3. Eric Hoover, "Captain Caperton," *Chronicle of Higher Education*, June 30, 2006. https://www.chronicle.com/article/captain-caperton/.

4. See Philip M. Sadler, ed., *AP: A Critical Examination of the Advanced Placement Program* (Cambridge, MA: Harvard Education Press, 2010). See especially "Whither Advanced Placement Now?," 233–43, and Janie Scull, Review, Fordham Institute, https://fordhaminstitute.org/national/commentary/ap-critical-examination-advanced-placement-program.

5. David Coleman, "Achieving the Social Mission of the College Board," October 24, 2012, https://www.youtube.com/watch?v=LWpgKb52C2M.

6. "College Board President: 'We Are Building an Iron Wall of Inequality,'" Aspen Institute, July 16, 2014, https://www.aspeninstitute.org/blog-posts/college-board-president-we-are-building-an-iron-wall-of-inequality/.

7. "College Board President."

8. "College Board President."

9. See also Susan F. Paterno, *Game On: Why College Admission Is Rigged and How to Beat the System* (New York: St. Martin's Press, 2021); Richard Phelps, "Does College Board Deserve Public Subsidies?," *Nonpartisan Education Review*, 2019, https://files.eric.ed.gov/fulltext/ED593681.pdf; Mercedes Schneider, "The College Board 'Nonprofit': Oh, the Money One Can Make!," deutsch29, February 27, 2019, https://deutsch29.wordpress.com/2019/02/26/the-college-board-nonprofit-oh-the-money-one-can-make/.

10. North Dakota Department of Public Instruction, "Advanced Placement Exam Fees Guidance, 2021–2022," accessed June 9, 2022, https://www.nd.gov/dpi/sites/www/files/documents/Academic%20Support/2021-2022%20AP%20Exam%20Fee%20Guidance.pdf; Massachusetts Department of Elementary and Secondary Education, "Massachusetts State Advanced Placement (AP) Exam Fee Subsidy and International Baccalau-

reate (IB) Program, 2021–2022," accessed June 9, 2022, https://www.doe
.mass.edu/ap/.

11. Kentucky Department of Education, "Advanced Placement (AP)," March
2, 2022, https://education.ky.gov/educational/AL/ap/Pages/default.aspx.

12. North Carolina Department of Public Instruction, "Advanced Placement,"
accessed June 9, 2022, https://www.dpi.nc.gov/students-families
/enhanced-opportunities/advanced-learning-and-gifted-education
/advanced-coursework/advanced-placement.

13. Tennessee AP Access for All, accessed April 26, 2022, https://tnapaccess
forall.org/; NYC Department of Education, "AP for All," accessed June 10,
2022, https://apforallnyc.com/.

14. Kristin Klopfenstein and M. Kathleen Thomas, "The Link between
Advanced Placement Experience and Early College Success." *Southern
Economic Journal* 75, no. 3 (2009): 873–91.

15. Department of Higher Education and Workforce Development, "Advanced
Placement Incentive Grant," accessed June 9, 2022, https://dhewd.mo
.gov/ppc/grants/advancedplacement.php; C. Kirabo Jackson, "Cash for
Test Scores," Education Next, last updated August 15, 2008, https://www
.educationnext.org/cash-for-test-scores/.

16. Jill Tucker, "S.F. Families Say the School District is Cutting AP Classes, with
Lowell Taking the Biggest Hit. Here's What's Really Going On," *San Francisco Chronicle*, February 24, 2022, https://www.sfchronicle.com/bayarea
/article/S-F-families-say-the-school-district-is-cutting-16942499.php.

17. Janee Wilson, "Schools: AP Coursework Offers Challenge, College Credit,"
Frontiersman, April 8, 2017, https://www.frontiersman.com/news/schools
-ap-coursework-offers-challenge-college-credit/article_49a93d36-1cd0
-11e7-92af-d3ff1ad66fbb.html.

18. Kara Grant, "The College Board Enlists High School Students to Lobby
Albany for Advanced Placement Funding," School Stories, May 15, 2020,
http://school-stories.org/2020/03/the-college-board-enlists-high-school
-students-to-lobby-albany-for-advanced-placement-funding/.

19. Thomas Germain, "The College Board is Sharing Student Data Once
Again," Consumer Reports, July 30, 2020, https://www.consumerreports
.org/colleges-universities/college-board-is-sharing-student-data-once
-again/.

20. Ohio Board of Regents, "Directive 2008–010," May 30, 2008, https://www
.ohiohighered.org/sites/default/files/Directive_2008-10.pdf.

21. Sidwell Friends, "Beyond AP," accessed June 9, 2022, https://www.sidwell
.edu/academics/upper-school/ap-announcement/rationale.

22. Torsheta Jackson, "Mississippi College is 'Lit' Over New National Chief
Reader," *Jackson Free Press*, June 2, 2021, https://www.jacksonfreepress.com
/news/2021/jun/02/mississippi-college-lit-over-new-national-chief-re/.

23. See, for example, "Louisiana Believes—AP ESSER," April 2022, https://
www.louisianabelieves.com/docs/default-source/achieve/esser-ii
-funding_-ap.pdf?sfvrsn=9d806718_4.

24. Amazon Future Engineer, "High School," accessed July 9, 2022, https://
www.amazonfutureengineer.com/high-school; "Amazon Donates $15
Million to Code.org to Create New Equity-Minded Advanced Placement
Computer Science Curriculum to Help High School Students in Underserved Communities Excel in Tech," February 24, 2021, https://press
.aboutamazon.com/news-releases/news-release-details/amazon
-donates-15-million-codeorg-create-new-equity-minded.

25. George Lucas Educational Foundation, "Knowledge in Action," Lucas
Education Research, accessed June 9, 2022, https://www.lucasedresearch
.org/grant-awards/knowledge-in-action/.

26. David Coleman, "There's More to College Than Getting into College,"
The Atlantic, May 22, 2019, https://www.theatlantic.com/ideas/archive
/2019/05/david-coleman-stop-college-admissions-madness/589918/.

27. Jay Mathews, "Decision by 7 Private Schools to Drop AP Courses Flunks
the Smell Test," *Washington Post*, July 15, 2018, https://www.washington
post.com/local/education/decision-by-7-private-schools-to-drop-ap
-courses-flunks—the-smell-test/2018/07/15/a27e9572-8571-11e8-8553
-a3ce89036c78_story.html.

28. Jay Mathews, "The Triumph of Advanced Placement: How Trevor Packer
Made Advanced Placement a Powerful—and Controversial—Force in
American Education," *Washington Post Magazine*, October 23, 2018,
https://www.washingtonpost.com/news/magazine/wp/2018/10/23
/feature/meet-the-man-who-made-advanced-placement-the-most
-influential-tool-in-american-education/.

29. Chester E. Finn and Andrew E. Scanlan, *Learning in the Fast Lane: The
Past, Present, and Future of Advanced Placement* (Princeton, NJ: Princeton University Press, 2019), x.

30. Dante Ciampaglia, "Introducing the College Board Foundation," *The Elective*, November 19, 2021, https://elective.collegeboard.org/introducing
-college-board-foundation.

31. "Strengthening Connections from HS to Postsecondary Education and
Work," YouTube, June 29, 2021, https://www.youtube.com/watch?v
=ZmkvFjUESQc.

32. Douglas Belkin, "For Sale: SAT-Takers' Names. Colleges Buy Student Data
and Boost Exclusivity," *Wall Street Journal*, November 5, 2019, https://
www.wsj.com/articles/for-sale-sat-takers-names-colleges-buy-student
-data-and-boost-exclusivity-11572976621; College Board, "AP Services
Terms and Conditions," accessed November 30, 2021, https://apcentral
.collegeboard.org/pdf/ap-services-terms-conditions.pdf; Thomas

Germain, "The College Board Is Sharing Student Data Once Again," Consumer Reports, July 30, 2020, https://www.consumerreports.org /colleges-universities/college-board-is-sharing-student-data-once-again.

33. College Board, "Why Springboard?", https://springboard.collegeboard .org/why-choose-springboard.

34. See Wendy Wall, *Inventing the "American Way": The Politics of Consensus from the New Deal to the Civil Rights Movement* (New York: Oxford University Press, 2009).

35. See Jill Lepore, *This America: The Case for the Nation* (New York: Liveright, 2019), and Martha Craven Nussbaum, *Not for Profit: Why Democracy Needs the Humanities* (Princeton, NJ: Princeton University Press, 2016).

36. Andrew Delbanco, *College: What It Was, Is, and Should Be* (Princeton, NJ: Princeton University Press, 2014); Johann N. Neem, *What's the Point of College? Seeking Purpose in an Age of Reform* (Baltimore: Johns Hopkins University Press, 2019).

37. Christopher Newfield, *The Great Mistake: How We Wrecked Public Universities and How We Can Fix Them* (Baltimore: Johns Hopkins University Press, 2018); Kathleen Fitzpatrick, *Generous Thinking: A Radical Approach to Saving the University* (Baltimore: Johns Hopkins University Press, 2021); Tressie McMillan Cottom, *Lower Ed: The Troubling Rise of For-Profit Colleges in the New Economy* (New York: New Press, 2018).

38. Anne Kim, "AP's Equity Face Plant," *Washington Monthly*, August 29, 2021, https://washingtonmonthly.com/2021/08/29/aps-equity-face-plant/.

39. Nicholas Lemann, *The Big Test: The Secret History of the American Meritocracy* (New York: Farrar, Straus and Giroux, 1999), 349.

40. Eric Rothschild, "Forty Years of AP," *College Board Review*, no. 177 (Summer 1995). After I'd finished this manuscript, I read about Scarsdale's reversed course: Joanne Wallenstein, "AT vs. AP," Scarsdale10583, https://scarsdale10583.com/schools/9734-at-vs-ap-what-best-serves -scarsdale-students.

41. See, for example, Jennifer Berkshire and Jack Schneider, *A Wolf at the Schoolhouse Door* (New York: New Press, 2020); Jake Jacobs, "Biden is Reigniting the Movement to Oppose Standardized Testing," *The Progressive*, March 22, 2021, https://progressive.org/public-schools-advocate /biden-movement-oppose-standardized-test-jacobs-210322/; and Chester Finn and Michael Petrilli, *How to Educate an American: The Conservative Vision for Tomorrow's Schools* (West Conshohocken, PA: Templeton Press, 2021).

42. "Barney Charter School Initiative," https://k12.hillsdale.edu/Programs /BCSI/.

43. See John L. Rudolph, *How We Teach Science: What's Changed, and Why It Matters* (Cambridge, MA: Harvard University Press, 2019).

EPILOGUE

1. "Ralph Ellison, the Art of Fiction, No. 8," interviewed by Alfred Chester and Vilma Howard, *Paris Review*, no. 8 (Spring 1955), https://www.theparis review.org/interviews/5053/the-art-of-fiction-no-8-ralph-ellison.

2. US News and World Report's High School Rankings rely on College Board data. Rankings rely on student participation in AP or IB (30 percent of a school's score, as of 2022) and AP offerings (10 percent of a school's score): Robert Morse and Eric Brooks, "How US News Calculated the 2022 Best High Schools Rankings," US News and World Report, April 25, 2022, https://www.usnews.com/education/best-high-schools/articles/how-us -news-calculated-the-rankings.

3. For one Black educator's recent experiences with a form of liberal educa- tion in K–12, see Anika Prather, "Living in the Constellation of the Canon: A Phenomenological Study of African American Students Reading Great Books Literature," PhD diss., 2017, University of Maryland, https://drum .lib.umd.edu/handle/1903/19437?show=full. For some possibilities and complexities of inclusive progressive education, see Craig Kridel, "Black Progressive Educators of the 1940s: An Overlooked Chapter of Progressiv- ism in American Education," *Kappa Delta Pi Record* 56, no. 3 (2020): 105–11; Jeffrey Aaron Snyder, "Progressive Education in Black and White: Rereading Carter G. Woodson's 'Miseducation of the Negro,'" *History of Education Quarterly* 55, no. 3 (2015): 273–93; and T. Fallace, "The Paradox of Race and Culture in Dewey's Democracy and Education," *Journal of the Gilded Age and Progressive Era* 16, no. 4 (2017): 473–87.

4. Roosevelt Montás, *Rescuing Socrates: How the Great Books Changed My Life and Why They Matter for a New Generation* (Princeton, NJ: Princeton University Press, 2021), 34.

5. Montás, *Rescuing Socrates*, 224.

Index